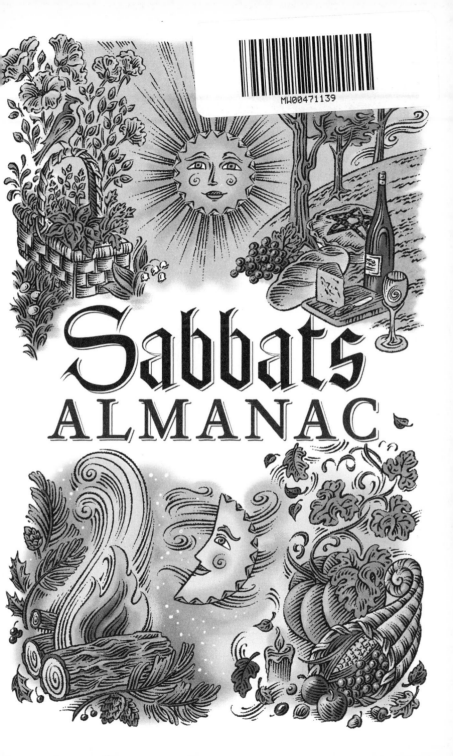

Sabbats
ALMANAC

Llewellyn's Sabbats Almanac:
Samhain 2011 to Mabon 2012

Cover art © Carolyn Vibbert/Susan and Co.
Cover design by Ellen Lawson
Editing by Ed Day
Interior Art: © Carolyn Vibbert/Susan and Co., excluding illustrations on pages 33, 75, 111, 147, 181, 183, 222, 224, 257, 295, and 297, which are © Wen Hsu

You can order annuals and books from *New Worlds*, Llewellyn's catalog. To request a free copy call toll free: 1-877-NEW WRLD, or order online by visiting our Web site at http://subscriptions.llewellyn.com

ISBN: 978-0-7387-1498-1

Llewellyn Worldwide Ltd.
2143 Wooddale Drive
Woodbury, MN 55125-2989
www.llewellyn.com

Printed in the United States of America

2011

JANUARY
S	M	T	W	T	F	S
						1
2	3	4	5	6	7	8
9	10	11	12	13	14	15
16	17	18	19	20	21	22
23	24	25	26	27	28	29
30	31					

FEBRUARY
S	M	T	W	T	F	S
		1	2	3	4	5
6	7	8	9	10	11	12
13	14	15	16	17	18	19
20	21	22	23	24	25	26
27	28					

MARCH
S	M	T	W	T	F	S
		1	2	3	4	5
6	7	8	9	10	11	12
13	14	15	16	17	18	19
20	21	22	23	24	25	26
27	28	29	30	31		

APRIL
S	M	T	W	T	F	S
					1	2
3	4	5	6	7	8	9
10	11	12	13	14	15	16
17	18	19	20	21	22	23
24	25	26	27	28	29	30

MAY
S	M	T	W	T	F	S
1	2	3	4	5	6	7
8	9	10	11	12	13	14
15	16	17	18	19	20	21
22	23	24	25	26	27	28
29	30	31				

JUNE
S	M	T	W	T	F	S
			1	2	3	4
5	6	7	8	9	10	11
12	13	14	15	16	17	18
19	20	21	22	23	24	25
26	27	28	29	30		

JULY
S	M	T	W	T	F	S
					1	2
3	4	5	6	7	8	9
10	11	12	13	14	15	16
17	18	19	20	21	22	23
24	25	26	27	28	29	30
31						

AUGUST
S	M	T	W	T	F	S
	1	2	3	4	5	6
7	8	9	10	11	12	13
14	15	16	17	18	19	20
21	22	23	24	25	26	27
28	29	30	31			

SEPTEMBER
S	M	T	W	T	F	S
				1	2	3
4	5	6	7	8	9	10
11	12	13	14	15	16	17
18	19	20	21	22	23	24
25	26	27	28	29	30	

OCTOBER
S	M	T	W	T	F	S
						1
2	3	4	5	6	7	8
9	10	11	12	13	14	15
16	17	18	19	20	21	22
23	24	25	26	27	28	29
30	31					

NOVEMBER
S	M	T	W	T	F	S
		1	2	3	4	5
6	7	8	9	10	11	12
13	14	15	16	17	18	19
20	21	22	23	24	25	26
27	28	29	30			

DECEMBER
S	M	T	W	T	F	S
				1	2	3
4	5	6	7	8	9	10
11	12	13	14	15	16	17
18	19	20	21	22	23	24
25	26	27	28	29	30	31

2012

JANUARY
S	M	T	W	T	F	S
1	2	3	4	5	6	7
8	9	10	11	12	13	14
15	16	17	18	19	20	21
22	23	24	25	26	27	28
29	30	31				

FEBRUARY
S	M	T	W	T	F	S
			1	2	3	4
5	6	7	8	9	10	11
12	13	14	15	16	17	18
19	20	21	22	23	24	25
26	27	28	29			

MARCH
S	M	T	W	T	F	S
				1	2	3
4	5	6	7	8	9	10
11	12	13	14	15	16	17
18	19	20	21	22	23	24
25	26	27	28	29	30	31

APRIL
S	M	T	W	T	F	S
1	2	3	4	5	6	7
8	9	10	11	12	13	14
15	16	17	18	19	20	21
22	23	24	25	26	27	28
29	30					

MAY
S	M	T	W	T	F	S
		1	2	3	4	5
6	7	8	9	10	11	12
13	14	15	16	17	18	19
20	21	22	23	24	25	26
27	28	29	30	31		

JUNE
S	M	T	W	T	F	S
					1	2
3	4	5	6	7	8	9
10	11	12	13	14	15	16
17	18	19	20	21	22	23
24	25	26	27	28	29	30

JULY
S	M	T	W	T	F	S
1	2	3	4	5	6	7
8	9	10	11	12	13	14
15	16	17	18	19	20	21
22	23	24	25	26	27	28
29	30	31				

AUGUST
S	M	T	W	T	F	S
			1	2	3	4
5	6	7	8	9	10	11
12	13	14	15	16	17	18
19	20	21	22	23	24	25
26	27	28	29	30	31	

SEPTEMBER
S	M	T	W	T	F	S
						1
2	3	4	5	6	7	8
9	10	11	12	13	14	15
16	17	18	19	20	21	22
23	24	25	26	27	28	29
30						

OCTOBER
S	M	T	W	T	F	S
	1	2	3	4	5	6
7	8	9	10	11	12	13
14	15	16	17	18	19	20
21	22	23	24	25	26	27
28	29	30	31			

NOVEMBER
S	M	T	W	T	F	S
				1	2	3
4	5	6	7	8	9	10
11	12	13	14	15	16	17
18	19	20	21	22	23	24
25	26	27	28	29	30	

DECEMBER
S	M	T	W	T	F	S
						1
2	3	4	5	6	7	8
9	10	11	12	13	14	15
16	17	18	19	20	21	22
23	24	25	26	27	28	29
30	31					

Contents

Introduction . . . 7

About the Authors . . . 8

Samhain

The Season of Death by Elizabeth Barrette . . . 14

Celestial Sway by Fern Feto Spring . . . 18

The Old Ways: Magical Bats by Patti Wigington . . . 22

Feasts and Treats by Susan Pesznecker . . . 26

Crafty Crafts by Ellen Dugan . . . 31

All One Family by Clea Danaan . . . 36

Samhain Ritual: Make Friends with Death
        by Elizabeth Barrette . . . 40

Yule

Winter Solstice: Joy and Tradition by Kristin Madden . . . 52

Celestial Sway by Fern Feto Spring . . . 59

The Old Ways: Io, Saturnalia by Patti Wigington . . . 63

Feasts and Treats by Susan Pesznecker . . . 67

Crafty Crafts by Ellen Dugan . . . 72

All One Family by Clea Danaan . . . 77

Yule Ritual: The Give-Away by Kristin Madden . . . 80

Imbolc

Imbolc: Welcoming the Light by Deborah Blake . . . 88

Celestial Sway by Fern Feto Spring . . . 95

The Old Ways: The Hearthfire by Patti Wigington . . . 99

Feasts and Treats by Susan Pesznecker . . . 103

Crafty Crafts by Ellen Dugan . . . 108

All One Family by Clea Danaan . . . 113

Imbolc Ritual: Cultivating Dreams by Deborah Blake . . . 117

Ostara

Spring Equinox: Nox and Lux by Natalie Zaman . . . 126

Celestial Sway by Fern Feto Spring . . . 132

The Old Ways: Labyrinth Magic by Patti Wigington . . . 136

Feasts and Treats by Susan Pesznecker . . . 139

Crafty Crafts by Ellen Dugan . . . 144

All One Family by Clea Danaan . . . 148

Ostara Ritual: Cleanse, Balance, Rest
by Natalie Zaman . . . 152

Beltane

Beltane: Portal of Transformation
by Jhenah Telyndru . . . 162

Celestial Sway by Fern Feto Spring . . . 168

The Old Ways: Legend of Rowan by Patti Wigington . . . 172

Feasts and Treats by Susan Pesznecker . . . 176

Crafty Crafts by Ellen Dugan . . . 180

All One Family by Clea Danaan . . . 185

Beltane Ritual: Between the Worlds by Jhenah Telyndru . . . 188

Litha

Midsummer: Otherworldly Magic
by Bronwynn Forrest Torgerson . . . 200

Celestial Sway by Fern Feto Spring . . . 207

The Old Ways: Native Sun Stories by Patti Wigington . . . 211

Feasts and Treats by Susan Pesznecker . . . 215

Crafty Crafts by Ellen Dugan . . . 220

All One Family by Clea Danaan . . . 225

Litha Ritual: Find, Claim, and Name Your Magical Tool
by Bronwynn Forrest Torgerson . . . 229

Lammas

Feast of the First Harvest by Kenny Klein . . . 236

Celestial Sway by Fern Feto Spring . . . 243

The Old Ways: Goddess of Grain by Patti Wigington . . . 247

Feasts and Treats by Susan Pesznecker . . . 250

Crafty Crafts by Ellen Dugan . . . 255

All One Family by Clea Danaan . . . 260

Lammas Ritual: Calling the Pagans Home by Kenny Klein . . . 264

Mabon

Summer's End by Dallas Jennifer Cobb . . . 276

Celestial Sway by Fern Feto Spring . . . 283

The Old Ways: Mabon Apple Magic by Patti Wigington . . . 287

Feasts and Treats by Susan Pesznecker . . . 290

Crafty Crafts by Ellen Dugan . . . 294

All One Family by Clea Danaan . . . 299

Mabon Ritual: Power of Dark by Dallas Jennifer Cobb . . . 302

Introduction

NEARLY EVERYONE HAS A favorite sabbat. There are numerous ways to observe any tradition. This annual edition of the *Sabbats Almanac* provides a wealth of lore, celebrations, creative projects, and recipes to enhance your holiday.

For this edition, a mix of up-and-coming writers—**Dallas Jennifer Cobb, Jhenah Telyndru**, and **Natalie Zaman**—join more established writers—**Elizabeth Barrette, Deborah Blake, Kenny Klein, Kristin Madden,** and **Bronwynn Forrest Torgerson**—in sharing their ideas and wisdom. These include a variety of paths such as Garden Witchery or Green Witchery as well as the authors' personal approaches to each sabbat. Each chapter closes with an extended ritual, which may be adapted for both solitary practitioners and covens.

In addition to these insights and rituals, specialists in astrology, history, cooking, crafts, and family impart their expertise throughout.

Fern Feto Spring gives an overview of planetary influences most relevant for each sabbat season and provides details and a short ritual for selected events, including New and Full Moons, retrograde motion, planetary positions, and more.

Patti Wigington explores the realm of old-world Pagans, with a focus on customs such as gathering healing herbs for Midsummer and little-known lore like the story of the Yule Goat—and their connection to celebrations today.

Susan Pesznecker conjures up a feast for each festival that includes an appetizer, entrée, dessert, and beverage.

Ellen Dugan offers instructions on craft projects that can also be incorporated into your practice.

Clea Danaan focuses on activities the entire family can share to commemorate each sabbat.

About the Authors

Elizabeth Barrette has been involved with the Pagan community for more than twenty-two years. She served as managing editor of *PanGaia* for eight years and dean of studies at the Grey School of Wizardry for four years. She has written columns on beginning and intermediate Pagan practice, Pagan culture, and Pagan leadership. Her book *Composing Magic: How to Create Magical Spells, Rituals, Blessings, Chants, and Prayers* explains how to combine writing and spirituality. She lives in central Illinois where she has done much networking with Pagans in her area, such as coffeehouse meetings and open sabbats. Her other public activities feature Pagan picnics and science-fiction conventions. She enjoys magical crafts, sabbat entertaining, and gardening for wildlife. Her other writing fields include speculative fiction and gender studies. One of her Pagan science fiction poems, "Fallen Gardens," was nominated for the Rhysling Award in 2010. Visit her blogs: *The Wordsmith's Forge*, http://ysabetwordsmith.livejournal.com and *Gaiatribe: Ideas for a Thinking Planet*, http://gaiatribe.geekuniversalis.com.

Deborah Blake is the author of *Circle, Coven & Grove: A Year of Magickal Practice; Everyday Witch A to Z: An Amusing, Inspiring & Informative Guide to the Wonderful World of Witchcraft; The Goddess is in the Details: Wisdom for the Everyday Witch; Everyday Witch A to Z Spellbook*; and *Witchcraft on a Shoestring*. Her award-winning short story, "Dead and (Mostly) Gone" is included in the *Pagan Anthology of Short Fiction: 13 Prize Winning Tales* (Llewellyn 2008). When not writing, Deborah runs the Artisans' Guild, a cooperative shop she founded with a friend, and works as a jewelry-maker, tarot reader, ordained minister, and an intuitive energy healer. She lives in a 100-year-old farmhouse in rural upstate New York with five cats who supervise all her activities, both magickal and mundane.

Life is what you make it, and **Dallas Jennifer Cobb** has made a magical life in a waterfront village on the shores of great Lake Ontario. Forever scheming novel ways to pay the bills, she practices manifestation magic and wildlands witchcraft. She currently teaches Pilates, works in a library, and writes to finance long hours spent following her hearts' desire—time with family, in nature and on the water. Contact her at jennifer.cobb@live.com.

Clea Danaan is the author of *Sacred Land: Intuitive Gardening for Personal, Political & Environmental Change* (Llewellyn 2005), *Voices of the Earth: The Path of Green Spirituality* (Llewellyn 2009), and *Magical Bride: Craft an Interfaith Wedding for a Goddess* (Wyrdwood Ebook 2009). *Sacred Land* was a 2007 *Foreword* Book of the Year Finalist (Mind/Body/Spirit) and received a 2008 Bronze Medal Independent Publisher Book Award for "Most Likely to Save the Planet." Clea's writings have been influenced by her studies in Creation Spirituality, body-based psychotherapy, expressive arts therapy, and energy work. She has an MFA in creative writing from National University. She has been gardening organically for over fifteen years and recently added a small flock of chickens to her suburban homestead near Denver. Most of her time is spent homeschooling a precocious kindergartner and nursing the baby. You can visit her at cleadanaan.blogspot.com and www.IntuitiveGardening.net.

Ellen Dugan, the "Garden Witch," is an award-winning author and psychic-clairvoyant. A practicing Witch for more than twenty-five years, she is the author of ten Llewellyn books: *Garden Witchery, Elements of Witchcraft, Cottage Witchery, Autumn Equinox, The Enchanted Cat, Herb Magic for Beginners, Natural Witchery, How to Enchant a Man* and her latest books, *A Garden Witch's Herbal* and *Book of Witchery*. Ellen wholeheartedly encourages folks to personalize their spellcraft—to go outside and to get their hands dirty to discover the wonder and magick of the natural world. Ellen and her family live in Missouri. For further information, visit her website at www.ellendugan.com.

Fern Feto Spring, M.A. is a counseling astrologer whose readings integrate intuition, practicality, compassion, and humor. With over 18 years of astrological experience, she incorporates flower essences and other healing modalities into her consultations. Besides her consultation practice, Fern teaches and gives talks on astrology and other topics nationwide. She has written for *The Mountain Astrologer*, astrology.com, and a variety of other publications. She also works as an intuitive consultant, conducting team-building and communications workshops for a number of businesses, schools, and nonprofit organizations. She lives and gardens avidly, if a bit wildly, in Fairfax, California, with her partner and her dog Sweetie. Her website is: www.wisestars.net.

Kenny Klein is an author, musician, performer, and fine artist. His books include *Through The Faerie Glass* (Llewellyn, 2010) and *Fairy Tale Rituals* (Llewellyn, 2011). He is also the author of *The Flowering Rod* (Immanion Press, 2008), a book about the role of men in Paganism and Wicca. Kenny is also a regular contributor to The Green Egg (www.greeneggzine.com), and to many smaller publications that you've never heard of. As a musician and performer, Kenny has performed at a disparate array of venues that include Pagan festivals, renaissance faires, and really not Pagan-ish music in country bars and at bluegrass festivals. He's even played on cruise ships (that was really really not Pagan-ish music). He has several CDs available, including the Pagan Dark Wave CD *The Fairy Queen* (with singer Lori Watley), and *Meet Me in the Shade of the Maple Tree*, the world's first CD of Pagan bluegrass music. As an artist Kenny is known for his customizing of collectible dolls (really). He also paints, but no one really cares about that. Visit Kenny at www.kennyklein.net.

Kristin Madden is an author and mother, as well as an environmental chemist and wildlife rehabilitator. She is the Director of Ardantane's School of Shamanic Studies. A Druid and tutor in the

Order of Bards, Ovates, and Druids, Kristin is also a member of the Druid College of Healing and is on the Board of Silver Moon Health Services. She has been a freelance writer and editor since 1995. Her work has appeared in *Whole Life Times, PARABOLA,* and many other publications. Kristin is the author of five books including *Mabon: Celebrating the Autumn Equinox* and *The Book of Shamanic Healing.* Kristin was raised in a shamanic home and has had ongoing experience with Eastern and Western mystic paths since 1972. Over more than a decade, she has offered a variety of shamanic and general metaphysical workshops across the United States. Kristin is active in both pagan parenting and pagan home-schooling communities locally and globally. She also served on a master's degree thesis committee for a program on the use of visual imagery and parapsychology in therapy with ADD/ADHD children.

Susan Pesznecker, a.k.a. Moonwriter, is a writer, college English teacher, nurse, and hearth Pagan living in northwestern Oregon. She holds a master's degree in nonfiction writing and loves to read, watch the stars, camp with her wonder poodle, and work in her own biodynamic garden. Sue is Dean of Students and teaches nature studies and herbology in the online Grey School of Wizardry (greyschool.com). She's the author of *Gargoyles* (New Page, 2007) and *Crafting Magick with Pen and Ink* (Llewellyn, 2009) and is a regular contributor to many of the Llewellyn Annuals and to Australia's *Spellcraft* magazine. Visit Sue on her Facebook page: http://www.facebook.com/susan.pesznecker.

Jhenah Telyndru is the founder and Morgen of the Sisterhood of Avalon www.sisterhoodofavalon.org and serves as Academic Dean and lead instructor of the Avalonian Thealogical Seminary. She presents retreats and workshops across North America, and facilitates Pilgrimages to sacred sites in the British Isles. Jhenah is the author of *Avalon Within: A Sacred Journey of Myth, Mystery, and Inner Wisdom* (Llewellyn, 2010), the creator of a unique system of trance journey postures found on the DVD *Trancing the Inner Landscape:*

Avalonian Landscape Postures, and has released a spoken word album of guided meditations entitled *Journeys to Avalon: Immrama to the Holy Isle.* Jhenah's writing has been featured in *PanGaia, Sage-Woman, Witches and Pagans, The Beltane Papers,* and *Circle Magazine.* She holds degrees in Archaeology and Social Science, and is currently earning her master's degree in Celtic Studies at the University of Wales, Trinity Saint David. Jhenah lives in Upstate New York with her husband, two children, three cats, and too many books. She welcomes your contact through her website: www.ynysafallon.com.

Bronwynn Forrest Torgerson is the author of *One Witch's Way,* Llewellyn 2008. She makes her home in Glendale, Arizona, with her soulmate husband Dan. She is the founder of HearthFire CUUPS, hosted by West Valley Unitarian Universalist Church, and an eight-year veteran organizer of Phoenix Pagan Pride Day. Her Pagan path is Norse Heathenry with a dash of eclectic Wicca thrown in.

Patti Wigington has been the host of About.com's Pagan/Wiccan website (http://paganwiccan.about.com) since 2007, and has published a number of short fiction stories and freelance magazine articles. She is the author of an alphabet book for children, a middle-grade novel, and two adult novels. Her work has appeared in *Llewellyn's Herbal Almanacs,* as well as a number of Pagan websites. She works as an educator in her local Pagan community. Patti lives in central Ohio with her husband, David, and children Caitlin, Zachary, and Breanna.

When she's not chasing free range hens, **Natalie Zaman** is trying to figure out the universe. Her work has appeared in *FATE, Sage Woman, newWitch,* and she currently writes a recurring feature called The Wandering Witch for *Witches and Pagans.* Natalie has also published work for children, and co-publishes, edits, and writes for broomstix.com, a project for Pagan children and their families. Her YA debut, *Sirenz* is being published by Flux in 2011.

Samhain

The Season of Death

Elizabeth Barrette

SAMHAIN FALLS ON THE night of October 31. One of the eight high holy days, it marks the beginning of the Pagan year. In some traditions, Beltane and Samhain divide the year into a "light half" and a "dark half." Like Halloween, All Hallows Eve, and Dia de los Muertos, the holiday of Samhain deals with issues of mortality, spirits, and darker aspects of magic. From this foundation come the familiar images of skeletons, ghosts, bonfires, the Moon, the besom, and mystical creatures such as cats and spiders.

Pagans do not consider these things "evil"—they belong to the cycle of nature as surely as night follows day. They can be mysterious, though, and sometimes that makes them seem daunting or difficult to face. Pagans typically believe that it is better to face challenges and work through them, rather than hide from them. Therefore many Samhain rituals create a safe space to explore our feelings about death and dying, or the dark emotions that everyone experiences, or the creatures and deities that represent mysterious forces.

If you are new to Paganism and the celebration of Samhain, you may want to study up in a bit more detail before working through the material in this *Almanac*. For Paganism in general, consider *Paganism: An Introduction to Earth-Centered Religions* by Joyce and

River Higginbotham; for Samhain and other sabbats, consider *Halloween: Customs, Rituals, and Spells* by Silver RavenWolf and *Celebrating the Seasons of Life: Samhain to Ostara* by Ashleen O'Gaea.

The Faces of Death

Most cultures and religions personify universal ideas and experiences in the form of gods, goddesses, folk heroes, spirits, or other archetypal figures. All that lives must die, so Death appears in almost every pantheon. Just as mortality takes many forms, the personifications also vary widely. The figure of Death shows what each culture considers the most salient features; common ones include hunger, cold, earth, lechery, negotiation, implacability, lamentation, patience, and compassion. Often Death embodies some kind of paradox or combination of opposing traits.

Some cultures consider dying a natural part of life, something to welcome in its proper time and manner. They are likely to portray representatives of Death as neutral or helpful figures. Ritual activities introduce people to issues of mortality and assist in forming a healthy perception of death; members of these cultures may thus be less vulnerable to the panicky aversion that turns an inevitable event into such an ordeal for some people. Other cultures take a more troubled view of dying, as something to be resisted by all means. They are likely to depict representatives of Death as negative or actively malicious figures. Although these cultures also have rituals dealing with death, those are often more oblique—and examples of "macabre" or "graveyard" humor are more prevalent, in an attempt to weaken a frightening image.

As contemporary Pagans, we enjoy a wide choice of religious experiences. Because we have only fragments from most of our ancient practices, we rely on those mainly for inspiration and create new activities for current use. Combining these two aspects of our culture gives us an "eclectic" approach, in which we can take corresponding examples from different sources and offer them together so that participants may choose whichever they find most compatible.

This Samhain ritual (detailed on page 40) brings together manifestations of Death from four different cultures. Each presents its own perspective on the transition from this world to the next. By exploring diverse representations of Death, participants may find one that feels like a good match, enabling them to contemplate mortality in a personally meaningful—if not necessarily comfortable, at least tolerable—way.

Yamantaka comes from Tibetan Buddhism, although related figures appear in other Buddhist and Hindu traditions. Buddhism considers life to be a state of suffering, caused by desires and attachments. Releasing attachments brings enlightenment and escape from the cycle of rebirth. Yama is a demon that causes a phobia of death, which contributes to trapping souls in unfortunate incarnations. Yamantaka defeats Yama, making enlightenment easier to reach. So Yamantaka directly confronts a key issue, the fear of death and the desperate attachment to life, teaching people to be more relaxed about transitions. This figure also has both meditative and martial qualities.

Baron Samedi comes from Haitian Vodou, with analogous figures in other Afro-Caribbean religions. This *loa* holds a great deal of power in a tradition that centers around ancestral spirits. Baron Samedi is associated not just with death but also with healing and bawdy sexuality. He can be a raunchy nuisance or a perfect gentleman—often both within the same ceremony. In Vodou, death is not an end but a transition; the ancestors remain part of family life. This culture treats death with festivity as well as solemnity, which helps make it less intimidating and more familiar. In addition to helping people understand mortality, Baron Samedi is often willing to exchange favors with his followers.

Erishkegal comes from the Sumerian tradition. She is best known for facing off against her sister, Inanna, in the myth of Inanna's descent to the underworld. Ancient Sumerians took a very bleak view of death and the afterlife, so their underworld is a place of little comfort. Yet, the Sumerian view also deals with acceptance and compassion. Erishkegal never turns anyone away from her realm—although she can get temperamental with people who treat her disrespectfully. She is helpful for coping with suffering and for setting aside life's burdens.

The Pale Horse appears in many different traditions as Death itself, or the mount of Death or Deathlike figures. The color can be white, ivory, light gray, dun, or even greenish. In other cases, the horse is merely a skeleton—a form sometimes created for parades. The shamanic power of the horse evokes the idea of death as a journey, of being swept up and carried away. The mood can vary from compassionate to terrifying, though. Horse lovers and adventurers may find this manifestation appealing.

If your group has a strong connection to a Death figure not represented here, feel free to make substitutions. You can keep the framework the same and just write a new section for that figure, using its cultural background for inspiration. Try to maintain diversity so that participants will have different manifestations of Death to choose from, rather than ones that share a similar flavor.

Celestial Sway

Fern Feto Spring

AS YOU COMMUNE WITH your beloved dead this Samhain season, don't be surprised if you hear powerful messages coming through from the other side of the veil. Both Mercury, the planet of communication and Venus, ruler of love and relationships are not only in Scorpio—the sign of death, spirits, and transformation—but this year they also form a powerful conjunction aspect. The dead will be talking up a storm this year, so a séance or other ritual will be particularly timely now, as there will be much to learn from the wisdom of those who have passed on.

You may need to prepare for some possibly confusing messages as Neptune forms a tense square aspect to these two planets throughout the Samhain weekend. Though the misty fog of Neptune can help you to commune with spirits more easily, the square aspect indicates that it's important to get clear on the type of spirits you are in communication with. It may be helpful to be very specific when reaching out to those on the other side, asking that you receive helpful, supportive information. With trickster energy in the air now, it's possible to run into a few ghosts who want to stir up mischief rather than offer support or insight.

Since this Samhain gains energy from the New Moon cycle, which began on October 26, this is also a good time to focus on the future, using the growing darkness to turn inward and dream up what is to come. This forward movement is supported in early November when both Venus and Mercury move into freedom-loving Sagittarius. This transition indicates that both our hearts and our minds are focused on exploration, expansion, and adventure. This may be a good time to take a fall trip to some unknown destination, or if you prefer to stick closer to home, this fire combo is an excellent planetary alignment for expansions of consciousness. Try taking a workshop or class that helps you to open your mind and experiment with new philosophies and belief systems.

A Full Moon in Taurus on November 10 brings a more grounded energy to the cosmos, and Mars' transition into Virgo on November 10 further supports an earthy balance to the strong fire arrangement of the planets. Mid-November offers the opportunity to integrate some of the otherworldly explorations we may have experienced as we danced between the veils of the world during the early days of the Samhain season. As we use these earthy energies to bring our experiences into the physical realm, we can more easily take any spiritual gifts we have received and gain some practical benefit from them.

Neptune, which has been retrograde (moving backwards) since June 2011, goes direct on November 9. The planet of spirituality, dreams, compassion, art, confusion, addiction, and deception will slowly began to move forward now. This cosmic transition gives us an opportunity to have more direct access to the Neptunian realm of life. We may find that our creative potential grows at this time, and we are more able to tap into our inner spiritual resources. It's also possible that we can gain a greater awareness of how we deceive ourselves and others, which can allow us to make future choices with a greater sense of clarity and understanding.

The Samhain season ends with a fire sign emphasis as Mercury goes retrograde in Sagittarius on November 24 and the New Moon forms a solar eclipse in Sagittarius on November 25. This double Sagittarius influence asks us to carefully review and meditate on what brings meaning to our lives, expanding our awareness of diverse beliefs and ways of being in the world. As the light dies away and the darkness grows, we are encouraged to follow a path inward, finding answers within ourselves and learning from our own accumulated wisdom and knowledge.

Mars in Virgo

Mars moves into Virgo on November 10, bringing energy and drive to our ability to perfect any projects or work we are currently focused on. In the sign of Virgo, Mars can be finicky and demanding, but this planetary combo is also a great opportunity to get things done! Use the earthy energy of Mars in Virgo to move forward on your plans and zero in on the details. For extra "oomph," perform a Mars in Virgo ritual on or around November 10.

Mars in Virgo Ritual

Write a list (Virgo loves lists!) of all the things you want to accomplish during the Samhain season. Big or small, jot all of your plans down. Then, prioritize them, putting tasks that will really support your higher goals and move you forward at the top of your list. When you have completed your list, put it on your altar and light a yellow candle (to invoke earth energy), and ask Mercury, Virgo's ruling planet to guide you through the list with skill and dexterity. As the candle burns, imagine in your mind's eye that you are completing the first task on your list. See yourself happily engaged in the job at hand and move through all the steps, watching them easily and effortlessly unfold. When you are done with your visualization, blow out the candle and take one step to get you started on that first item on your list. You can return to the list and light the candle each time you want to start on the next item. When you have completed all the list tasks, burn the list and thank Mercury for his help.

Full Moon in Taurus

The Samhain season Taurus Full Moon on November 10 brings our awareness to the need to find balance between the spirit world and the physical realm. Use this Full Moon energy to find your own balance as you commune with the dead and the living during this potent time.

Taurus Full Moon Ritual

On the night of the Full Moon, reflect on any messages you may have received from your beloved dead on Samhain Eve and write these down on small slips of paper. Bury the slips of paper in a potted plant, setting the intention that as the plant grows, you will receive further insight and guidance from the spirit realm that will help you in the physical and manifest realm.

New Moon Eclipse in Sagittarius

The New Moon eclipse in Sagittarius on November 25 is the last lunation of the Samhain season. This New Moon offers a new beginning in the realm of exploration, adventure, belief systems, and shifts in consciousness. A square from Mars in Virgo indicates that we may have to integrate details and a step-by step approach into our plans. Use this New Moon energy to take advantage of everything you have learned in the seed-planting time of Samhain to dream big, expand your options, and look at the big picture for the year ahead. Incorporate the messages and guidance you received from your ancestors and the beloved dead into your visions for the future, letting the wisdom of the past inform your plans for the road ahead.

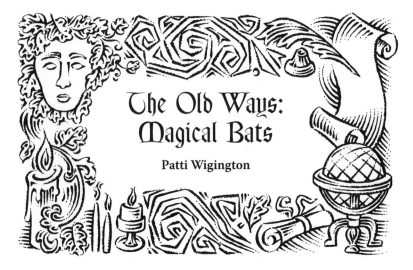

The Old Ways: Magical Bats

Patti Wigington

EVERY YEAR, WHEN OCTOBER rolls around, it's not uncommon to see bats all over the place, tucked into the Halloween décor aisles between the plastic skulls and the cats wearing Witch hats. Sometimes the bats are scary, other times they're cute or just silly—but what's the deal with bats being associated with Halloween anyway?

In the Middle Ages, it was believed that bats not only carried diseases, but that they talked to the dead as well. Add to that the fact that they only come out at night and that for years, no one knew how to classify them, and you've got a flying nocturnal creature that gives people the heebie-jeebies!

Let's look back to the beginning to figure out where all this scary bat mythology comes from. Back in the days of ancient Rome, the writer Phaedrus collected a series of folktales much like Aesop's fables. In one, "The Birds and the Bat," Phaedrus describes the bat as a neutral party in the battle between land animals and birds—in fact, the bat is smart enough to wait until he knows which side is winning. When the god Mars steps in and declares birds to be the victor, the bat knows exactly which team he wants to play for. The bat joins the birds and rejects his earthbound friends despite the fact that scientists consider the bat a mammal, and not a bird at all.

During the Middle Ages, particularly in England and Western Europe, the bat was believed to spread disease, most likely because of its similarity to the rat, which, of course, was on occasion blamed for spreading the plague. During this time, folks also believed strongly in witchcraft, and bats were often associated with black magic and sorcery. In parts of northern England and Scotland, it was believed that a Witch could summon a bat to carry a message to the devil.

The Mayans honored a god called Camazotz, a monstrous creature with the head and wings of a bat. Camazotz was associated with not just death and darkness, but with human sacrifice. When Cortez and his Conquistadores got to the Yucatan Peninsula, bringing with them their European sensibilities, a god such as Camazotz must have seemed frightening indeed!

For some North American tribal cultures, the bat was a trickster, much like the coyote, who appears in a number of cautionary tales. However, other Native American tribes associated the bat with intuition and clarity of vision.

There have been a number of legends portraying bats as night-flying bloodsuckers. While there are three species of bats that consume blood in their diet, they don't attack humans. Instead, they choose to get their snacks and meals from small rodents, birds, and other mammals that don't move quite fast enough.

When Bram Stoker wrote his legendary tale *Dracula*, he created the idea of a shapeshifting vampire who morphed into a bat to escape after sucking the blood of his victims. Dr. Elizabeth Miller of the Florida Bat Conservation Center writes that Stoker was inspired by a newspaper article in which a victim was allegedly drained of blood by a vampire bat. Dr. Miller points out that Stoker conveniently ignored the relatively small size of the vampire bat.

While people in Western societies often see the bat as a harbinger of death, interestingly, Eastern cultures have another view. In China, the bat represents happiness and long life. In fact, a group of five bats indicates a five-fold blessing: financial security, good health, longevity, a virtuous life, and a natural death.

In ancient Egypt, bats were seen in a positive light as well. It was believed that hanging a bat over a doorway would help prevent such maladies as baldness, poor eyesight, and even fevers. Dried parts of bats were used in healing rituals to treat these and other ailments.

One of the most fascinating aspects of the bat is the gift of echolocation. It's like radar for bats—a built-in GPS system. By bouncing sounds off their surroundings, bats are able to fly in complete darkness. A few quick high-frequency calls returned as echoes help bats not only fly, but locate and identify their prey at night.

How did bats come to be associated with Samhain and its mundane holiday, Halloween? No one really knows for sure. It may be that bats are connected with Halloween because to some people, bats are just plain scary-looking. Let's face it, they've got those beady little eyes, paper-thin wings, and ratlike claws…and they fly in total silence.

Perhaps the bat's nocturnal ways and association with death are what has linked it so closely to the Samhain season. Another theory is that in late October, the air has gotten cool enough that we light outdoor fires, which lure insects in close with their light. Those insects, in turn, draw in hungry bats looking for dinner. Usually by the time November is in full swing, North American bats are migrating south, so you may see more bat activity around this time of year.

Despite their odd appearance, bats are truly beneficial creatures. In addition to their mystery and magic, they provide some practical assistance as well. A single bat can consume up to 1,000 mosquitoes in just one hour, according to *Mother Earth News.* That's 1,000 mosquitoes that aren't biting you! Not only that, bats pollinate hundreds of species of fruits and flowering plants, including wild bananas, cactus, and agave. Their droppings—called guano—make an excellent organic fertilizer, and there's even an enzyme in bat saliva that pharmaceutical companies use in anti-clotting medications.

When it comes to magic, bats are clearly associated with death, spirits, and communication. How can we use these aspects of the bat in magical workings?

• When you see a bat flying about in the night, ask it to carry a message for you. Have you lost a loved one recently? Send the message to the bat, and ask it to deliver to the person on the other side of the veil.

• Carry a bat talisman or charm to open yourself up to messages from the spirit world. Use it to meditate when you're trying to communicate with someone who has crossed over.

• Are you having trouble seeing a problem or its solution clearly? Call upon bat energy to help you gain some clarity in the situation— and trust your intuition!

• Have you ever found a dead bat lying on the ground? Allow the wings to dry out completely and then grind them into powder. Sprinkle the powder around your home to keep malevolent spirits out.

• Invoke bats during astral projection, and take advantage of their blind-flying abilities to navigate through the astral planes.

• Build a bat house on your property to attract bats. Call upon them when you wish to improve your own communication skills— whether it's speaking or listening.

• Make a bat amulet and charge it with magical energy so that when you wear it, you'll never get lost.

Next time you're outside for an autumn evening walk, or sitting in your back yard at dusk, take a look up at the sky. Watch near the trees, and chances are good you'll start seeing bats flitting about. They move silently, in order to surprise their prey, and dart about the sky looking for sustenance. They won't hurt you—in fact, they'll probably ignore you completely. But take a moment and think about the mysterious, magical power of the bat.

Feasts and Treats

Susan Pesznecker

SAMHAIN IS DEEP AUTUMN. Imagine crispy-cold evenings with leaves blowing underfoot and the deep smell of woodsmoke. Long, dark nights with clouds scattering overhead. Chilly mornings that lift damp fingers to a veiled Sun. It's a time of change, and for many who practice earth-based traditions, it's the turning point of the year and a time to reach through the veil and communicate with otherworldly realms. The fiery herbs in this menu—chili, cayenne, pepper, cinnamon, cloves, and allspice—are intended to warm the soul and enliven the spirit.

Disguise-Your-Own Chili

Chili is a hearty dish, and your guests will love adding their own toppings. Vary the flavor with different ground meats, beans, or firm tofu. For extra heat, add more spices and a teaspoon of ground cumin.

Prep time: 30 minutes
Cook time: 2+ hours
Serves: 4

1 lb. lean ground beef
1 yellow onion, diced

1 clove garlic, minced
1 16-ounce can black beans, rinsed
1 16-ounce can garbanzo beans, rinsed
1 28-ounce can diced tomatoes
1 16-ounce can tomato sauce
1 8-ounce can tomato paste
½ teaspoon salt
2½ teaspoons chili powder
¼ teaspoon cayenne
½ teaspoon black pepper
¼ teaspoon red pepper flakes

Toppings:
Sweet onion, diced
Sweet peppers, diced
Cheddar cheese, grated
Jalapeños (canned), diced
Avocado, peeled and diced

Crumble the meat into a 3- to 4-quart saucepan and cook over medium heat until it starts to brown. Add the diced yellow onion and cook until the meat browns completely, i.e., brown bits begin to stick to the bottom of the pan. This develops the flavor.

Spoon off excess fat. Stir in the garlic, beans, tomatoes, tomato sauce, tomato paste, and spices. Simmer over medium-low heat for 2 to 3 hours, stirring occasionally. At this point, serve immediately or refrigerate for 1 to 2 days.

Arrange toppings in small dishes. Serve the chili in deep bowls and have your diners add their choice of toppings. Don't forget to set a place for the ancestors.

Cornbread

Good cornbread is autumn comfort food! Bacon drippings and a heavy cast iron pan work together to create a rich crust. Crumble the bread over chili or slather thick slices with silky honey butter.

> ***Prep time:*** 10 minutes
> ***Cook time:*** 30–40 minutes
> ***Serves:*** 4–6

Bacon drippings (or vegetable oil)
½ cup unsalted butter, melted
⅔ cup sugar
1 teaspoon salt
2 eggs
1 cup buttermilk
½ teaspoon baking soda
1 cup medium-grind cornmeal
1 cup all-purpose flour

½ cup unsalted butter, softened
Honey

Measure all ingredients in advance and have at room temperature. When ready to cook, preheat oven to 375 degrees F. Grease a cast iron skillet (or 8-inch square pan) with bacon drippings. Place the pan in the oven to preheat.

Melt butter and pour into a large bowl. Stir in sugar and salt. Add eggs and beat briefly until blended. Add buttermilk and baking soda, and stir to mix.

Add cornmeal and flour; stirring just until the dry ingredients are incorporated—there will be a few lumps. Pour into preheated pan and return immediately to the oven.

Bake 30 to 40 minutes until a toothpick inserted near the middle comes out clean. Cool 10 minutes and then cut into squares and remove from pan.

Make honey butter: In a small bowl, combine softened butter with ¼ to ½ cup honey and beat with fork until smooth. Taste and add more honey if needed.

Cranberry Upside-Down Cake

This beautiful jewel-like dessert makes a lovely breakfast cake as well. Serve with whipped heavy cream.

Prep time: 15 minutes
Cook time: 20 minutes
Serves: 6–8

8 tablespoons unsalted butter (divided)
1 cup white sugar (divided)
1½ teaspoons ground cinnamon
¼ teaspoon ground allspice
1¾ cups raw cranberries, rinsed and dried
1 large egg
1 teaspoon vanilla extract
1¼ cups all-purpose flour
1½ teaspoons baking powder
¼ teaspoon salt
½ cup milk

Topping:
½ cup heavy cream
1 tablespoon sugar
¼ teaspoon vanilla

Measure all ingredients in advance and have at room temperature. Preheat oven to 350 degrees F with rack at center position.

Rub the bottom and sides of a round, 8-inch cake pan with 2 tablespoons soft butter. In a small bowl, whisk ½ cup sugar with the cinnamon and allspice. Sprinkle this over the bottom of the pan; arrange cranberries in a single layer on the sugar base.

With a mixer, cream remaining 6 tablespoons butter and ½ cup sugar until light and fluffy. Add egg and vanilla; beat until combined.

In another bowl, whisk together flour, baking powder, and salt. With mixer on low, add flour mixture to butter mixture in three batches, alternating with the milk, until well combined.

Spoon the batter over the cranberries in the prepared pan, smoothing the top. Place pan on a baking sheet; bake until a toothpick inserted in the center comes out clean, 30 to 35 minutes.

Cool on a wire rack for 20 minutes. Run a knife around edge of cake; invert onto a decorative platter.

Forgo chemical-based frozen "whipped topping" and choose the real deal! Pour ½ cup heavy whipping cream into a chilled medium bowl. Using a portable mixer, beat at high speed until it thickens. Add 1 tablespoon sugar and ¼ teaspoon vanilla extract. Beat until soft peaks form.

Hot Mulled Cider

This cider provides a warm finish to your autumn feast.

Prep time: 10 minutes
Cook time: 30+ minutes
Serves: 4–8

2 quarts fresh cider (or apple juice)
Fresh lemon, several thin slices
2 cinnamon sticks
4–6 cloves, whole
2–3 star anise, whole
Generous grating of fresh nutmeg
Optional: Sugar, extra cinnamon sticks, brandy or spiced rum, caramel ice cream topping

Combine the first six ingredients in a large saucepan. Bring to a near boil, then lower heat, cover, and simmer gently for at least 30 minutes before serving. Taste and sweeten if needed.

Ladle into warm mugs, garnishing with a cinnamon stick and brandy or spiced rum, if desired. Stir in a spoonful of caramel for caramel apple cider.

Crafty Crafts

Ellen Dugan

Introduction to Arts and Crafts

In creating, the only hard thing is to begin:
A grass blade is no easier to make than an oak.
—James Russell Lowell

THE SABBAT-THEMED CRAFTS suggested in this almanac are fairly simple to do. Most can be made inexpensively and are suitable to make with your coven or your family. Watch for sales, use coupons, and remember: in the arts and craft world, seasonal decorations and supplies tend to show up at stores a season or two ahead of time.

In other words, come late July or early August you will find the biggest selection of fall flowers and accessories for your projects. Likewise for Yule, the best pieces of floral stems and ornaments and winter holiday crafts are likely to be found by late September or early October, before they are picked over.

Have fun putting the craft back in your witchcraft. And remember, it's not about how much money you spend on your arts and crafts, what's important is spending time creating something enchanting to help celebrate the wheel of the year with the ones you love.

Samhain Crafts

Theme of the Season: Completion
Colors: Orange, white, and black
Scents: Cinnamon, pumpkin, clove, and patchouli
Energy: Mystery and magick

Goth and Glittery Pumpkins

Supplies

A clean pumpkin, real or artificial. (An elaborately decorated artificial pumpkin can be used year after year.)

Newspaper to cover the work surface

Black dimensional fabric paint (puff paint)

Black glitter

Wet paper towels to neaten up any paint if necessary

A clean, flat surface where you can let this pumpkin dry undisturbed for several hours

A soft brush to brush off any loose glitter—AFTER the paint is dry

Instructions: Choose your pumpkin. Orange is a classic; however, there are fabulous shades of white and green pumpkins now. You could work with any of those—be creative and see what you can conjure up. Just choose a pumpkin with an interesting shape and a good-sized stem. Make sure the pumpkin is clean and dry.

With a ballpoint pen, lightly draw a spiderweb or other design, such as stars, flying bats, a pentagram, or abstract designs and swirls. Once the design is plotted out, set the pumpkin on a flat, clean, paper-covered surface, such as a table, so you can paint on it easily.

Using a bottle of black dimensional fabric paint (puff paint), follow the spiderweb lines or design lines that you have sketched on the pumpkin. Once you have the spiderwebs/design drawn on with the fabric paint, apply a generous amount of paint to the ridges of the pumpkin stem and onto the very top (around the stem area) of the pumpkin itself.

While the paint is still wet, sprinkle the black glitter over all of the painted areas. Pour any unused glitter back into the container. Let the paint dry completely (this takes several hours), then brush off any excess glitter with an old soft paintbrush.

Note: While I was making this project my cat jumped up in the middle of the kitchen table, and I dropped the half-painted pumpkin—an arts and crafts disaster! Paint smeared horribly, glitter flew, the cat bolted—it was a moment. However, I quickly took the pumpkin to the kitchen sink, grabbed some wet paper towels to wipe all the wet smeared puff paint off the pumpkin, and then dried the pumpkin on a kitchen towel. The pumpkin was now clean except for the spiderweb design that I had drawn on with a ballpoint pen. I could easily start again.

So if you make a huge mistake, don't worry. Just keep a few wet paper towels handy and neatly wipe up any goofs made with the puff paint. Dry the pumpkin thoroughly. Once I had everything cleaned up, I put the cat in a bedroom, shut the door, and started again. Lesson learned.

After I was finished with the project, and had the pumpkin safely up and out of kitty reach, I let the cat out. I did discover later that my little calico cat was sporting black glitter on her front paws. I wiped it up with a soft wet cloth, which she endured with only a sigh of feline disgust.

Variations on your pumpkins: You could use green puff paint and emerald glitter. That would be stunning on ghostly pale pumpkin. Or try deep purple on orange pumpkins in various festive Samhain designs. Or you could work with white and silver, and make your orange pumpkin look like it's been frosted, or glamoured up!

Lunar images or triple moon symbols would be stunning done in metallic silver on a white pumpkin. Or even a frosted magickal look on a green pumpkin in white puff paint and iridescent white glitter. Black glitter on a pale green pumpkin would be gothic and fabulous as well. See what you are inspired to create!

Time: One hour to design and paint

Drying time: One day

Cost: Between $10.00 and $20.00 depending on the pumpkin you purchase. I used a small artificial white pumpkin that I bought on sale for only $6.00. The puff paint cost $2.50 and the black glitter $2.50. Have fun and blessed be.

Samhain Witch Hat Personalized Place Cards

Here is a fun project for your coven or your family. This would even make a good Halloween project for a scout troop or a class project. These are fun and inexpensive and add an amusing, tongue-in-cheek touch to your Samhain festivities and dinner table!

Supplies

2-inch terra cotta flowerpots
Outdoor terra cotta paint (Patio Paint) in black, 2-ounce size
Outdoor terra cotta paint (Patio Paint) in white or yellow (optional)

Paintbrush

Sharpened pencil

Thin sheets of crafting foam (fun foam) in black and yellow

Scissors

Tacky glue (thick white craft glue)

Black iridescent glitter

Silver or white paint pen (for personalization)

Instructions: Paint the entire pot black and allow it to dry (about 5 minutes). You can choose to make white dots on the pot by dipping a sharpened pencil into white paint and dotting the surface. Or you could carefully paint a white crescent-moon shape or a star on the hat.

Trace a circle from the black foam about ½ inch wider all around than the pot opening. (Hint: Use an appropriate-sized lid or cup to get a perfect circle.) Cut it carefully out.

To make a buckle for the band of the hat, cut a small rectangle of yellow foam that measures about ⅛ inch taller than the band on the pot. Cut out a smaller rectangle from the center. Glue the foam buckle to the band. Allow the glue to dry.

Use the white or silver paint pen to write the name on the colored band if desired. Or for a little more pizzazz, draw out various spiral, moon, and star designs on the hat with the tacky glue and sprinkle with black glitter. (The glitter makes the hats look more like Witch hats.) Allow the glue and glitter to dry thoroughly before using for decorations on your Samhain/Halloween table.

Time to create: 30 minutes, plus 30 minutes to 2 hours of glue drying.

Cost: Under $12.00 for two Witch hat place cards—the little terra cotta pots cost about a dollar a piece. A 2-ounce bottle of patio paint costs $2.50, and it goes a long way. Sheets of fun foam are 99 cents apiece. I used the leftover glitter from the Goth pumpkin project, so you can keep this project very affordable if you are making several Witch hat place cards.

All One Family

Clea Danaan

ONE DAY MY DAUGHTER was peeling a hard-boiled egg. She said, "I wonder why eggs have so many parts: there is the shell, then the skin part, then the egg inside." I said, "Well, each part has its purpose." She turned to me and asked, "Do people have a purpose?" I smiled and said yes, that every person had a purpose, though we don't always know what that purpose is. "I thought so," she said, "but I just wondered." These are the kinds of everyday encounters that can instill in our children the sacredness of life and help launch deeper discussions. They also introduce the idea of metaphor; the egg is real, and it is also a story about purpose. Just like the Wheel of the Year.

The Wheel of the Year is a metaphor, a story about meaning, unfolding, growth, and journey. As a Pagan parent, I am always offering my children both the literal interaction with life (the garden, the egg) and the story (Samhain, magic, purpose) that will guide them as they grow physically, emotionally, and spiritually. Through play and daily living we live the Wheel.

The cycle of the planet around the Sun brings us through eight sabbats, each both a literal and a metaphorical guide to our spiritual journeys. To Pagans, Wiccans, Druids, and others who center their spiritual path in the Earth, the Wheel is our sacred text. As Pagan parents, we can draw on the spiral of the sabbats as we raise our children. It is a curriculum for life, a how-to guide for the evolution of our material and spiritual selves on Earth.

For many Pagans the Wheel begins with Samhain, as the Goddess descends into the underworld and the earth rests. Where I live in eastern Colorado, we often get our first snow around Samhain. The garden is done producing, the chickens are laying fewer eggs, and the summer bounty has already been preserved. I use Samhain as a resting point between the busyness of summer and fall and the bustle of Thanksgiving and Yule. Samhain has always been a favorite holiday of mine, and I enjoy sharing the traditions with my children.

In some ways Samhain is the easiest Pagan holiday to celebrate publicly because many of its symbols and practices have been embraced by secular culture for Halloween and the Catholic All Hallow's Eve. However, the American Halloween portrays death as a frightening, freakish specter. This puzzles my young daughter. She has grown up with the Wheel of the Year as danced by the garden. She knows that plants die to make new life. She has said goodbye to three beloved chickens. We discuss lovingly and matter-of-factly how three of her grandparents are spirits now, just as she was before she joined this family. To her, death is not frightening, just interesting, a phase of the journey about which she has many questions, but no fear.

One simple and powerful symbol of death is the annual show of leaves turning yellow, brown, and red, then falling to the ground where we play with them and pile them on the garden beds. My children rejoice in the colors of autumn as mums and pumpkins arrive at the grocery store and in the garden. We carve jack-o'-lanterns several times in October, for it is a craft and a ritual we all enjoy. Carving pumpkins and the other perennial ritual of costume-making provide doorways to discuss the meaning of the holiday. Gourd lanterns guide us and our ancestors through the literal and metaphorical darkness. Meanwhile, costumes and masks allow us to explore aspects of our inner selves. Many popular Halloween costumes also depict death and the ancestors. The season is all about going within to the darkness, into our shadows, and meeting ourselves and those who have gone before.

Children (and adults) came to understand part of who they are by exploring their roots, and Samhain can be a perfect time to delve into family history by sharing stories from the past, poring over photo albums, and even crafting a family tree. This can be simple as a big piece of poster board showing three or four generations, or you could begin a family history project using online or print genealogy resources. Include your poster or other projects on your family altar.

Samhain is also a time to discuss, depending on the ages of your children, the Halloween symbol of the Witch versus real Witches. My daughter and I tend to have these talks in the car en route to our various activities. We talk about how real Witches are normal people who believe that the earth is sacred (and discuss what sacred means) and who practice magic. Then, of course, we discuss magic. I stay away from lecturing; my daughter's natural curiosity and keen questions guide the conversation, and we move on when she changes the subject. As my children grow older, these talks will grow more in-depth, including the history of Halloween symbols and their meaning to us as Pagans. I always tie these discussions to real examples in her life, like the rituals we follow in the garden and at the dinner table.

For my family, our Samhain rituals include giving thanks and saying goodbye to the past year. We turn the compost, searching for bugs and discussing how the bugs eat the dead plants to make healthy soil, that will nourish plants that will die to nourish us. We thank the garden and the compost for their gifts to us. Other families might perform a Samhain ritual with an altar, salt, water, and invocation of gardening goddesses like Demeter or Proserpine. We cook pumpkin pie and bread, honoring how a plant can offer so many gifts and discuss how spices and plants have magical qualities: cinnamon and pumpkin offer protection, love, and abundance. We light candles at the dinner table and say prayers for our loved ones living and dead. As my children get older, I introduce new aspects of ritual, such as anointing candles or casting a circle. For now, most of our sacred practice is tied to an everyday activity like eating and gardening. Food is sacred and the land is sacred. These are the foundations of our path.

Children learn through doing, through play, and through stories. Samhain is a time of the fall-to-winter play, which tells the story of the Goddess entering the underworld. Some stories to share include the Greek myth of Persephone and Hades, the Sumerian myth of Innana's descent, and the Celtic story of the Morrigan. Some children may want to act out these stories; younger ones can do puppet shows while older youth may want to put on family pageants with elaborate costumes. Either would be fun activities for a Halloween party and can be followed up with discussion about the myths and where children see themselves in the stories.

Samhain is also a time of letting go, a lesson all of us revisit again and again. For Samhain, make rituals out of whatever you and your children are letting go of, be that a loved one, warm days, or a beloved summer shirt. Write poems or spells together that honor the importance of whatever you say goodbye to. Let it be an age-appropriate discussion of how it hurts to say goodbye and how that can be a new beginning at the same time. Light a candle and take time for reflection as you read your poem or recite your spell. Invite silence as well.

You also may want to read popular culture Halloween stories and discuss the symbology behind them if it's age-appropriate. Draw pictures of the season's sacred symbols—apples, pumpkins, masks, etc.—and discuss them. On Samhain night, make an ancestor altar together, with pictures of loved ones, sacred symbols, seasonal decorations, and a candle or two. Include your family tree. Introduce the meaning of the four elements and Spirit. Older children and teens may want to create altars for themselves, with seasonal images and symbols from their own lives like gifts from friends, poems they've written, and other treasures. Let the family or personal altars be a place to honor and discuss "darker" emotions like sadness, grief, or fear. These practices, as simple or complex as appropriate, will form the foundation for more complex learning and spiritual growth as your children grow through the spiraling Wheel of the Year.

Ritual: Make Friends with Death

Elizabeth Barrette

Setup: This ritual may be performed indoors or outdoors. If indoors, dim the lights in a room and clear a space large enough for the celebrants to circle around the altar table. If outdoors, start after dark in a clear space of yard or meadow. Ideally, build a fire in the center and set the altar table nearby; you may also want to use tiki torches at the quarters for extra light.

Cover the altar table with a black cloth. Arrange four candles (one each of gold, black, indigo, and white) in candleholders at the four quarters of the altar table, along with a lighter and a snuffer. Include symbols of death for each of the four spirits: a painting or a skull for Yamantaka, a skeleton or a top hat for Baron Samedi, a clay statuette or piece of lapis lazuli for Erishkegal, and a figure of a horse or bit of horsehair for the Pale Horse. Under the altar table, store an apple, a platter, a knife, a bottle of pomegranate juice, and a chalice.

Celebrants may wear ritual garb or simply dress in black. Symbols of the season, such as skeleton shirts or skull jewelry, are also appropriate. Everyone should form a circle around the altar table at the start of the ritual.

High Priestess: Welcome to our Samhain celebration. Please take a moment to center yourselves. Quarter Callers, please cast the circle, beginning with the East.

Caller for the East: *[Turns to face the East. Lights the East candle, saying:]*
I call to the East, breath of life, from first breath to last.
Breathe life into our ritual on this holy night.
Hail and well met!

All: Hail and well met!

Caller for the South: *[Turns to face the South. Lights the South candle, saying:]*
I call to the South, fires of the funeral pyre.
Lend your spark to guide the good spirits to our circle on this holy night.
Hail and well met!

All: Hail and well met!

Caller for the West: *[Turns to face the West. Lights the West candle, saying:]*
I call to the West, waters of the well of souls.
Draw up those with whom we would speak on this holy night.
Hail and well met!

All: Hail and well met!

Caller for the North: *[Turns to face the North. Lights the North candle, saying:]*
I call to the North, womb of the Earth.
Bear us in life as in death, and hold our circle on this holy night.
Hail and well met!

All: Hail and well met!

High Priest: *[Steps to the altar. Delivers the statement of intent.]*
Tonight is Samhain, when the veil between worlds grows thin.

We celebrate both life and death, for neither can exist without the other.

Our passage through this world begins at birth and ends at death, just as the warm season begins at Beltane and ends at Samhain.

Our passage through the otherworld begins at death and ends at birth, just as the cold season begins at Samhain and ends at Beltane.

The wheel always turns, and although we cannot see the whole at once, still we know that the unseen part of the Wheel is ever present.

Many voices whisper to us the fears of the unknown, and encourage us to dread the approach of death.

Around the world, the ways of the Wise teach us to face the hidden, embracing the mysteries instead of fleeing from their power.

Tonight we hail the spirits of Death and thank them for their guidance, that we may meet them with friendship rather than enmity when our journey through this world reaches its end:

In the East, Yamantaka; in the South, Baron Samedi;

in the West, Erishkegal; and in the North, the Pale Horse.

Let us welcome them into our celebration tonight.

High Priest steps back into the circle.

High Priestess: *[Steps to the altar and lifts the symbol of Yamantaka over her head, then says:]* I call upon Yamantaka, Conqueror of the Fear of Death. *[Replaces the symbol on the altar and steps back into the circle.]*

Yamantaka: *[Steps to the altar, saying:]*

I am Yamantaka, Conqueror of the Fear of Death.

I am the Enlightened One who defeats Yama, the fear-demon of mortality.

My many faces are terrible and my many arms bear fearsome weapons so that I may struggle against Yama as he oppresses human souls.

I dance my victory upon the back of panic.

Yet within my center lies calm, for I am an aspect of wisdom.

I have mastered my desire and released it; the force of attachment has no hold on me now.

I am a buddha, no longer trapped within *samsara*, the cycle of rebirth; it is my choice to visit the material world or the spirit world at will.

All of my lives are visible to me, as the spokes within a single wheel; because death has no power to rob me of my experiences, so too it lacks the power to sway my heart with terror.

Face me. Sit with me. Meditate upon my image.

I may look ugly, but I will show you how to defeat the fear-demon.

I will teach you that death is only a point on the great wheel.

High Priest: *[Steps to the altar and lifts the symbol of Baron Samedi over his head, then says:]* I call upon Baron Samedi, Gentleman Death. *[Replaces the symbol on the altar and steps back into the circle.]*

Baron Samedi: *[Steps to the altar, saying:]*

I am Baron Samedi, Gentleman Death. I am the skeleton in the top hat and tail coat, the inspiration for the *calacas*.

I am the driver of the black coach that waits around the corner.

To those who face death with dignity, I am the guide who opens the door at the bottom of the grave and leads them into the next world where the Ancestors wait.

Do not mistake me for a stuffy old god, though—I too was human once.

I know what it is to live on the edge, party hard, spit in the face of loss.

To those who wring out the last drop of satisfaction from life, who slide into the grave sideways with a drink in one hand and a smoke in the other, I am the designated driver waiting to take them Home after the party is over.

Understand that I have two faces, for I see two worlds—and the face I show to you will be the one you need, not necessarily the one you wish to meet.

Invite me into your home. Pour me a drink. We'll talk.

I may seem odd, but I'll be your ally on the Other Side.

I'll teach you that death is just a crossroad along the way.

High Priestess: *[Steps to the altar and lifts the symbol of Erish-kegal over her head, then says]:* I call upon Erishkegal, Queen of the Great Below. *[Replaces the symbol on the altar and steps back into the circle.]*

Erishkegal: *[Steps to the altar, saying:]*

I am Erishkegal, Queen of the Great Below.

I am the mistress who dwells in Irkalla, the House of Dust.

Here there are no shining gods and no fine trappings.

Here there are only columns of lapis and floors of clay, muddy water in the river that separates the worlds.

But here also there are no lies, no place for deception to hide.

What you see is barest truth, the pure white bones of the soul.

My gatekeepers greet those who approach and relieve their burdens.

The spirits of the dead descend to my realm for me to swallow, and I turn away none who come unto me.

The murdered, the starved, the plague-stricken, the frozen, the soldiers moaning away their end in forgotten fields, the widows and the widowers, the little children cut down too soon, the victims stoned by those who would not let them be as they are, the suicides, the abandoned heroes, the senescent elders—they come to me and I take them in, though I groan from the weight.

Oh, oh, my belly! Oh, oh, my liver! Oh, oh, my inside and my outside!

Hear me. Heed my cries. Know that you are not alone in your suffering.

I may sound like a demon, but I will swallow your pain in the end.

I will teach you that death is a doorway to sympathy and surcease.

High Priest: *[Steps to the altar and lifts the symbol of the Pale Horse over his head, then says]:* I call upon the Pale Horse, Bearer of Death. *[Replaces the symbol on the altar and steps back into the circle.]*

Pale Horse: *[Steps to the altar, saying:]*

I am the Pale Horse, Bearer of Death. I am the mount of myths and gods.

As the world has changed, I have changed with it, yet still I serve.

I have led the Wild Hunt through the woods of madness.

I have carried the fallen warriors over the bridge to Valhalla.

I have marched in parade ahead of the Danse Macabre.

I am storm and mist and shadow. I am bone and fire.

I am the sharpness of the blade and the truth in the bard's word.

The moon is in my hooves and the wind is in my teeth.

Whether I appear caparisoned in battle, or bare as a skeleton, still I remain the same spirit first painted upon cave walls.

Though the night be dark, I can see through it.

Though the forest be dense, I can pass by it.

Though the road wear thin, I can follow it.

Wherever you go, I can find you, no matter how lost you feel.

I will always come for you. I will never leave you alone.

Come. Reach out your hand. Touch my mane and know that I am here.

I may feel wild to those who do not know me, but I will wait for you to ride.

I will teach you that death is a journey, and joy in the running.

High Priestess: *[Steps to the altar and says:]*
Come forward and pay your respects to one or more of these honored representatives of death.

Praise them for their service, as we will all meet death in our own time.

Let them know that you wish to learn what they have to teach you.

[When all the celebrants have spoken and returned to their places, High Priestess steps back into the circle.]

High Priest: *[Steps to the altar and says:]*
Each year, souls depart from this world to the next.
Let us remember those who have gone beyond.
Speak the names of those you have lost,
and share a little of how they enriched your lives.

[High Priest begins by naming any public figures the group wishes to honor. Then the other celebrants name those they have lost personally. When everyone has spoken, High Priest steps back into the circle.]

High Priestess: Now we partake of cakes and ale, as a reminder to nourish our bodies and our spirits. Tonight we have chosen apple and pomegranate, two sacred fruits associated with both life and death.

High Priest: *[Steps to the altar. Places the apple on the platter and slices it horizontally, showing the star, saying:]* Hidden within the core of each apple lies a pentacle, symbol of magic and mystery.

[Cuts the apple into pieces and distributes them to the celebrants, saying:] "Taste the fruit of death in life." *[Returns to the circle.]*

High Priestess: *[Steps to the altar. Fills the chalice with pomegranate juice, saying,]* The pomegranate gives of its seeds, symbol of rebirth and power.

[Offers the chalice to each of the celebrants in turn, saying:] Taste the juice of life in death. *[Returns to the circle.]*

High Priest: *[Steps to the altar and says:]*
Thank you all for joining us here tonight.
May your bodies and your spirits be refreshed by our celebration.
[Lifts the symbol of the Pale Horse over his head, saying:]
I give thanks to the Pale Horse, Bearer of Death.
Return to your journey with our regards.
Hail and farewell!
[Replaces the symbol on the altar, as the Pale Horse rejoins the circle.]

All: Hail and farewell!

High Priestess: *[Steps to the altar and lifts the symbol of Erishkegal over her head, saying:]*
I give thanks to Erishkegal, Queen of the Great Below.
Return to Irkalla with our regards.
Hail and farewell!
[Replaces the symbol on the altar as Erishkegal steps back into the circle.]

All: Hail and farewell!

High Priest: *[Lifts the symbol of Baron Samedi over his head, saying:]*
I give thanks to Baron Samedi, Gentleman Death.
Return to the Other Side with our regards.
Hail and farewell!
[Replaces the symbol on the altar as Baron Samedi steps back into the circle.]

All: Hail and farewell!

High Priestess: *[Lifts the symbol of Yamantaka over her head, saying:]*

I give thanks to Yamantaka, Conqueror of the Fear of Death.

Return to your meditations with our regards.

Hail and farewell!

[Replaces the symbol on the altar as Yamantaka steps back into the circle.]

High Priest: Quarter Callers, please release the circle beginning with the North.

Caller for the North: *[Turns to face the North. Snuffs the North candle, saying:]*

I give thanks to the North, womb of the Earth.

Bear us onward in our walk through life to death.

Hail and farewell!

All: Hail and farewell!

Caller for the West: *[Turns to face the West. Snuffs the West candle, saying:]*

I give thanks to the West, waters of the well of souls.

Hold our tears of sorrow and joy until we rejoin those who have gone before.

Hail and farewell!

All: Hail and farewell!

Caller for the South: *[Turns to face the South. Snuffs the South candle, saying:]*

I give thanks to the South, fires of the funeral pyre.

Bank your coals until we meet again.

Hail and farewell!

All: Hail and farewell!

Caller for the East: *[Turns to face the East. Snuffs the East candle, saying:]*

I give thanks to the East, breath of life, from first breath to last.

Calm the air as we close our ritual tonight.
Hail and farewell!

All: Hail and farewell!

High Priestess: The circle is open, but unbroken.

All: Merry meet, and merry part, and merry meet again!

Adaptations

This ritual is designed for a medium-size group, but can be adapted for other contexts. There are ten roles: the High Priest and High Priestess, the four Quarter Callers, and the four representatives of Death. A smaller group can collapse some of the roles: High Priest and High Priestess can be done by one person; the four Quarter Callers may also call the representatives of Death. Condensed down to four people, each would call a quarter and a representative, while one or two would also do the High Priest(ess) roles. Note that if you're reducing the number of participants, you may want to omit the shifting of positions in and out of circle as individuals speak.

For a solitary ritual, you'll be reading all the lines yourself. You can leave out the "All" responses and most of the position shifts. Condense the naming of the dead into a single section of public and private people important to you.

For a large group ritual, really try to do it outdoors; if that's not possible, get a big open space like an empty meeting hall. A bonfire in the center is ideal. Instead of one big altar, set up four smaller altars, one at each quarter. Don't put candles on the ground where people will step on them; use tiki torches or keep the candles on tables. Don't wear solid black; break it up with white for visibility. Use tools large enough for people to see at a distance in dim lighting. Keep all the roles separate. The altars will help prevent celebrants from bunching up during the interaction phase. You may also want to use two or four sets of materials for the "cakes and ale" activity; switch those roles to the Quarter Callers if necessary, with each caller serving one quadrant of the circle.

Notes

Yule

Winter Solstice: Joy and Tradition

Kristin Madden

IMAGINE A PLACE WHERE blue twilight lasts for weeks in the fall. During winter, the sun may not rise above the horizon for more than a month, though occasional iridescent clouds seem to glow from within during the few hours of daylight. On Winter Solstice, you may experience the Aurora Borealis twisting and crackling its way across the sky. Snow covers the ground and temperatures often hover between −10 and −20 degrees F. Schnapps and Jul glögg may help to keep you warm. Real reindeer pull sleds, and you can feel the ground shake from more than a mile away when a herd approaches.

These are the images that were passed on to me from my Swedish and Sami relatives (the Sami are indiginous peoples inhabiting the northernmost parts of the Scandinavian countries and a small portion of Russia). The ongoing darkness and cold of winter was very real to them and, each year, their stories spurred my imagination. Winter Solstice, as the harbinger of growing light to come, was a time of great celebration.

Most of us understand the generalities of the Winter Solstice season. We know that, because of the earth's tilt, this is the shortest day and longest night. We have been taught that this is the first day of winter. We read that cultures around the world have midwinter celebrations, often involving a "child of light," a promise of better things to come. We can name a half-dozen or so winter deities and recite a long list of seasonal symbols. And we get the reasons behind this on an intellectual and an emotional level. Yet, something deep within us remembers the challenges our ancestors had to face, particularly during cold, dark winters.

While many of us love winter recreation and snow, we also love to return to a comfortable home and be able to enjoy a warm meal, and perhaps a hot beverage. For most of us, shorter days have little impact on our daily lives. We have indoor plumbing, temperature-controlled environments, and an abundance of food throughout the year. Few of us, as adults, rely on family to any real extent and many people live thousands of miles away from their blood relations. Perhaps this is why so many of our modern celebrations have become rather hollow. With busy modern lives, it can be easy to simply pick up a card or send an email gift certificate and get on with the seemingly endless to-do list.

In my opinion, these connections to tradition and community are some of the greatest values that the holidays offer us. Winter Solstice, in particular, brings us back to our roots and a long tradition of sharing with our communities. Yuletide is an ideal, filled with families coming together to share in a joyful time filled with fabulous feasts and gifts of everything we could dream of. No matter what your religious tradition, this season is the culmination of another long year and the promise of a better tomorrow.

Take a moment to consider your Yule season traditions. What is most special to you about this time of year and why? You may have a very traditional set of practices handed down through generations. Or perhaps your "traditions" have developed within your own lifetime. Are your Winter Solstice customs limited to spiritual observances, or do they encompass a wider part of your life at this time of year?

As a child, my Jul (Yule) was based firmly in far northern Scandinavian customs. Our food and music was predominantly Swedish, but most of our rituals and decorations were often handed down from the Sami side of the family. I have wonderful memories of family, dancing, feasts, gifts, and countless stories of the ancestors from those years. It was the perfect combination of spirituality, community, and good old American commercialism. I was, after all, an American kid.

My husband and I have developed our own Winter Solstice traditions that we continue to create with our son. Our combined cultural heritage is meshed with more personal symbols and practices. These days, our teenaged son puts up the holiday tree and decorates it with ornaments we have made, along with gift ornaments from friends and family. Each ornament has a story or other memory associated with it. Altars and additional decorations are placed around the living room, and these have their stories as well. As you can imagine, reminiscing greatly increases the time it takes to decorate. The beauty of this is that the decorations are not just for show, nor are they merely pretty things purchased from a store. They have great meaning for us, as individuals and as a family. The process of decorating for a holiday becomes a renewal of the bonds of family.

Some of these traditions have found their way into the Yule ritual at the end of this section. While it is difficult to comprehend the depth of any tradition without having been raised in that culture, I do believe that some degree of knowledge regarding their stories and origins offers a deeper connection to these practices and may make them more effective for the practitioner. In the hopes that you can better understand and use this ritual, I would like to share some of those stories with you.

Evergreens are strewn about the altar. In many areas, these are the only remaining signs of life in the plant world at this time of year. Evergreens are a part of every great commercial holiday tale. It's almost a requirement that a winter holiday story must have snow and pine trees. And who can forget Charlie Brown's little Christmas tree that just needed love? In addition, the festival of Beiwe, a Sami sun goddess, occurs in Finland on the solstice. Among other things, Beiwe brings green plants back for reindeer to feed upon.

At the center of the altar sits the Yule log. Versions of this can be found in several European cultures. When I was a child, we used a piece taken from the freshly cut Christmas tree and burned it in the fireplace after the solstice. Now we have a piece of birch that is reused year after year, sometimes with the addition of new ribbons or boughs that have naturally fallen from evergreens.

A brass ring may seem like an odd addition to a Yule custom. Brass rings can be found in the ancient bear ceremonies and the drum divination techniques of the Sami people. In some areas, a brass ring would be hung in the opening of the *lavvu* (similar to a teepee) to catch and hold the light of the solstice moon. Not only does this connect us with our ancestors and with other people participating in the same custom, we love the idea that this special shiny ring holds a bit of that moonlight, as well as the growing sunlight, warming our home and energizing our lives. In modern vernacular, grabbing the brass ring implies winning a prize or gaining blessings. It is a symbol of luck and fortune that we take into the new year with us.

A wooden bowl filled with water or birdseed is my adaptation of an ancient tradition, not limited to the Sami or Swedes, of leaving offerings to the spirits and the "little people." In some areas, Sami people filled birch bark boats with fruit and other foodstuffs to appease the spirits. In Sweden, a bowl of special porridge is left out for the *Jultomte*, or the *tomten*, a type of fairy folk.

My grandfather was a state park ranger for 32 years and I followed him everywhere, as often as I could. He taught me to walk quietly and gently on the land, with great respect for all living things. From time to time, old superstitions were woven into his teachings for me. For example, whistling around Christmas Eve can be dangerous because it attracts the attention of the *stallo*, a kind of giant. We took our roles as stewards very seriously. Our tradition of putting out offerings of food and water was as much rooted in the idea of stewardship as it was an appeasement to the winter spirits. The offerings were always something that could be used safely by our local wildlife.

Because this is the time of greatest darkness in our world, it is an appropriate time to explore the darkness within each of us and seek illumination to guide us through those challenges. In a ritual setting, we embark on a traditional shamanic journey, with the addition of a little modern magic to solidify and manifest the experience. There is another method of working with your shadows that I have been using in my classes around the country for many years. It is a fairly simple, yet powerful, walk. While you might be more comfortable doing it during warmer months, the bracing chill of winter makes this exercise all the more powerful. Be sure to take care of yourself afterwards with a hot bath or a warm mug of eggnog.

Shadow Walk

When possible, perform this exercise out in nature in an area where you feel safe and able to freely express your feelings. Choose a direction and begin walking slowly. As you walk, call to mind a time when your actions were motivated by fear or anger. This may have been a time when you snapped at someone, agreed to an unethical act, or were too afraid to act when you felt you should have.

Permit yourself to fully experience anything that may come up. As you walk, allow memories, thoughts, actions, and nonactions to flow freely. Give yourself permission to express the emotions that come up and move through them. Do not become mired in guilt or regret. Experience, express, and move on.

When you feel you are ready to end this exercise, or feel a beneficial change in your energy, focus your attention on something nearby that attracts you and walk over to it. Fully appreciate this object. Allow your being to be filled with the wonder of its existence. Thank this object and focus your attention on something else that attracts you. Continue to repeat this process of appreciation and gratitude until you feel happy and connected to all things.

❧

Most modern people associate winter holidays with gifts, at least in Western culture. You can see Christmas and Hanukkah decorations in stores well before the American Thanksgiving feasts. Sadly, this Season of Giving has become very commercial and less focused on gifts from the heart that require any real thought. The Give-Away part of our Winter Solstice ritual is an attempt to return to the beauty and magic of the season.

At some point in our history, all of our ancestors needed their communities in order to survive. Certainly, this was true for my ancestors above the Arctic Circle, but somewhere in your heritage, your forebears had similar struggles. The truth is that many modern people continue to have those same struggles but often without a strong and supportive community behind them. That is where the Yule Give-Away comes in. The idea is to remember that we are all connected and we need each other to survive. Our prayer is that everyone involved will share in that Winter Solstice promise of a happy and healthy new year. Collecting donations and ritually blessing them is our way of magically contributing to the cycle of blessings throughout our world.

As a prelude to the Yule feast, we end our ceremony with our own version of cakes and ale. It is very similar to how some of my native American friends from Alaska end their sweat lodge ceremonies, which is not surprising, given the similarities among circumpolar traditions. We pass around a plate of salmon and berries, offering thanks to our ancestors, spirit allies, spirits of place, and all those that shared in our ceremony. In this way, sacred space is opened and we return to normal awareness, ready to move on to the real feast.

Like the presents we share, the feast is a Give-Away to each other. In the ritual, we deal with the macrocosms of the spirit realm and the global community. During the feast, we bring all of that home to the microcosm of family and friends. Once again, this simple act strengthens the bonds of relationship and embodies the promise of a bountiful new year. In my family, the feast is a smorgasbord of traditional and modern favorites. Dessert is also a mix of old and new but the Risgryngrot is always a part of it. This is a special dish, traditionally a rice porridge, that bears within it that promise of joy to come. One bowl contains either a raisin or an almond. The person that finds the surprise gets to make a wish.

Winter Solstice celebrations can be as elaborate or as simple, as modern or as traditional, as you choose. Like the other holidays, this one must hold meaning and joy for you in order to feed your soul and keep you connected to your spiritual life. Whatever type of celebration you choose, it is likely that it incorporates at least a few of these same seasonal meanings. Winter Solstice is all about navigating through the darkness, remembering that we need each other to find our way, and emerging into the light, stronger both as an individual and as a community. Through our Winter Solstice rituals, we continue the circle of light and life throughout our world.

Celestial Sway

Fern Feto Spring

THE DARK OF THE year takes place at the dark of the Moon this Winter Solstice. As we stand witness at the crossroads, celebrating the birth of the Sun King, we are encouraged to journey deeply inwards, following the thread of the returning light. A New Moon in Capricorn follows the Winter Solstice on December 24. This lunation offers both opportunity and surprises with two outer planets showing up to provide a little excitement. Lucky Jupiter, in Taurus, forms a harmonious trine to the moon, and the trickster planet Uranus creates tension and excitement with a square aspect with the moon. Celebrations with friends and family create a chance to plant the seeds of new beginnings and pave the way for exciting changes ahead.

Jupiter's direct station in Taurus occurs on December 25, heralding a Solstice season of abundance and earthy goodness. This is a great year to spend extra time relaxing, as the sign of Taurus brings many opportunities for sensual pleasures. A winter walk in the woods followed by a delicious feast will help you to honor the sign of the bull, as you surround yourself with all the bounty of Mother Earth.

The outer planets cooperate with this pleasure-loving solstice energy as Saturn, the planet of reality, structure, and form, is in a roughly trine position to Neptune, which rules spirit, flow, and acceptance. This cooperative alignment between the physical realm and the unseen realm help us to more deeply understand how to integrate the worlds of spirit and matter during this darkest time of the year. Solstice 2011 presents us with plenty of opportunities to ground our spiritual work in the real world, allowing us to see more clearly the benefits of cultivating our relationship with the divine.

The season continues in January with a Full Moon in Cancer on January 9. This Full Moon welcomes the start of the New Year with a heightened awareness of our dual roles at home and at work. A trine to Mars in Virgo preceding the Full Moon emphasizes the need to move back out in the world, returning our energy to our external plans and projects. As the light of the year grows, we also begin to gain momentum, setting goals and completing tasks that may have been forgotten over the holiday season.

Mercury's transition into the sign of Capricorn just before the Full Moon helps to focus our minds, giving us a greater ability to see the big picture and offering the chance for us to communicate in more practical and efficient ways. Mercury in Capricorn encourages us to plan ahead, forming long-term goals and ambitions.

Venus moves into Pisces on January 14. The planet of love and resources is now in a sign where it is considered "exalted," which allows it to operate from a place of great power and strength. Venus in Pisces expresses love from a wellspring of compassion and acceptance, welcoming all into its encompassing embrace. Forgiveness and understanding are possible now, as the barriers that appear to separate us disappear and we come to a greater understanding of what "one love" really means. As Venus enters Pisces, she forms an energizing sextile aspect to Jupiter in Taurus, indicating that opportunities to expand our resources are available now if we put in the work and effort necessary to take advantage of these potential gifts from the universe.

New Moon in Capricorn

The New Moon in Capricorn, which occurs two days after the Winter Solstice, on December 24, heralds a time of new goals and plans for the future. We can make the most of this New Moon energy by setting intentions that focus our energy and help us to leave behind anything that stands in the way of moving forward. A trine from Jupiter and a square from Uranus give this lunation an extra "sparkle" that make it a prime Moon for doing Solstice magic.

New Moon in Capricorn Ritual

Use the communal energy of the Winter Solstice to infuse your magical workings with appreciation for all the special people in your life. As you join together with loved ones to welcome the birth of the sun, draw on the New Moon to plant the seeds of new beginnings. Gift-giving magic is a great way to maximize the abundance of the Jupiter trine and navigate any unexpected events that arise from the Uranus square. As you plan your gifts this year, take some time to charge them with this potent New Moon energy. Since the New Moon actually occurs on Christmas Eve at 1:06 pm, you may want to plan ahead, so you have time to infuse your gifts with magical intention directly after the New Moon (or within eight hours).

You can easily charge your offerings by gathering your gifts together before distributing them and focusing your intentions of love, joy, abundance, and peace (or whatever you feel is most appropriate). To further build the energy, you may want to sing festive songs or even create a special chant that you sing as you wrap and prepare your offerings. Light a candle as you work, which will harness the power of fire and help your wishes manifest with ease. You can also write blessings that reflect what you wish for each person and include these as part of your ritual. As you direct your energy and intentions toward these offerings of love and spirit, you can be sure that you will receive what you have given out three-fold in the days to come.

Full Moon in Cancer

A Full Moon in Cancer lights up the New Year's sky on January 9, bringing our awareness to the polarity between work and family, public and private, inner and outer, and our home environment versus our role in the world. Though our hearts may be with our loved ones now and we'd rather stay home and nest, the pull of the outer world is strong as planetary forces urge us to get back to work and plan for the future. Mars in Virgo supports the Sun in Capricorn with a flowing trine aspect, as these two earth signs work together to encourage us to focus on our goals and pay attention to the details.

Venus in Pisces

Venus in Pisces starts the new year off right on January 14 with an infusion of gentle love and compassion. You can greet the beginnings of 2012 and honor this planetary shift by focusing on opening your heart and cultivating forgiveness in your life. Venus placed in the sign of the fishes helps us to forget our differences with others and blur the boundaries that separate us.

Venus in Pisces Ritual

As Venus moves into Pisces, make a list (on biodegradeable paper), of all those who you have bitterness and resentment toward. Place this paper into the ocean or other large body of water, asking for help and blessings from the spirits, gods, and goddesses of the sea. Ask them to gently help you to release and let go of any anger, pain or memories that are preventing you from going forward with your life. Remember that you don't need to forget any harm that others have caused and that self-protection and caution can still be maintained, but that you can let go of and release any emotions that may be stopping you from moving on.

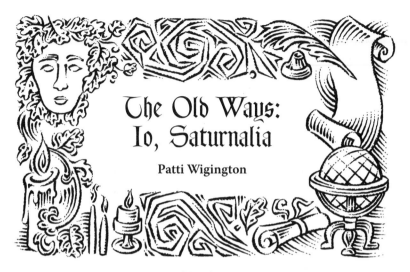

The Old Ways:
Io, Saturnalia

Patti Wigington

NO ONE THREW A party quite like the citizens of ancient Rome, and from the records they left us, it looks like they'd have a festival at the drop of a hat. Nearly every deity had his or her own celebration each year, so Rome was a constant buzz of celebration, worship, and festivities. One of the most popular festivals each year was Saturnalia, and it's one that has survived in the record books as well, so we're able to learn quite a bit about what it meant, and how it was celebrated.

Saturn was one of the many Roman agricultural deities. Typically associated with sowing and animal husbandry, Saturn was seen as a righteous and benevolent real-life ruler from long ago, who taught the people of Rome's seven hills how to till the ground, plant crops, and reap the benefits of the harvest. While Saturn reigned, there was no war, no bloodshed, no infighting between the tribes that lived in the mountains. Everyone was equal under Saturn's guidance, and he was known as a good god and a kindly king. At last he vanished, and shrines were erected in his memory.

Later, during the golden age of Rome's classical days, Saturn was revived as a god of feasting and revelry. His festival, which consisted of seven days of merrymaking, took place not only in the homes of Rome's citizens, but in the streets and public squares. Celebrations often got out of hand, and there was all sorts of debauchery. In fact, by the time Christianity moved into Rome during the reign of Emperor Constantine, the word Saturnalia was used to describe an orgy, rather than a specific holiday.

Businesses typically closed down for Saturnalia celebrations, starting on December 17, and court proceedings were held only on a very limited basis. Like many other Roman festivals, there was a great deal of feasting going on during Saturnalia. Fresh foods from the winter fields were brought in, and gifts were exchanged with friends and family. Pliny the Younger tells us that although these presents were small, they were often useful items such as dice, combs, writing tablets, scented oils, cups, and even the occasional hen or pig.

In addition to banquets and gifts, Roman citizens decorated their homes in honor of Saturn. Boughs of greenery were hung over doors to welcome guests, and fragrant branches were strewn about the homes of masters and slaves alike. Tin shapes were cut out and hung from trees and bushes—a precursor to today's Christmas tree ornaments. In an activity that seems to have been a forerunner to today's Christmas caroling, naked groups of revelers would roam the streets during Saturnalia, singing the praises of the god himself, and clapping their hands.

Sacrifices were made in Saturn's name at his shrines—typically white animals such as ewes, cattle, or goats. There is some conjecture that human sacrifices may have been made as well during Rome's Imperial age, although it was illegal by that time.

Sir James G. Frazer points out in *The Golden Bough* that festivals that fell at the end of the year were often "used to observe an annual period of license, when the customary restraints of law and morality were thrown aside." Certainly, one of the best-known aspects of Saturnalia was the opportunity given to slaves by their masters for this short period each December.

Rome's republic was built on a very rigid class system. There were citizens and there were slaves. A citizen was someone (typically male, although a few women held limited citizenship) who was afforded high social status and all the rights that came along with it. Citizens could vote, own land, hold office, and join the Roman legions. Slaves, on the other hand, were property. They could be bought, sold, traded, or beaten at the whim of their master and mistress. However, most Roman citizens understood that well-treated slaves were far more productive—and less likely to rebel—than those who were abused.

During Saturnalia, the roles of master and slaves were reversed for one glorious week. The lines between the classes were done away with, and slaves sat at tables with their masters, spoke to them like social equals, wore the red woolen pileus hats of freemen, and did as little work as they could get away with. Masters set aside their formal togas and wore casual clothes instead. They allowed slaves to speak as insolently as they pleased without fear of punishment.

Interestingly, although the roles of slaves and masters were reversed in outward appearance, Tacitus writes that there were still some fairly strict boundaries. While a citizen might serve food and drink to his slave during Saturnalia, the meal was still prepared by domestic slaves in the kitchen. A slave might wear the cast-off clothes of his master for that week, but was always aware of his rightful place in the order of things. Keeping these limitations in place allowed Roman citizens to maintain their power and control. No one wanted their slaves getting wild ideas about the benefits of freedom and citizenship.

Reigning over all the mayhem and celebration of Saturnalia was the Lord of Misrule. This figure was supposed to be a representative of Saturn in his guise as the benevolent, merry king. Ostensibly, he was chosen to be honored by all during the week of Saturnalia, indulging in every possible vice the Romans could come up with. However, Frazer points out a less happy interpretation of the role. He says that Roman soldiers at Durostorum celebrated Saturnalia by choosing a young man to be Lord of Misrule, and then dressed him in the finest clothes. For thirty days, they plied him with food, wine, and women, and then once the festival was over, slit his throat on the altar of Saturn. Tacitus writes that the Lord of Misrule was a household position, and that each home had its own Lord to order people around during Saturnalia.

As the Roman civilization fell, festivals like Saturnalia came to a halt. Christian rulers like Constantine declared such activities as too barbaric and Pagan to participate in, and for a time, Saturnalia was cancelled completely. However, during the Middle Ages, Winter Solstice festivals began to come back into fashion. Italy's Carnevale may owe some of its customs to Saturnalia traditions. A few British winter celebrations incorporate a Lord of Misrule even today, although in this day and age one would hope the "merry monarch" isn't being sacrificed at the end of the party.

In ancient Rome, the traditional Saturnalia greeting is "Io (*e-o*), Saturnalia!" So, the next time someone wishes you a Merry Christmas or some other variant on Happy Holidays, feel free to offer back an Io, Saturnalia! After all, back in the days of Rome's glory, it was Saturn who was the reason for the season.

For Further Reading:

Sir James George Frazer, *The Golden Bough*, 1890.

Pliny the Younger, *Epistles*.

Lucian of Samosata, *The Complete Works of Lucian*. Translated by H. W. Fowler, 1905.

Tacitus, *Historiae* (Histories).

Feasts and Treats

Susan Pesznecker

IN MILLENNIA PAST, OUR ancestors feasted as they marked the winter solstice and rejoiced in the promise of light's return. The menu, below, is a Yule feast. Set the table with a multitude of candles; turn the lights low and imagine yourself back with the Ancient Ones, celebrating the ebbing darkness!

Roast Prime Rib with Yorkshire Pudding

Prime rib is pricey, but as a once-a-year treat, there's nothing better. Adding to the sumptuousness is a pan of crispy Yorkshire pudding, a mega-popover baked in the beef juices.

Prep time: 20 minutes (plus time for the roast to come to room temperature before cooking)

Cook time: 2½ hours

Serves: 6–8

Notes: Use a roasting pan and rack, and use a meat thermometer for best results. Internal temperature is the most accurate way to check doneness; going by time alone can yield a disappointing result.

4-rib (9–10½ lb.) prime rib roast
Pepper
3 eggs
¾ cup flour
¾ cup milk
½ teaspoon salt

Leave roast at room temperature for 2 to 4 hours *before* roasting. This helps the meat roast evenly.

Preheat to 450 degrees F. Set the oven rack one setting above the lowest.

Place the roast—ribs down and fat layer up—on a roasting rack and set in a roasting pan. Sprinkle liberally with pepper.

Put the meat in the oven and roast/sear 15 minutes; then, reduce heat to 325 degrees F. Total cooking time will be about 1¾ to 2¼ hours, or about 20 minutes per pound.

While the meat roasts, prepare the Yorkshire pudding batter. In a medium bowl, blend the eggs, flour, milk, and salt. Whisk until smooth then return to the refrigerator to chill. (Ideally, do this 24 hours in advance: colder batter will puff up better in the hot oven.)

Begin testing with the thermometer about 45 minutes before you believe the meat will be finished. An internal temperature of 125 degrees F indicates a rare roast, 135 degrees F medium rare, 145 degrees F medium, and 155 degrees F well-done. (Note: cooking a gorgeous piece of beef like this well-done is arguably a sacrilege!)

Remove the roast from the oven and tent with foil. Make Yorkshire pudding.

Increase oven heat to 425 degrees F. Spoon about ½ cup pan drippings (beef fat and juices) into in a 13 × 9-inch glass baking dish. Place in oven to heat for 5 to 8 minutes.

When the glass pan is smoking hot, remove it from the oven and swirl to coat with melted fat. Pour in the chilled Yorkshire batter and return to the oven to bake for 20 minutes. The pudding will puff up and brown nicely.

Slice the beef and serve with squares of roasted pudding.

Twice-Baked Potatoes

Simple and delicious, these can be made ahead and provide a nice complement to the rich roast meat.

Prep time: 15 minutes
Cook time: 1½ hours
Serves: 6

6 baking potatoes
6 tablespoons butter, melted
½ cup sour cream, room temperature
½ cup heavy cream, warmed
2–3 tablespoons fresh chives, chopped
Salt and pepper
Toppings: grated cheese, crumbled cooked bacon, sliced green onions

Wash the potatoes and poke each one 2 to 3 times with a knife. Bake in a preheated 450 degree F oven for 1 hour.

Cool potatoes for about 15 minutes. Cut in half, scooping the flesh into a large bowl. Save the shells/skins.

Mash the potatoes with the butter and sour cream. Add hot cream as needed for a soft, fluffy consistency. Stir in chives and add salt and pepper to taste.

Pile the mashed potatoes into the shells and add toppings as desired. At this point, either bake at 350 degrees F for 20 to 30 minutes, or cool, wrap, and chill for later use. To reheat, bring to room temperature for an hour then bake as above.

Rumpleminze Pie

This variation on the traditional Grasshopper Pie is pale pink and light as air—a perfect ending to the feast.

Prep time: 30 minutes
Serves: 8

5 tablespoons melted unsalted butter
1½ cups finely crushed chocolate wafer crumbs
30 large marshmallows
⅔ cup whole milk
1 cup heavy cream
1½ ounces white crème de cacao
1½ ounces Rumpleminze (peppermint liqueur)
Red food coloring
Garnishes: grated chocolate, chocolate syrup

Combine butter and chocolate crumbs and press into a 9-inch pie plate. Bake at 325 degrees F for 10 minutes. Cool thoroughly.

Combine milk and marshmallows slowly in a double boiler over hot water. Stir until completely smooth. Remove from heat and cool to room temperature.

Whip the cream; fold into marshmallow mixture. Add the liqueurs and 1 drop of red coloring; blend well. Pile into pie crust and freeze. Thaw 10 to 15 minutes before cutting and serving. Garnish as desired.

Eggnog

"Nog" is British slang for strong ale. In the time before refrigeration, alcohol was used to extend milk's shelf life. This nog is rich, decadent, and warming.

Prep time: 20 minutes
Serves: 8+

6 eggs, separated
¾ cup sugar, divided
2 cups heavy cream
4 cups milk
2 cups brandy or bourbon
1 tablespoon vanilla
Freshly ground nutmeg

In a large bowl, beat the egg whites with ¼ cup sugar until soft peaks form.

In a second large bowl, beat the cream until thick.

In a medium bowl, beat the egg yolks with ½ cup sugar until thick.

Add the cream to the yolks then fold this mixture into the egg whites. Gently blend in the milk, alcohol, and vanilla. Pour into a serving bowl and chill in freezer for at least 2 hours before serving.

To serve, grate nutmeg over the bowl.

Bonus: New Year's Gin Fizzes

Welcome in the new calendar year with this hair-of-the-dog drink—served at breakfast in my family!

Prep time: 10 minutes
Serves: 4

½ cup light cream
½ cup gin
½ cup orange juice
1 teaspoon lemon juice
½ teaspoon lemon zest
¼ cup sugar
3 egg whites
2 cups cracked ice

Combine all ingredients in a blender. Blend on high speed until thick and frothy. Serve in chilled highball glasses.

Crafty Crafts

Ellen Dugan

Theme of the Season: Birth and illumination
Colors: Red, green, white, silver, and gold
Scents: Cranberry, pine, bayberry, and cinnamon
Energy: Wonder, peace, and family

Polished Yule Ornaments

Plain glass ornaments are given a glowing coating of color by using... are you ready? Metallic and glittery fingernail polish!

Supplies

Six glass ball ornaments, whatever color you desire
Metallic or glitter fingernail polish in your chosen colors
Satin ribbon to hang the Yule ornaments on the tree
String to hang the ornaments up while they dry
A curtain rod or plant hook for drying

Instructions: To begin, figure out a spot to hang the ornaments to allow them to dry and not smudge the polish.

Tie a loop through the ornament hanger using sturdy string. Then after you finish painting it, you can hang it up in your chosen spot and allow it to dry, *before* you add it to your Yule tree or other decor.

Hold onto to the metal top of the ornament—where the hanger is—while you paint the ornament. Next, decide what design to paint on the ornament: sacred spirals, stars, swirls, pentagrams, dots, stripes, etc.

Using the brush included with the fingernail polish, paint the ornament. You can cover the whole ball or just work on the desired designs. The polish might pull some of the paint off the ornament, but that's okay. It will only make the silver show through and it will look more unique.

Consider creating silver ornaments with white sparkling polish or white ornaments with silver and gold polish. Various shades of reds and greens and metallic tones are gorgeous, too! For example, think of a red ornament with a shade of burgundy glittery polish. Think tone on tone, contrast, and color. Be creative and make these one of a kind and magickal for your home's décor.

Keeping the polish in thin smooth coats will ensure faster drying time and fewer smudges. After you have finished painting the ornament, carefully hang the ornament by the string and allow it to dry. Leave it alone and untouched for at least 30 minutes.

Once the ornament is completely dry, remove the string, and thread it through a pretty satin ribbon in any color you wish. Now add it to your Yule tree or to your mantle decorations. You could even arrange these one-of-a-kind polished ornaments in a large clear glass bowl or apothecary jar and use them for a centerpiece on your mantle, a shelf, a coffee table or the kitchen table.

Time to create: 5 minutes per ornament

Drying time: 30 minutes to one hour

Cost: Generally $10.00 to $20.00 for six polished ornaments A box of six glass ornaments will run around $6.00. Look for inexpensive nail polish in glittery colors. Also, before you purchase any fingernail polish for the project, see what you have at home.

A Victorian Kissing Ball for Yuletide

A Victorian "Kissing Ball" creates a very festive mood. These decorated balls of evergreens, holly and herbs—and sometimes a sprig of mistletoe—are a festive decoration that invites kisses and good cheer.

Originally made of fresh mistletoe, kissing balls were hung in the parlor or entryways of the house to remind guests to share the love at the holidays. Today, a kissing ball can be made with boxwood, fragrant rosemary, evergreens or holly, and ivy. It's up to you.

Personally I would go with whatever plant material you can get your hands on most affordably. Also, you should note that real holly berries and or mistletoe foliage and berries are, while traditional, in fact, toxic. If you have small children or pets, you may want to either use a pretty *artificial* sprig of mistletoe, or artificial red berries to promote safety.

Supplies

Greenery: Suggested greenery—boxwood, pine, rosemary, spruce, holly, and ivy

1 green Styrofoam ball about the size of a softball

Floral wire

2 yards of festive red Yuletide ribbon

Scissors

3 or 5 small clusters of artificial holly berries clusters to add some color. (If you use artificial berries you won't have to worry about pets or children accidentally eating them if they fall off the kissing ball.)

Wire cutters or heavy pruners to snip the stems and wires

Low temperature glue gun and glue sticks

Floral pins or plain straight pins to anchor the ribbon into the foam

A small silver bell (optional)

Instructions: Gather the greenery, which you may be able to do on a walk through your own yard by pruning a branch or two. If not, you may want to visit a local florist for some small fresh clippings or

check a holiday tree lot. They trim off live branches and may have some cast off pieces of evergreen that you can get for a song!

If you want your kissing ball to last indefinitely, or you are allergic to pine (like I am), you can purchase artificial greenery. That way you have the kissing ball to reuse every year.

To begin, stick the stems into the green stryofoam ball—you do not want to have any bare spots—so you will be using a lot of greenery. **Tip:** Don't pull the stems in and out of the Stryofoam, it will make big holes that nothing will fill in. Put the stem in and leave it. You can always trim the outer ends off a bit shorter *after* it's in place. Take your time and completely cover the surface of that foam ball. It should look a bit shaggy and wild. Don't bonsai-trim the ball to death—just go for a rough circular shape.

Once your ball is full (and trimmed if necessary), you will want to begin with the embellishments. Add a few small clusters of artificial berries and tuck them into the ball. Use floral pins, hot glue, or straight pins to secure them.

Next, using your ribbon, wrap it vertically around the ball to meet at the top center. Overlap the ends of the ribbon on top of the ball and hot glue it in place. Secure the ribbon with floral pins or straight pins. Tie a small bow and pin that directly into the top center of the overlapping ribbon. Be sure it is firmly secured. This bow will become your hanger. Or you may wish to use a piece of cording or a piece of floral wire. Pin this bow down and use one of the loops from the bow to hang the ball up from the ceiling, doorframe, archway, or chandelier.

If you wish, add a small silver bell to the bottom of the kissing ball and let it dangle. Happy Yuletide!

Time to create: 1 hour

Cost: $15.00 to $25.00. The cost of this project can go down dramatically if you use fresh greenery from your own yard. Also, it's easy to catch a sale on floral supplies, sprays of artificial holiday greenery, and ribbon at the arts and crafts store.

All One Family

Clea Danaan

YULE HONORS THE REBIRTH of the light, the rebirth we each go through ourselves daily, monthly, yearly, and as souls on an infinite journey toward non-dual consciousness. It is our own light that is reborn at Yule. On the longest night of the year, we turn to our deepest comfort: family. Then as the sun is reborn, we too feel a lightening and a return of hope.

This is the time to tell stories around the fire, to rejoice at having made it through the darkness once again, and to make plans as a family for the year to come. I like to make resolutions now rather than at the Gregorian New Year; the light is returning and I feel alive in my own rebirth. Keep in mind this season the image of rebirth. What does it mean to you? To your children? What does the returning sunlight symbolize for you? By focusing on rebirth and the return of ourselves into the light, we resist getting sucked into the spending frenzy of the holidays. This is an antidote to the seasonal depression that affects thousands this time of year.

It can be hard, in a culture that so worships stuff, to spend little and focus on the heart. We like to give things, lots of things, piles of wrapped gifts and cool treats and fabulous trinkets. We also love to get a bunch of great stuff, and so do our kids. I think, though, that we do our children a disservice when we focus on the size of the box, the pile under the tree, and the credit card bill. In regard to all spending, my credo is to love what I buy and buy what I love. This is all the more true at Yuletide. It helps me, and my family, to remember the theme of rebirth and light. The gifts we buy or make need to honor the light in those to whom we give. If this is not a part of your larger family culture, it can be introduced in non-preachy ways such as a card saying something like, "This token of my love will bring love and light throughout the coming year."

For young children, a family rule about gifts can help. A friend of mine created a little axiom to guide their gift giving. Yule gifts in their house include the following: "Something you want, something you need, something to play with, and something to read." They make a point to give to gift and food drives as well. Their children enjoy the gifts they receive and give thanks for their blessings.

Of course Yule is not just about gifts. Yule trees, candles, wreaths, the big elf Santa Claus, snowflakes and icicles, and the Saturnalian bounty of food and beverages all epitomize the holiday. It is a fun and easy sabbat to include the whole family in decorations, preparations, and rituals.

Real Yule trees are important to me—my love of nature and my German heritage make an artificial tree out of the question. We found a tree lot in the middle of downtown Denver that brings in sustainably harvested trees from Colorado woodlands and which gives their proceeds to local charities benefiting children. Their prices are affordable and the trees are open and natural looking— the best kind, in my opinion, to find fairies in. One year we planned to be away on Yule and Christmas (which we celebrate with family), so we decorated our tree for the fairies and ourselves, and then just before we left for our trip we took off the indoor decorations, took the tree outside, and redecorated it with berries, seed-infused pine cones, and little bits of yarn for the birds. As we set it outside, we said a little blessing for the animals and the land.

Many of our indoor decorations are handmade by either me or my daughter. We have a parade of salt-dough ornaments starting from when she was two years old; each year we add more, saving our favorites. For salt dough, mix one cup of salt with two cups of flour and a half cup of water. Knead until smooth. You can color portions using food coloring or natural dyes like beet juice and coffee, or leave the dough plain to paint later. Cut out shapes with cookie cutters or sculpt into shapes. Use a straw or skewer to poke a hole at the top for hanging. Bake at 325 degrees F for an hour and a half, let cool, then decorate with paint, glitter, etc. These ornaments will last forever, and are less likely to be eaten off the tree by the family dog than are cookie ornaments!

With older children, salt-dough ornaments can be more than just a craft when you add in a little magic. Mix any herbs or spices into the dough to draw on their magical qualities and scent—for example, cinnamon is a good choice for protection and health, plus it smells nice. You might also anoint the finished ornaments with oils like pine, calling in prosperity, healing, and long life. For a long-lasting amulet, write a simple spell or blessing on a small piece of paper, then press it into the soft dough of your ornament before baking. Give these amulets as gifts or hang them on the tree to bless your family for years to come.

When crafting rituals for your family for any occasion, remember that the magic comes from within. Tools, whether trees or ornaments or wands, are merely guides to help you focus your intentions. The most powerful rituals can be had while gathered as a family around a shared meal, maybe lit by a little candlelight, with some seasonal music playing. Within this circle share your love and connection by telling stories about how each of you has made a difference in each other's lives. Your souls have been reborn in this life together, and at Yule we celebrate that light as we gather together as one family.

Yule Ritual: The Give-Away

Kristin Madden

Items Needed

3–5 small evergreen boughs

Altar cloth in dark green, red, or white

Yule log: small, with 3 candle-sized holes carved out along the top

Candles: 2 red and 1 white

Fireproof container and dried pine or cedar (alternative: pine or cedar incense and an incense holder)

Matches or lighter

Black pieces of paper

A gold or silver marker

Brass ring: one for each participant or one for the ritual location/covenstead

Wooden bowl containing water or bird seed

Additional seasonal objects of your preference

Donations of clothes, toys, or canned food

Plate containing berries and canned or freeze-dried salmon and small spoons

Drums

Tape of shamanic drumming or ritual drummer

Set up the altar so that you face north when you face the altar. The Yule log is placed in the center. Insert the white candle in the middle hole of the log and the red candles on either side of the white candle. Lay the evergreen boughs over the log and around the altar. Place the brass ring in front of the log, the smudge or incense to the left, and the wooden bowl to the right. Additional seasonal objects may be placed around the altar where they feel right to you. Have the donations and plate of salmon and berries off to the side. Invite ritual participants to take their places around the circle, entering at the north and moving clockwise.

Light the smudge or incense. Cense the altar and carry the smudge around the circle.

Cleanse the space through sound. Drum a heartbeat rhythm first to the sky, inviting in the spirits of the heavens. Then drum to the ground, inviting in the spirits of the earth. Then drum at the center of your body, inviting in the Great Spirit, your ancestors, and your spirit allies. As you drum, invite these beings to share in this circle and ask for their guidance and protection. With the drum (or drums), walk the perimeter of the circle three times, drumming the heartbeat rhythm. As you walk, see and feel the space purifying and energizing. Feel your own personal power rising and strengthening.

If you choose, stop at each of the cardinal directions and allow any rhythm that feels appropriate come through as you invite in the spirits of that direction. It may help to envision those spirits that you work with. As you drum, invite them to share in this circle and ask for their guidance and protection.

Return to the altar and light the candles, beginning with the white candle. (Speak all italicized lines in this ritual).

With light, life returns to our world

In the darkness, there is always light, if we are only open to the possibility

May these lights help guide us through the dark times and illuminate our inner selves

Prepare for a shamanic journey to obtain illumination into some of the challenges you currently face. Allow each person a moment to decide on a specific focus for this journey. Then invite them to go to the altar, write that focus on a piece of black paper with the marker, and return with the paper to their places in the circle. Each person will hold the paper during the journey.

Turn on the shamanic drumming tape or invite your ritual drummer to begin to drum for the shamanic journey. If you have a drummer, ask him or her to give the return signal at 15 to 20 minutes and then continue to drum for another minute or two to allow journeyers to return gradually. Remind participants that the sound of the drum will lead them into relaxation and open the way for the journey. If their minds wander, they can return their attention to the drum and allow it to return them to journey. If they feel uncomfortable and wish to leave the journey, direct them to imagine following the sound back to the drum and to the physical room where they can simply enjoy the healing vibrations of the drum until the others complete their journeys.

Holding the piece of paper, focus on the intent of your journey. Feel yourself relax as the bonds of this time and space fall away. Ask your spirit allies for guidance and protection as you seek to illuminate an area of your life that is frustrating you. Be specific that you seek answers and solutions. Then allow the journey to unfold. If you need to use your imagination, do so, knowing that it springs from the same source as inspiration. When you have received the answers you seek, or when the return signal is given, thank your guides for their assistance, and return to the here-and-now. When all participants have completed their journeys, all should take a few moments to take notes or consider what they received. Then have them return to the altar one by one, and burn the black pieces of paper, envisioning these challenges eliminated and their energies transformed.

I release the hold that this shadow had on me
I choose to move through and beyond this
I free myself to accept the blessings of the returning light in my life

Take up the brass ring or rings.

Through these circles of sacred metal
We receive and hold the light of the solstice moon and of the re-
turning sun
May it inspire and illuminate us throughout the year
And remind us of the spark within, whenever shadows threaten

The ring or rings should be hung outside the front door or in a prominent window at this point, or as soon as possible after the ritual is complete. Say:

In times of darkness and challenge, our ancestors worked together to create and support community so that all might have the chance to survive and prosper. We don't always remember that we are vitally interconnected with other humans and with all those beings that share our world. For this reason, it is fitting that we offer a give-away each year at this time of the longest night. First, let us offer a gift to the animals and the spirits of this place.

Take up the bowl of water or seed.

Brothers and Sisters in spirit, we thank you for your presence in our lives. We send you blessings, that you might continue to enjoy this life and that we might all live on in peace and harmony.

The bowl should be placed outside at this point, or as soon as possible after the ritual is complete. If a private yard is not available, sprinkle the water or seed in a location where plants or animals may use it in safety.

Now let us remember that our connections to each human that shares our world. Close your eyes for a moment and imagine that you are standing in a circle with a great many other people. Become aware of your connections to each other and to the Earth. Feel the harmony and community and love in this circle.

Look to your left and smile at the person holding your hand. Recognize this as a kindred spirit. Just like you, this being is seeking his or her own way toward completion and happiness. Before looking away, notice that this person wears a crucifix.

Look beyond this person and smile at the next person in the circle. Recognize this as a kindred spirit. Just like you, this being is seeking his or her own way toward completion and happiness. Before looking away notice that this person wears a pentacle.

Smile at the person on your right. Recognize this as a kindred spirit. Just like you, this being is seeking his or her own way toward completion and happiness. Before looking away, notice that this person's forehead bears a colored dot.

Look around the circle and see individuals of all races, religions, and lifestyles. Their paths may not be right for you but you see Divinity within each of them. In each of them, you recognize a piece of yourself. Just like you, they are following their hearts and striving to be better people in order to create a better world for all people. Understand that we are each reflecting a piece of the beautiful and diverse tapestry of life and we need each other.

Become aware of people all over the world that see you as a kindred spirit. Feel your connection to each person who wants to create a global community of unconditional love and personal responsibility.

Now extend your awareness to the world beyond the circle of humanity. Feel your connections to the plants and animals of this world. Feel your Oneness with the land and sky and know that we are all connected. Now return your awareness to the circle and to yourself.

❧

Invite everyone to take up their donations and bring them to the center of the circle. Request that everyone with a drum begin to drum a heartbeat rhythm. Call upon each member of the circle to focus the harmony and community from the meditation into these donations. Ask for the blessings of spirit allies as you contribute to a healing cycle of relationship within our world. Chant over the donations, three times.

We give of ourselves freely
We receive blessings freely
May these gifts continue the cycle of love

Place the donations to the side and take up the plate of berries and salmon. Be sure to take the donations to an appropriate place as soon as possible after the ritual.

As we give so do we receive. Let us now share in the gifts of earth and sea.

Pass the plate and spoons around the circle. Each time a person takes a spoonful, they should offer thanks to a deity, spirit ally, ancestor or participant and gradually close the circle. When the plate is empty, give one final blessing to all involved and end the ritual.

Notes

Imbolc

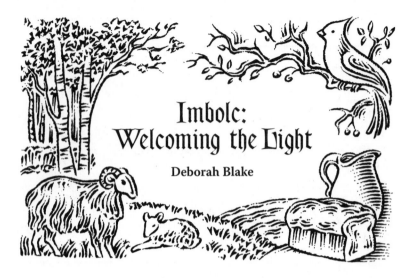

Imbolc: Welcoming the Light

Deborah Blake

FOR MANY PEOPLE, FEBRUARY 2 is known as Groundhog Day, a minor secular holiday when the groundhog's shadow—or lack thereof—predicts the coming of spring. What most folks don't realize is that this day is derived from the Pagan sabbat of Imbolc, a quarter-cross holiday that falls midway between Yule and Ostara.

Imbolc—also known as Imbolg, the Festival of Lights, Candlemas, or the Feast of Brigid—celebrates the first tiny stirrings of spring and the return of light and warmth to the world. It is a time for cleansing and purification; shaking off the melancholy of winter and preparing for the year ahead. It is also a time to set goals, both magickal and mundane, for the coming year, and to start changing your focus from the internal to the external. Time, in short, to come out of hibernation and greet the returning sun.

At this point in the Wheel of the Year, the goddess is a young mother, and the god is growing from the newborn infant of Yule into robust childhood. Many celebrations focus on the goddess alone, or may include one of the young sun gods, such as Eros.

Imbolc was originally a Celtic holiday, often associated with the goddess Brigid (or Brigit, or Bridgid). Brigid is a triple goddess, the patroness of healing, smithcraft, and the arts. From her comes fertility and inspiration, poetry and fire. So who better to jump-start our energies and help us to move into a new year?

Brigid's symbols are the forge and the fire (both in a physical sense, as in smithcraft, and in a spiritual sense, as in the fire of creativity), and if we are willing to enter her fires, we can come out renewed and transformed.

Of course, depending on where you live, the coming spring rejuvenation has to be taken on faith. In chilly upstate New York, for instance, there is often a blanket of snow on the ground, the temperatures still hover in the twenties, and it is hard to imagine that the warmth and light will ever return. But that is part of the reason for the holiday—to remind us that far underneath our feet, buried deep in the earth, the seeds for rebirth are growing and stirring. And so we too must begin to look toward the future, and what we hope to achieve in the year that lies ahead.

Imbolc Correspondences

The Celtic origins of the word *Imbolc* means "in the belly." Some say that this refers to the fire in the belly that we get as we are fired up by inspiration and hope. Others say it comes from the young lambs born at this time of year, carried in the bellies of their mothers as we are carried in the belly of our Mother, the earth. The birth of the new spring lambs signaled the start of a new season, while also providing a steady supply of milk to eke out the remaining lean months before the growing season returned.

Food: Because of the connection with ewes and nursing lambs, dairy products are a central theme of this holiday. Appropriate foods are milk, cheese, seeds, lamb, and early spring herbs and greens. Poppyseed muffins or mini-cheesecakes make perfect offerings for cakes and ale. One of my coven's favorite dishes for our Imbolc feast is Tres Leches Pie, which is made with three different forms of milk (whole milk, cream, and butter—yum!). We also like cheese fondue, creamed spinach (which combines a dairy product and an early spring vegetable), and Moussaka, a Greek dish made with lamb.

Colors: White is the primary color of this sabbat, probably because of the association with milk and lambs (although where I live, it can also be because of all the snow on the ground). Other colors commonly used are silver, pale yellow, and lavender. Some people will also use other pastel colors, such as light green and light blue, but I prefer to wait until Ostara for these.

Stones: Amethyst, bloodstone, garnet, ruby, and turquoise (all of which can be used for healing, interestingly enough)

Incenses: Basil, carnation, cinnamon, jasmine, myrrh, neroli, rosemary, and sweat pea

Animals and Totems: Lamb, ewe, all burrowing animals (including the groundhog and snakes), firebird (the phoenix that rises from the ashes of the old year and soars into the new), dragon

Symbols: Candles, bonfires, cauldrons, Brigid Wheel, Brigid Cross, seeds and grains, brooms (to sweep clean), all white and yellow flowers, daisies

Imbolc Exercises

Welcoming Back the Light

One of the things I like to do at Imbolc to symbolize the returning of the light and coming out of the darkness of winter is start my celebration by turning off all the lights in the house. If you observe the holiday with friends or a coven, gather in a central room like the kitchen or living room and turn off the lights as you go through the house. Otherwise, you can start in front of your altar or in whichever room you prefer.

Spend a few moments standing in silence, taking this opportunity to appreciate the quiet, internal nature of the dark months and their gifts of introspection and rest. Then send your awareness down into the earth, and feel the roots and seeds beginning to awaken; slowly, hesitantly, but as always, part of the cycle of life. Light one central candle to celebrate the return of light and life, and your own light that shines out into the world. (If doing this as a group, let each person light a small taper or tealight.) Then walk through the house and turn on the lights, one by one, or if it is safe to do so, light a candle in each room. Don't forget to thank the gods for helping you to make it through the winter darkness, and out into the light on the other side.

Purification and Cleansing Imbolc Bath

Another good way to celebrate this sabbat is by taking a purification bath (a shower will do if you don't have a tub, or you can use a basin of water and just soak your feet if you prefer).

The intent here is to wash away any negative energy that might interfere with your moving forward into the new year, leaving yourself clean and fresh and open to potential.

You can use one of the herbs listed on the preceding page under incenses, or choose one that is particularly appropriate for purification. I like rosemary, lemon, or geranium essential oils for this, combined with lavender if I have been feeling stressed and tense. It is also nice to add some sea salt to the bath water for cleansing, grounding, and healing. If you have to use a shower instead, you can make a simple sea salt purifying scrub by combining sea salt, oatmeal, and a few drops of essential oil.

Prepare the bathroom by lowering the lights and placing a few candles around the tub if it is safe to do so (watch out for flammable bathroom fabrics like shower curtains, as well as small children and pets). If you can't use a real candle, a small "faux" candle or lantern can take its place.

If you want, you can play some quiet background music with drums or flutes to put you in the proper state of mind. Undress slowly, making sure that you have fresh new clothes to put on when you are done. Then add your salt and herbs or oils and step into the water. If using a tub, you can visualize a serene pond in the midst of the forest, and if taking a shower, see yourself stepping under a sparkling waterfall. Spend however long you need, allowing the water to wash away all the debris of the cold, dark months, then step out feeling refreshed and reborn.

Meditation and Divination

Imbolc is a good time to tap into our creative and intuitive selves. If you have an artistic bent, try setting aside some space on this day to paint or draw or write. Find inspiration in the sabbat celebration and pen a poem to Brigid that you can dedicate to her on your altar.

Even if you aren't creative, you can use the inspirational energy of Imbolc for meditation and divination. The first coven I belonged to, run by the high priestess who taught me much of what I know, always did a labyrinth meditation and divination ritual at Imbolc. I found this tradition so rewarding, I continued it when I started my own coven, Blue Moon Circle.

This can be done on your own or with a group. If you are doing it with a group, I highly recommend having everyone drum for a while to build energy and induce a light trance state. If you are doing it by yourself, you can either drum or put on a tape of drums or other light rhythmic music in the background.

Start by writing a number of words and phrases on small pieces of parchment or plain white paper. These can say something inspirational, or be words that would provide guidance on your path or a suggestion of a direction to go in. For instance, Blue Moon Circle uses words like *growth*, *prosperity*, *focus*, *cooperation*, or *patience*. (Don't even ask me how many years in a row I ended up with patience—it's a running joke in the coven now.)

If you are doing this divination on your own, and you are seeking answers to a particular issue or issues, then put in only words or phrases that pertain to your specific circumstances. Otherwise, keep it general.

Once you have written down the words and phrases, fold the pieces of paper so that you can't see what is on them and place them in a small cauldron or bowl. You will also need a candle, some chalk, string, or masking tape, and your drum or music.

Draw a labyrinth pattern on the floor using chalk, string, or masking tape. This can be as simple as a circle that spirals inward or as complicated as you desire. If you are doing this with a large group, you may want to make a labyrinth large enough for two people to use at a time—one going in and one coming out, so the process doesn't take all night. Or you can skip the labyrinth altogether and just do your meditation sitting on the floor.

Place a table or altar at the center of the labyrinth (or the space you are using), put the bowl of paper slips on the table and light the candle in a fire-safe container. Then start your music or your drumming. This should be tranquil and rhythmic in order to bring on a relaxed and meditative state.

Think about the year to come, and the path you will be walking. Send out a silent request to the gods for guidance on your journey. Then when you are ready, walk slowly inward on the labyrinth until you get to the center. Pull out a slip of paper and see what message the universe has sent you. Then go back and sit down, listen to the music for a while longer, and think about what the word or phrase you chose might mean for you. (If doing this as a group, everyone drums while each person takes a turn walking the labyrinth. There is no speaking.)

When you are done, thank the gods, blow out the candle, and put the slip of paper on your altar or somewhere you can see it on a daily basis (like taped to your mirror or refrigerator).

Creating a Focus Board

I think Imbolc is the perfect time to set goals for the upcoming year. Unlike New Year's Day, when many folks traditionally make resolutions (which they then break almost immediately), Imbolc is one month after the major holiday season. This allows you some time to recover from the hustle and bustle, and gives you the dark time to look inward to see which direction you want to go and what you need to work on.

So by the time you sit down at Imbolc, you should know what your goals—both magical and mundane—are for the seasons ahead. Blue Moon Circle likes to spend an evening together making focus boards that will help us remember where we were heading and what we are hoping to achieve.

Focus boards are easy, cheap, and fun to make. But more than that, they serve as a concrete manifestation of your goals; something that as Witches, we know can be very powerful.

All you need is a piece of sturdy paper (like posterboard, or even part of a cardboard box), some pictures (we cut ours out of magazines, but you can also use catalogs, download pictures from online, take some photos, or even draw a picture with crayons or colored markers), cut out or written words, glue, a pair of scissors, and anything else you want to add to your board. If you want to get fancy, you can use multicolored glitter and add runes or other symbols. Or you can just cut out pictures and words, and leave it at that. You are tapping into the creative energy of Imbolc, so let yourself go a little wild if you want to.

You may want to start out with a list of your goals for the year. I usually have two sets: one for my writing goals, and one for my personal life. This year's focus board had a section dedicated to health and happiness, one for prosperity, another for love, and a large space filled with words like *agent, success,* and *book signings.* (Luckily, I have a lot of writing magazines, so it was easy to find words and pictures that fit my needs.)

Simply cut out and glue on anything that represents your goals for the year. If you are doing this project with others, feel free to have snacks and talk about what you want to achieve over the course of the year. Or you can be quiet and meditative, if you so choose.

When you are done, hang your focus board where you will see it often, so it can keep you focused on your goals.

Celestial Sway

Fern Feto Spring

BRIGID, THE CELTIC GODDESS of fire, awakens the spark of life within us as we slowly emerge from the dark cave of winter. The Imbolc season is a time to honor Brigid's spirit, celebrating the growing light with flowers, feasting, and poetry. We are once again born to the world and initiated into the cycle of life. Like green buds growing from the soil, the fertility of springtime fills us with new possibilities and energy.

Aquarius, the visionary sign of the truth-teller, is the astrological guardian of this time. The water bearer awakens our need for community and returns our attention to the big picture. As we move away from Capricorn's focus on survival and progress, Aquarius reminds us that we are all in this together and encourages us to work collectively for solutions.

Imbolc 2012 begins on a waxing Moon, which then blossoms into a Full Moon in Leo on February 7, featuring an opposition to the communication planet, Mercury. This lunation offers us the opportunity to integrate our heart's desire with our dreams and visions for the future, though we may need to first fine-tune our message and check in with others along the way. Brigid reminds us that in order to make an impact with our words and ideas, truth must be spoken with heart and reflect our deepest desires.

Mars, the planet of action and courage, is now moving backwards through the sign of Virgo (January 23 to April 13). We may need to refine and clarify our efforts at this time, taking extra care to perfect and finesse whatever actions we want to take. Use this period to tend and nurture the Brigid's flame that lives inside you, allowing the gentle warmth to temper and shape the blade that you later want to wield out in the world.

Venus moves into Aries on February 8 and then forms a conjunction with energizing Uranus on February 9. Relationships are bold, passionate, and full of surprises as the planet of romance meets the trickster archetype of the zodiac. This is a time to take risks, experiment, and innovate in the realm of both love and resources. As we move forward toward the warmth of springtime, this planetary alignment provides a little excitement to inspire us and ignite our inner flame.

A New Moon on February 21 occurs in the early degrees of Pisces and forms a conjunction with Pisces' ruling planet, Neptune. This lunation heralds the arrival of a new astrological era, as we transition from the airy realm of Aquarius into the oceanic waters of Pisces. The dreamtime beckons and reality takes on a hue of magic and mystery as Neptune initiates us into a fairy world beyond imagination.

Jupiter, which is in the early degrees of Taurus, is now approaching a harmonious trine aspect with Pluto in Capricorn. Though this aspect isn't exact until March 13, the slow-moving nature of the planets involved means that their energy pervades the entire span of the Imbolc season. Jupiter in Taurus is like the King of Disc: sensually regal, confident in his ability to manifest, and a master of the physical realm who knows how to work in harmony with the Earth.

With a jolt of energy from Pluto in Capricorn, Jupiter in Taurus takes on a unique depth and power. This combo can literally move mountains and transform landscapes. Prosperity and abundance take on new heights as these earthy powerhouses meet in a complementary dance of progress and growth. This lucky alignment welcomes in the springtime with a wealth of possibility and new opportunities.

Full Moon in Leo

The Full Moon in Leo on February 7 nurtures Brigid's flame of creative passion and inspiration as we seek to know and understand our heart's desire. The Sun and Mercury form an opposition to the Moon, which asks us to balance Leo's desire for personal recognition and praise with an awareness of our greater role in our community—a reminder of what we have to share that will benefit the collective. Communication may demand more work now as we struggle to express our unique vision for the future, but if we remember to infuse our words with Leo's solar warmth, we may find that we reach a larger audience.

Venus in Aries

Venus in Aries brings boldness, moxie, and passion to the Venusian arts of love, beauty, resource cultivation, social gatherings, and fashion. Uranus' addition to this lively energy is like a stick of dynamite thrown into a keg of gunpowder. Expect fireworks and a few explosions in all Venus-related arenas during this time period (roughly February 8 to 12). New relationships started now are quirky, unexpected, and contrary to everyone's expectations. Existing relationships may go through interesting permutations, with a roller coaster ride of ups and downs that leave you breathless. Brigid's warrior energy encourages us to bravely confront the truth in matters of the heart, taking up a shield when necessary, but courageously forging ahead despite any unexpected curveballs that come our way.

You can use this fiery combo to your advantage by working with the energy it presents rather than fighting against it. Ritual offers one way to tap into the cosmic fireball offered by the Venus/Uranus union in Aries.

Venus/Uranus in Aries Ritual

Pick any day from February 8 to 12 to perform your ritual. On that day, choose an outfit to wear that is sexy, but different in style from anything you usually wear. This will appeal to Venus' strong affinity for fashion and Uranus' need to shake things up and be unusual. Set out an offering of honey, cayenne, and cinnamon to honor the sweetness, heat, and energy of this planetary alignment. Set an intention for your ritual—questions you may want to ponder: Does my love life need an infusion of passion and excitement? What risks might I take in regard to my finances/resources that could bring about new opportunities? Does my personal style/wardrobe need a change? How do I feel about my skills and resources? Is my self-esteem strong or in need of a boost? Once you have an area of intention for your ritual, meditate on this intention and write it down, draw it, or make a collage or other visual representation to place on your altar.

Then light a red candle and invoke Venus and Uranus, asking them to bless your ritual with their union in the sign of Aries. Ask for the planets help in bringing new energy, passion and enthusiasm to your love life, finances or personal appearance. Burn a bit of the candle every night until the next New Moon.

Jupiter in Taurus

Jupiter in Taurus brings an energy of expansion and abundance to the realm of resource cultivation, sensual pleasures and all things related to the earth and the environment. During the yearlong span of this transit it is a good time to focus on cultivating stability, comfort and a sense of gratitude or appreciation for the simple pleasures of life. To welcome in the springtime during the Brigid/Imbolc sabbat, go on a hike, cook a delicious meal with seasonal produce, or spend time enhancing the beauty and comfort of your home with spring flowers and symbols.

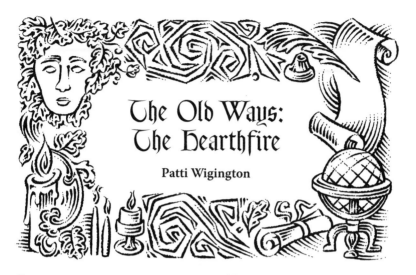

The Old Ways: The Hearthfire

Patti Wigington

BRIGHID IS WELL KNOWN as a goddess of the hearth in many Celtic-language cultures, but how did she come to be so? To first understand her role as a hearthfire goddess—and subsequently, domestic patron—we first have to look at the different aspects of Brighid herself. Unlike many deities, Brighid takes on multiple personas. In fact, she is even incorporated into the Christian pantheon as a saint.

Brighid has a number of different origins, depending on which source you're reading. According to the Irish mythological cycles, Brighid appears in some stories as a daughter of the Dagda. In some variations, she is one of three sisters who are also named Brighid, but in other stories she is a single goddess with triune features. In other words, she is a whole comprised of three separate, but complementary, parts. She became associated with fire in Ireland partly due to her role as a goddess of the smithy—after all, without fire, blacksmiths could hardly do their job.

One of the most fascinating parts of Brighid's tale is the overlap between her role as a Pagan goddess of fertility and fire and her status as a Christian saint of the same name—who was also associated with fire.

Celtic scholar Peter Beresford Ellis relates the story of Brighid, the daughter of a slave named Broiseach (a Pict who was once baptized by St. Patrick) and Dubhtach, a Druid priest from Leinster. Her birth and childhood were, according to legend, filled with Druidic symbols—young Brighid was nursed on the milk of magical cows, for example. Her birth itself was unusual, because Broiseach gave birth as she crossed the threshold into Dubhtach's house—meaning Brighid was born neither inside nor outside, which is a common theme seen in many Celtic legends.

Because of her piety and holiness, Brighid the nun was regarded as a saint even during her lifetime. She was never formally canonized by the church, or if she was granted sainthood by a local bishop, those records have been lost to time.

Despite her Druid upbringing, young Brighid converted to Christianity and around AD 470, founded a religious community at Kildare. Legend has it that this order was built on the site of an old school run by female Druids. Kildare was the site of a sacred perpetual flame, originally lit in honor of the goddess Brighid, but when Brighid the nun moved into town, the flame was moved to her abbey. No longer tended by Pagan priestesses, it was instead kept burning day and night by the nuns of Brighid's order. The sacred flame of Kildare remained alight until many of the monasteries were closed in the sixteenth century. In 1993, the town of Kildare relit Brighid's sacred fire, and it is tended regularly by the Brigidine Sisters in their center, Solas Bhride.

Lady Gregory writes in her Book of Saints and Wonders that Brighid was associated with fire from the very beginning. She says Brighid was born on the first day of spring to a servant woman, and that "it was angels that baptized her and that gave her the name of Brigit, that is a Fiery Arrow," almost in a parallel to the Greek Artemis, or Rome's Minerva. In many interpretations, the Celtic name of Brighid is read as Exalted One, tying in to Brighid's role as a goddess of light.

One of the best-known parts of the Brighid legend is the custom of smooring the fire. Alexander Carmichael, a British folklorist who collected thousands of poems, stories, and prayers in his Carmina Gadelica, writes that in the Highlands of Scotland and other damp, chilly areas of the British Isles, people developed a custom of keeping peat fires inside at night if wood couldn't be obtained. This, presumably, would prevent the fire from going out in the early morning mist. Plus, peat was nearly always on hand, while wood might not be readily available.

This process of keeping a peat fire at one's house involved putting the embers down for the night so your house wouldn't burn down while you slept. Although the fire wasn't completely extinguished, it was smothered enough that it presented no danger, and the embers would still be hot enough for use the following morning. This was done in a ceremonial fashion each night, which the Scots called smooring—in Gaelic it appears as *smaladh.*

Carmichael describes the ritual as simple, yet artistic. Embers from the peat fire are spread in a circle on the hearth—which in many cases was right in the middle of the floor. The circle of embers is then evenly divided into three parts, with a small pile left in the center, called the *Tula nan Tri*, or Hearth of the Three. Peat bricks are placed between each of the three sections, touching the center pile, and as each brick is laid down, a prayer is offered. The entire thing is then covered with ashes so that the embers will be contained, but not fully extinguished, and the lady of the house offers a final prayer.

A popular smooring prayer invoked Brighid and the Virgin Mary in tandem, calling out:

I will build the hearth as Mary would build it
The encompassment of Bride and of Mary,
Guarding the hearth, guarding the floor,
Guarding the household all.

Today, many of the legends of Brighid are a blend of tales about Brighid the Pagan goddess and Brighid the Christian saint. Both were associated with healing, fertility, domesticity, and the hearthfire. Sometimes, it's hard to distinguish where the stories of one end and the other begins.

Although it's not very practical—or safe—to leave a fire burning in the middle of your floor overnight these days, many people who follow a Celtic path choose to honor Brighid at Imbolc by recreating the smooring ritual in one fashion or another. You can do this either in your fireplace, or with a safely tended candle.

Regardless of how you choose to honor Brighid, take a moment at Imbolc to remember her long history, and honor her as a goddess of the hearthfire.

For Further Reading:

Carmichael, Alexander. *Carmina Gadelica.*

Ellis, Peter Berresford. *A Brief History of the Druids*, New York: Carroll & Graf Publishers, 1994.

Ellis, Peter Berresford. *The Celts: A History.* New York: Carroll & Graf Publishers, 1998.

Gregory, Lady Augusta. *A Book of Saints and Wonders,* 1906.

The Mabinogion. Translated by Lady Charlotte Guest. New York: Dover, 1997.

Feasts and Treats

Susan Pesznecker

ALTHOUGH IMBOLC MARKS THE start of spring on the Wheel of the Year, winter persists until the Spring Equinox in mid-March. For most of us, there's still plenty of cold weather as well as colds-and-flu season to deal with. Our hearty menu will warm you from the toes up while scaring away a lion's share of winter viruses. One of Imbolc's most potent symbols is the candle: Set your table with candles to break winter's darkness and welcome in the coming spring.

Hot Cinnamon-Beef Noodle Soup

This warming soup has now become one of my favorite home remedies for colds and any type of upper-respiratory bug. It's along the lines of the famous Vietnamese beef noodle soup, *pho* (pronounced "fuh"), but with more heat. The first few sips may widen your eyes, but this soup warms you all over and is absolutely delicious. The fiery herbs dilate your airways and enliven your senses, while the garlic and onions have antiseptic healing properties. For medicinal purposes, eat while it is as hot as possible and breathe in the steam.

Prep time: 30 minutes
Cook time: 2 hours
Serves: 6

1 teaspoon oil

6 green onions, cut into 1½-inch lengths and smashed slightly

6 cloves garlic, peeled and thinly sliced

4 slices fresh ginger (each the size of a quarter)

1½ teaspoons hot chile paste

2 cinnamon sticks

1 teaspoon anise seed, crushed slightly

8½ cups water

½ cup soy sauce

2 pounds lean chuck or stew meat, trimmed of fat and gristle and cut into 1½-inch cubes

6–10 ounces fresh spinach, washed and stems trimmed

A handful of washed basil leaves, chopped lightly just before using

½ pound flat Chinese wheat flour noodles, udon, or other flat noodle (such as fettuccine), cooked until almost tender, rinsed, and drained

3 tablespoons minced green onions

Additions: lime wedges, basil leaves, fresh bean sprouts

Heat oil in a large (8+ quart) kettle over medium to med-high heat.

Add the scallions, garlic, ginger, chile paste, cinnamon sticks, and anise seed, and stir-fry until fragrant, about 30 seconds.

Add the water and soy sauce and bring to a boil.

Add the beef and bring back to a boil.

Reduce heat to low, cover, and simmer for 1½ hours, or until beef is *very* tender. Skim now and then to remove surface foam or fat.

Remove the ginger slices and cinnamon sticks and discard.

Add the spinach and basil and bring to a boil.

Divide the noodles among 6 *large* pre-warmed bowls. Ladle the soup mixture over the noodles, and sprinkle with the 3 tablespoons green onions.

Serve the additions in small bowls to add as desired.

Spiced Winter Fruit Compote

In times past, fruits were often dried as a means of storage, and compotes were used to make use of these fruits. Serve this warming, spiced fruit blend as a surprising side dish: It will beckon to spring and provide a sweet counterpart to the highly spiced soup.

Prep time: 10 minutes

Cook time: 6–8 hours in the slow cooker

Serves: 6+

16 ounces dried pitted plums*

8 ounces dried apricots

8 ounces dried pears

8 ounces dried apples

4 ounces dried cranberries

4 cups water

½ cup sugar

½ teaspoon vanilla

½ teaspoon ground cinnamon (or ½ cinnamon stick)

1 teaspoon grated lemon zest

2 tablespoons fresh lemon juice

Inspect dried fruit for any spoilage, pits, etc. Combine all ingredients in your slow cooker and cook on low heat for 6 to 8 hours, until fruit is tender.

*Weighing dried fruit at the bulk section at a grocery store (or buying prepackaged) is an easy accurate method.

Spiced Gingerbread

Grandmothers have made gingerbreads for centuries, stirred up in stoneware bowls and baked by the fire. This one is made extra-zippy with abundant warming spices and the grounding protective magick of dark molasses.

Prep time: 15 minutes

Cook time: 1 hour

Serves: 9+

1 cup dark molasses

½ cup unsalted butter (or non-transfat shortening), room
temperature

½ cup sugar

1 egg

2½ cups flour

2½ teaspoons ginger

2 tablespoons candied ginger, chopped coarsely

1 teaspoon coriander

1 teaspoon nutmeg (freshly grated is best)

1½ teaspoons cinnamon

¼ teaspoon cloves

⅛ teaspoon cayenne

½ teaspoon salt

1 cup boiling water

1 tablespoon baking soda

I medium apple (tart yellow or green); peeled, cored, and finely
chopped

Whipped heavy cream or vanilla ice cream

Preheat oven to 350 degrees F. Grease and flour a 13 × 9-inch pan.

In a large bowl, cream the molasses, butter, sugar, and egg until
fluffy.

In a medium bowl, stir together the flour, gingers, coriander,
nutmeg, cinnamon, cloves, cayenne, and salt. Add to creamed mixture and mix just until blended.

Dissolve baking soda in the boiling water. Add to cake mixture
and blend well. Stir in apples.

Pour into prepared pan and bake for about an hour. Start testing
at 50 minutes: a toothpick inserted near the center should come out
clean. Serve warm with whipped cream or ice cream.

Double-Hot Chocolate

Simple, delicious, and oh-so warming. And chocolate keeps the Dementors away!

Prep time: 15 minutes
Cook time: 15 minutes
Serves: 8

4 ounces semisweet chocolate (chips or bars)
¼ cup light corn syrup
½ teaspoon vanilla
¼ teaspoon cayenne
1 cup heavy cream, chilled
4 cups whole milk

Melt chocolate and corn syrup over low heat. Refrigerate 30 minutes, until cool. Stir in vanilla, cayenne, and cream. Beat until soft peaks form.

Heat milk until very hot. To serve, spoon the chocolate mixture into 8 cups. Fill with hot milk and serve.

Bonus: GG's Hot Toddy

My medicine-woman grandmother used this to treat respiratory illnesses. It feels and tastes wonderful when you're sick.

Into a warmed mug, squeeze the juice of half a lemon

Stir in 1 tablespoon honey and 1 jigger (1 ounce) whiskey or rum. Blend well.

Fill mug with boiling water and stir again.

Drink while it is as hot as possible.

Customize as desired, adding molasses instead of honey, a pinch of ginger, cayenne, lemon peel, etc.

Crafty Crafts

Ellen Dugan

Theme of the Season: Introspection and wisdom
Colors: White and purple
Scents: Mint and sandalwood
Energy: Kindness, memories, and preparation

Creating a Coven Scrapbook

Imbolc is a time of introspection and indoor activities. I find this a perfect time of year to create a coven scrapbook. All of those pictures you have been taking of your group at the sabbats and Full Moons—what are you doing with them? Are they sitting in a box collecting dust or tucked into various photo envelops and stacked up somewhere? Why not use those photos and create a coven scrapbook to have as a memento of your group and a document of your journey together. I should probably warn you...scrapbooking is happily addictive. And when you make a coven or magickal scrapbooking you really get hooked.

Supplies

Various themes of scrapbooking papers for your pages—plain colors and printed

Photos of your coven

Glue stick (acid free)

Double-sided tape (acid free)

Various stickers and page embellishments

Scissors

Scrapbook album or three-ring binder and clear page protector
sheets

Creativity

Instructions: Start with a sheet of base paper the size of your finished page. Lay out the photographs and other accessories BEFORE
you glue or tape anything in. Take your time and lay out your pages
first. (To keep it simpler, scrapbook one coven gathering at a time.)
Personally, I work on four to six pages in my scrapbook at a time,
but feel free to go at your own pace.

Be sure to note which pages will be opposite or facing each
other when you open the book and work your pages around that.
After you have it all figured and plotted out, then you can attach everything. When the pages are done, slip them into their protective
sheets and enjoy!

Part of the fun of this project is that you will always be working
on it and adding new pages as your group celebrates the sabbats and
esbats together. And, of course, you get to hunt for seasonal papers
for your scrapbook pages. Watching for treasures for your magickal
scrapbook is half the fun! Oh, and you do not have to stick with just
plain colored cardstock for your pages either. Think outside the box
for a moment and consider some of these various themes.

Use gothic-looking papers in black, white, and red. Or look
to the Wheel of the Year for your scrapbook inspiration. For example, I am always on the lookout for sabbat-themed paper, or
any nature theme paper that may work for a sabbat or esbat. The
truth is that nature- or floral-themed paper works very well. Some
of these scrapbook papers are photographic and very real looking
while some are more artsy and clever, such as autumn leaves for
Mabon, pumpkins or witty Halloween papers for Samhain, and old-

fashioned, holly- and ivy-themed paper or the classic pine bough paper for Yuletide.

Then there's snowflake and wintry looking paper for Imbolc. For Ostara, I watch for paper with green grass and colored eggs or spring flowers. For Beltane and Midsummer I work with botanical, floral, garden, or songbird designs scrapbook paper. Finally for Lughnasadh, I watch for sunflower and summer flower paper. You should also consider Celtic, faery tale, and steam punk themes. Don't forget the vintage old-world scrapbook papers—fantastic vintage looks in shades of faded black, sepia, and ivory and tan. That old world theme is gorgeous for a magickal scrapbook.

Now you can write in a permanent marker on your pages, or use peel and stick lettering, in various fonts and scripts. I tend to do both. I use the fancy letters at the top of the page to title the page with something like "Imbolc 2012," and then for the captions underneath I will either write out by hand, or print them out in a pretty script on a sheet of computer parchment paper.

Then I tear the edges around my parchment paper captions, and glue-stick it in. Torn edges of papers are gorgeous (and practical, if you have a hard time cutting a straight line like I do). The rough frayed edges of the torn papers makes your scrapbook look more antique, witchy, and vintage. If you look, you will find books full of letters that you can cut out and paste in to your scrapbook. Hit the scrapbooking aisles at an arts and crafts store and see what you can find on sale!

Keep your eyes peeled for seasonal stickers and 3-D page embellishments—everything from autumn leaves, pumpkins, faeries, decorated trees, snowflakes, summer suns, flowers, cats, witches, to colored eggs. Watch for gears, clockworks, and botanical stickers too. Any of these will add a bit of textural panache to your coven scrapbook.

If you like, you can add pages from rituals, spells, or mementos from gatherings to your pages. For example, one of my coven sisters makes handmade cards at the sabbats and passes them out to each

of us. Over the years those gorgeous cards have found their way into my coven scrapbook.

Here is another tip: If you can't find any Pagan artwork to add to your scrapbook, do an "image" search online with Yahoo images or Google images. Print up a few smaller bewitching images, cut them out and add them to your scrapbook pages. I have found some great pictures of full moons rising through bare tree branches. Then I printed it out about four inches square and added it to a winter full moon page in my coven's scrapbook.

Also use your sense of humor. Look up 1950's retro black and white photos of "pinup Witches." They are glamorous and cool. Or hunt down Vintage Witches, wizards, and fortunetellers from old Victorian art.

Also, if you have a coven logo or pendant that you all wear, make a title page for your coven scrapbook and have the logo or a big group picture there. The sky is the limit.

Next you will need to decide if you want to invest in a big 12 by 12-inch album or use a large three-ring binder with pages that measure eight and a half by eleven inches. If you go the three-ring binder route, you will need to invest in a few packages of affordable clear page protector sheets. Just make sure they are listed as archival safe for your photos.

For my personal coven scrapbook, I use a three-ring binder. Well okay, I have three different binders by now from all the coven gatherings over the years. They are treasured memories and it is fun to look back and see how everyone has changed over the years.

Time: Hours and hours …

Cost: About $25.00 to start a coven scrapbook

If you already do scrapbooking or altered books, you will probably have some supplies in the house that you can raid! Watch for sales and talk to other scrapbookers. They always know where to go to find the "good stuff!" Blessed be.

All One Family

Clea Danaan

AT IMBOLC, WE REJOICE in the life that grows within as the light grows stronger. This time of quickening always ignites my urge to spring clean. I smudge the house and patio with sage and copal, organize the closets, and plant the first peas on a warm February day. At a mile high here in Colorado, Imbolc can bring heavy, wet snow or a teasing blast of 80 degrees, freezing again at night. I have to be careful not to get too excited on these warm days and plant too much. Peas are the only cool-season seeds safe to put in the ground this early. But, oh, do my green thumbs get itchy!

The first year we had our hens, we saw the increase of light as an increase of eggs as well. I wondered if the chickens could feel what I could: the pulse of life awakening in the earth, the hints of spring to come, the smell of warmth sneaking in on the wind. It's still so brown here in February that when the first spikes of crocus peek out of the mulch, I feel like crying with joy. I miss green desperately this time of year. My longing brings a poignant significance to my Imbolc celebration.

As Imbolc honors the growing light, it is traditional to celebrate it by making candles. February 2 is also the Roman Catholic holiday Candlemas, so one year I called together my spiritually diverse group of friends for some candlemaking. I pulled out the box of spent candles and bits of beeswax I had been collecting for years, and purchased a spool of wick. I gathered jam jars and empty candleholders. Friends brought their odds and ends and also new candle-making supplies like dyes and wax. We melted wax in clean aluminum cans in pans of simmering water, then poured the melted wax into jars. Mothers and their children took turns in my small kitchen making their Imbolc candles. We sprinkled herbs into some and dyed a few with old crayons. I saved a corner of the kitchen for the kettle and boxes of tea and mugs, and we all tried to keep an eye on the kids running wild on a lovely springlike afternoon. My kitchen smelled fabulous afterward. The scent of melted beeswax is truly divine.

My Catholic friend brought her candles to mass with her that evening, and my family lit ours for our Imbolc feast. I couldn't imagine a better way to celebrate light, friendship, community, and the gifts of the land. If you can't make candles, be sure to purchase new ones for your celebration. You might anoint them with fire or Imbloc oil from a Pagan shop, or simple say a prayer of thanks for the returning light as you touch the fresh wick with your match.

Another name for Imbolc is Oimelc, meaning ewe's milk. This is lambing season, when the milk of ewes begins to flow. Before the times of refrigeration and grocery stores, this would have meant the return of life-giving milk and cheese. Our bodies remember this time, and celebrate the lengthening and warming days with a sense of relief. By February, our ancestors were either very hungry or really sick of root vegetables and weevil-filled flour. You might celebrate Oimelc with a log of local sheep cheese and a salad of whatever greens grow wild on your land. In Colorado I can usually pull together an Imbolc salad of dandelion and violet greens; at lower elevations look for wild sorrel, lamb's quarters, chickweed, and other spring weeds for your salad. If you live in an apartment, you can still find edible weeds in the nooks of allies and parks. Stay away from anywhere that has been sprayed. Ask a local herbalist for help identifying edible weeds.

For your Imbolc meal or ritual, pour a glass of your favorite milk—cow, goat, human, or even almond—and raise it in honor of the returning light and the flowing milk. Discuss the blessings of milk with your family. It's a brilliant substance, made just for the species it feeds. Human milk contains a wealth of omega-3 fatty acids, lactoferrin, and oligosaccharides for digestive health, antimicrobial proteins, living white blood cells and immunoglobulins, and highly absorbable vitamins and minerals. Other mammal milk is naturally perfect for each respective species, though goat and sheep milk contain proteins most similar to human milk. Whatever milk you have access to this Imbolc honors the gifts of the Goddess, so drink a little and pour some on the earth in thanks.

Milk makes us who we are—compassionate mammals—and comes, of course, from mammary glands, nestled in mama breasts. This is a good holiday to honor our breasts, be you Mother, Maiden or Crone (gentlemen, I discuss the honoring of men and boys at Midsummer). Breasts are naturally honored in my house, where I have been lactating for five years now. My daughter knows she will one day have breasts, though thinks little of the fact. If your daughter is nearing menarche, this Imbolc might be a good time to discuss her budding sexuality and what it means as a giver of life. This needn't mean childbearing; creativity and compassion come in many forms. A lovely gift for an adolescent or tweener girl would be some breast salve. Steep calendula, clover, and dandelion flowers in olive or almond oil; strain; blend in beeswax to desired consistency, and finish off with a drop or two of lavender essential oil. (See Susun Weed's *Healing Wise* or Rosemary Gladstar's *Family Herbal* for more on making salves.) Breastfeeding mothers and crones can also benefit from this gentle salve. Another great breast salve for mothers is lanolin (sheep again!), through which we connect with our sister ewes. All women can honor their breasts by sending them love and light at each self-examination of their breasts. Let us take back the image of the breast as a sex symbol and a cancer petri; let us honor our breast tissue as life-giving and pleasurable.

Finally, Imbolc is a time to honor the life that grows within yourself. What projects and dreams do you gestate? In a family, new projects and goals are ever-evolving. As you sit around the altar or dinner table with your new Imbolc candles and a glass of milk, discuss with your family what is quickening for each of you and for the whole family. Stare into the flame of the candle and imagine your dreams being carried to the spirits on the rising heat or on the smoke of incense. Good incense choices for Imbolc include any with fire energy, like copal, dragon's blood, or frankincense. Now go outside and give the gift of milk and thanks to any bit of green you can find peeking through the snow or brown, or if you live in a more temperate climate, give praise to whatever flowers bloom on this blessed Imbolc.

Imbolc Ritual:
Cultivating Dreams

Deborah Blake

I RECOMMEND READING THE entire ritual through before starting. It will go much more smoothly if you know exactly what to expect at each section of the rite.

When and where? It is best to do this ritual at dusk, or full dark.

Who? This ritual is designed to be used by either a group or a solitary Witch. I have written it out to include the "welcome and explanation" speech that would customarily be given by the High Priest and/or High Priestess leading the ritual. Solitaries can leave that part out, or read it aloud to themselves. All "group" instructions will be printed in bold, so that solitaries can spot them easily. As necessary, substitute the word *we* for *I*. If doing a group ritual, the quarter calls would usually be read by various group members, and the High Priestess and High Priest would invoke the gods and cast the circle.

Items Needed

White candles (one per participant and/or each room in your home)
Goddess and god candles (white or silver for the goddess and yellow
    or gold for the god)

Quarter candles (red, yellow, blue, green—or whatever colors you usually use)

Sage smudge stick (you may substitute the cleansing incense)

Salt and water in separate containers and a small bowl to mix them in

Pieces of paper cut into star shapes (one for each participant)

Pen(s) or pencil(s)

Crocus bulb (one for each participant)

Small pot of dirt (one for each participant)

Pitcher with milk

Chalice

Seedcakes or any dessert using dairy (mini-cheesecakes are perfect, as are cheese pastries)

Table to use as altar and a cloth to cover it

Matches or lighter, and a snuffer to put out candle as the end of the ritual

Optional: White cloth or sheet

Before Starting: Turn off as many lights as you can, leaving the room in darkness or semi-darkness. Put all your supplies on the altar except the pot(s) of dirt, which should be under the altar, hidden by the cloth if possible. (This symbolizes the dark of winter and the ground waiting in hibernation for spring to come.)

If doing this as a group, you may wish to proceed in from another room, passing through a white curtain (a sheet works fine) to represent coming out of the depths of winter into the light. In that case, you can have one candle already burning on the altar. (You can even have the white cloth on the floor, and crawl underneath it on your way into the room to symbolize coming out of winter hibernation.)

Cleanse yourself and your sacred space with the sage smudge-stick. As the smoke wafts over you and around the circle space, visualize a glowing golden light washing away all negativity, and surrounding you with clarity and serenity. **Pass the smudge stick around the circle.** Take a few slow, deep breaths to help you ground and center.

Mix your salt and water together in a small bowl. If you want, you can say aloud: *"Salt into water, water into salt. Wash away all negativity, leaving only the positive and beneficial."* Anoint yourself at forehead, lips, heart, and center, then sprinkle the salt and water mixture around the outline of your circle.

Cast the circle by walking around the perimeter deosil (clockwise) with an athame or your finger pointed at the ground, while saying: *"I cast the circle round and round, from earth to sky, from sky to ground. I conjure now this sacred place, outside time, and outside space. The circle is cast, I am (we are) between the worlds."* Visualize the inside of the circle filled with light.

Invoke the four quarters by standing to face each direction (starting with the east), then lighting the appropriate candle after you have called that quarter. Quarter callers state the following:

East (yellow candle): I look to the east and invoke the power of air—cold breezes which chill the body, yet blow away the cobwebs of the year behind me **(us)**. With the coming of the light, may you bring me **(us)** clarity and creativity. [Light candle]

South (red candle): I look to the south and invoke the power of fire—the warmth of hearth and home which shelters me **(us)** from the winter cold outside. With the coming of the light, may you bring me **(us)** passion to warm my life **(our lives)** in the seasons ahead. [Light candle]

West (blue candle): I look to the west and invoke the power of water—perfect crystals of water frozen into snow, each one different from the rest. With the coming of the light may you help me **(us)** to become more comfortable with my own **(our own)** individuality. [Light candle]

North (green candle): I turn to the north and invoke the power of earth—frozen beneath me **(us)** now, yet hiding still unseen the first small stirrings of life, readying itself for the warmth ahead. With the coming of the light, may you help me **(us)** give birth to the seeds of new beginnings that lie within me **(us)**. [Light candle]

Invoke Goddess: On this night I (**we**) dedicate my (**our**) ritual to Brigid, triple goddess of smithcraft, poetry, and healing. She is the fire of creation, of creativity and of life itself and I (**we**) welcome her gladly into my (**our**) circle this night. Bright blessings at midwinter to all! Brigid has returned with the sacred flame, watching over home and hearth. This is a time of rebirth and fertility, and as the earth grows full of life, may I (**we**) find abundance on my (**our**) path. [Light candle.]

Invoke God: On this night too, I (**we**) honor Herne the hunter, Lord of the animals and keeper of the dark places. He who reminds us that in the light there is always dark, and in the dark, light. I (**we**) welcome him gladly into my (**our**) circle this night. [Light candle]

Welcome speech for group ritual, spoken by high priest or high priestess: Imbolc is a time of darkness and cold when winter lies heavy on the land and the days are short. But even in the midst of the darkness the days are slowly lengthening and moving towards spring, warmth, and rebirth. Sometimes it seems as though spring will never come. So too, we often have dreams that seem like they will never come to fruition. We work hard at them, and in our hearts we know that they may be just around the corner, like spring. But it can be hard to keep the faith when things seem dark. Tonight, we will reaffirm our dreams as we celebrate the coming of spring.

High priest/high priestess reads, or you can read aloud or visualize to yourself if doing as a solitary: Close your eyes and feel the silence of the winter around you. The world is dark and quiet, the land slumbers. Follow the sound of your breathing—slowly, in and out. Then feel your breath going down your spine and out into the earth below. Reach down and touch the energy of the earth. Can you feel it stirring, rising from its slumber? Slowly, ponderously, the ground begins to warm. Roots send their first tentative fingers trembling toward the surface, and growth. Seeds shudder and then lie still, waiting for the right moment to burst into life. The Wheel of the Year turns, and the light grows brighter again. So too does our own light grow brighter. Open your eyes and see the light return!

Open your eyes, and light the candle(s). **(If doing as a group, each person will take a turn, going around the circle, until everyone has lit a candle.)**

High priest/high priestess reads, or you can aloud to yourself or simply follow the instructions if doing as a solitary: Each of us will take a star and write on it our deepest dreams—the ones that are so important yet seem impossibly far away in this moment. Then we will wrap those stars around a bulb. Bulbs contain within them the seeds of life yet to blossom, and so we will plant them to symbolize our dreams. When it is your turn, feel the chill of the earth in which you will plant. Then use the warmth of your hands to warm the soil as the sun does in spring. As you plant your bulb, focus on sending the energy of your desires into the bulb, the earth and into your dreams. And know that soon, our dreams will come true, as surely as the spring will warm the cold and light the darkness.

Write your dreams and goals for the year on the piece of paper and follow the instructions above, planting the bulb in the pot(s) of soil hidden underneath the altar.

Hold your pot of soil with its bulb and planted wishes, and say the following spell:

> *I wish upon the stars above*
> *And on the moonlight's gleam*
> *I ask the gods to send their love*
> *And help fulfill my dream*
> *Hard I've worked to get to here*
> *This magic time and space*
> *I know my dreams are drawing near*
> *At Fate's own measured pace*
> *Bring to blossom dreaming's fruit*
> *I ask from heart and soul*
> *As flowers spring from planted root*
> *Let me achieve my goal**

Take a moment of silence to visualize your dreams coming true.

Once the bulbs are planted, they should go back underneath the altar, as if being placed in the earth until the spring is truly here. After the ritual, the bulbs can be placed outside if your part of the country is warm enough. Otherwise, they can be kept inside, either permanently or until it is warm enough to put them outside. Spring Equinox is the perfect time to do this, if you can!

Cakes and Ale

Hold "cakes" up to the sky and say: *"I (we) give thanks for the blessings of this food, fruit of the earth, and symbol of the earth's bounty. May it sustain me (us) until the next harvest comes around.* [Eat a bite of cake. If you wish, you can put a piece on the altar as an offering. **Pass around the circle**.]

Hold chalice up and pour milk into it. Say: *"Like the milk that sustained my (our) ancestors in times of old, may this blessed liquid sustain me (us) now.* Drink the milk. [Note: if someone is allergic to milk, they may substitute another beverage.] **Pass around the circle.**

Pass speaking stick if holding a group ritual. Now is the time for people to share their dreams and goals, if they wish to.

Dismiss the quarters (starting with North) by turning toward each direction and snuffing out the candle after saying thank you.

North: *Powers of earth, I (we) thank you for being here today and protecting my (our) circle. Stay if you will, go if you must, in perfect love and perfect trust. So mote it be.*

West: *Powers of water, I (we) thank you for being here today and protecting my (our) circle. Stay if you will, go if you must, in perfect love and perfect trust. So mote it be.*

South: *Powers of fire, I (we) thank you for being here today and protecting my (our) circle. Stay if you will, go if you must, in perfect love and perfect trust. So mote it be.*

East: *Powers of the Air, I (**we**) thank you for being here today and protecting my (**our**) circle. Stay if you will, go if you must, in perfect love and perfect trust. So mote it be.*

Thank the god and goddess for their help by lifting your hands in the air and then snuffing out each candle after speaking.

Goddess: Great Brigid, I (**we**) thank you for your presence here in this circle today, and always. Guide me as I walk the path seeking balance and growth, and help me to achieve my goals. Farewell, and blessed be.

God: Great Herne, I (**we**) thank you for your presence here in this circle today, and always. May your wind always be at my back (**our backs**), encouraging me (**we**)to move forward in a positive and productive way. Farewell, and blessed be.

Open the circle by walking widdershins (counterclockwise) around the circle, or simply visualize the sacred space opening up and returning to the mundane world. **For a group ritual, you can all join hands and recite the Wiccan Rede, or simply say: *"The circle is open, but never broken. Merry meet, merry part, and merry meet again!"* Let go of each other's hands, and the circle is open.**

If you want, have a feast to celebrate the Sabbat, featuring related foods like lamb (if you're not a vegetarian), cheese fondue, or even ice cream. Don't forget to follow up your magickal work with concrete action in the mundane world.

*First published in *Everyday Witch A to Z Spellbook*

Notes

Ostara

Spring Equinox: Dox and Lux

Natalie Zaman

EVERY WINTER IT'S THE same. As I plod my way through February and then March, it becomes harder and harder to believe that warm spring breezes are right around the corner. The merrymaking of Yule and the stirrings of promise celebrated at Imbolc seem far away. As one biting day roars into the next, it appears there's no end in sight to the cold and the dark.

This time of the year is particularly challenging for me. Between children and work, I'm up early and often keep late nights. Every time I step outside, it's gloomy and freezing. One winter morning, when I was driving my daughter to swim practice and was certain that I hadn't seen the sun for weeks, the "a-ha moment" came.

On the one hand, I was rushing from activity to responsibility to obligation, while on the other I was professing to be on a path that connected me with nature and divinity—all of this supposedly bringing me an immense sense of satisfaction and peace of mind that somehow, I was "doing it all." I can honestly say I felt anything but satisfied—and forget peace of mind! This was not the way to do things. But the universe has a way of bringing things to light at the time when you can use them to exact positive change. Looking back, it made perfect sense that my inspiration to adjust my way of life came at Ostara, the Spring Equinox.

🌱

Signals that this is a time for transformation and renewal occur on both the mystical and scientific planes.

Ostara, named after the Saxon goddess Eostre (her symbols are the hare and the egg), is the sabbat that celebrates the return of spring, the re-emergence of life, the return—thank goddess—of warmer days. From Yule to this moment, the days have been getting longer. A day of equal light and dark kicks off the festivities, and the countdown to the goddess season commences.

Scientifically speaking, here's what's happening (in the Northern Hemisphere): Earth is moving steadily along its elliptical orbital path, the North Pole tilted towards the sun. Somewhere between March 19 and 22, the sun will shine directly on Earth's equator. This is the Vernal, or Spring Equinox, a single moment in time, calculated down to the minute—NOT a day of equal light and dark that is the essential element of the sabbat.

Equinox is a Latin word meaning "equal night," and the name for the brief brush of the sun on Earth's equator. The *Equilux,* "equal day," is the actual 24-hour period where day and night are closest to being equal (exactitude is a rarity). The equilux always falls in the vicinity of the equinox, but which day and how close in time day and night will be depends on location.

To determine the equilux in your part of the world, visit the U.S. Navy's Sun and Moon Data Calculator (http://aa.usno.navy.mil) and plug in the date of the Spring Equinox—for 2012 it's March 20—and the largest city nearest to where you live. This will provide you with a chart with the times for sun and moon risings and settings and moon phases. Take a look at the difference between the sunrise and sunset times in minutes. When I did the calculation for New York City, the sun will rise at 6:58 a.m. on the equinox, and set at 7:08 p.m., a 10-minute difference. Keep going backwards one day at a time until you find the smallest difference between sunrise and sunset. For the metro New York area, the equilux will be on March 16, 2012, when there's only a one-minute difference between day and night. You can also use this resource to determine the Autumnal Equilux.

So when does one celebrate Ostara—on the equinox or the equilux? The answer lies in what resonates with you. I know folks who keep Ostara on the day of the equinox, and others who begin their celebrations when they encounter their first warm day, or spot their first budding tree or flower of the season. I've been making an effort to align the physical and the spiritual, so if life allows (and it's been known not to cooperate on numerous occasions), I opt for the equilux. Search your heart. Whenever you choose to honor this turn of the wheel, the important thing is to imbibe the spirit of the season, work with it, and live it.

The Ultimate Balancing Act

I've come to know the sabbats as times to regroup from the subtle changes that take place as season melts into season. This is doubly so at Mabon and Ostara when we're coming out from seasons of extremes. In the autumn, I breathe a sigh of relief as the summer—hot, active, and maddeningly unstructured—comes to an end. Spring is the light at the end of a long, dark tunnel.

It was at Ostara, the sabbat of renewal and transformation, that I decided to meld my magical and mundane lives into one unified existence. I knew that this could mean major changes in how I was living; it would mean giving up some things and tweaking others, but I was certain that the sacred and the everyday were meant to go hand in hand—the ultimate balancing act.

In our house, Ostara has become a time of renewal and re-establishing balance inside and out. I've found that especially with home-making tasks, the coalescence of magical and mundane occurred quite naturally. This is nothing new; magic has always had practical applications.

As soon as there's a change in the air, a ritual "airing out" of the house commences. Unless there's a blizzard (and on the East Coast, that is a very real possibility, even into April), the windows are opened. Each room is cleaned and smudged. We go through pantries, closets, and drawers to see what has accumulated. Part of living wholly is living green: creating as little waste as possible, reusing and recycling, and living in sync with the seasons and environment.

Clothes that no longer fit are either up-cycled into something new, or prepared to be donated to charity—with blessings of health and happiness for the future owners. Items that are beyond repair are given a new life as rags for cleaning. Inevitably we can amass a collection of outgrown toys and books that can be given a second life at shelters and centers. No drawer, closet, or cupboard is left undisturbed.

Apart from necessaries like milk and eggs, grocery shopping is brought to a halt. Food that's been languishing in the freezer and cabinets (that scone mix that looked so interesting, unused jars of jam, and lonely bags of frozen vegetables) are pulled out and finally consumed. According to Hugh Fearnley-Whittingstall in his book *The River Cottage Year* (a terrific resource for eating seasonally), this is an old "Shrove Tuesday" custom. The "shrove" of Shrove Tuesday is undoubtedly Christian, but the notion of "waste not, want not" and using up the remnants of the larder in preparation of the anticipated restocking that will happen once the garden is producing again is far older.

Here I found myself presented with another challenge. Like many people, I came to the Craft from another tradition. When I first started down this path, I wanted nothing to do with my former faith, but this attitude left me feeling bereft. I didn't want to abandon the customs I'd grown up with and shared with my family—and I didn't have to. Maintaining past traditions and connecting them to my evolving philosophy helped me to reconcile past religion to present and future spirituality. Knowing those dear to me that have passed on are still with me, the sweet whiff of an Easter lily, and chocolate eggs are all touchstones to the past, and a link to the divine (I challenge anyone to question the divinity of chocolate.).

Ostara and Easter celebrate the renewal of life (though by different means!). Nowhere is this more evident that what's happening outside. For us, it's time for animal dwellings to be refurbished. The herb bundles fixed above hutch and coop doors are refreshed with springtime wishes for health and fecundity. Thyme (the herb I've had the most success growing) is good for protection, and combined with human hair helps to keep foxes away. Eggs are left with the chickens to hatch, or if our hen population is low, we'll order chicks from the preservation center (to the delight of our mail carrier).

It's also time to prepare the garden. In central New Jersey, we don't dare put anything in the ground until well after Beltane, but there's still plenty of work to do. Plots are tidied up. Ashes from the Yule log, saved for this moment to bring the positive energy from the past year, are mixed into the soil. Going forward, the ground will be turned and mixed with compost on a regular basis until it's time to plant.

Plastic fruit containers with hinged lids and coffee cups with dome tops have been saved for a second life in beginning the garden. They make great mini-terrariums that create an ideal environment for starting the herbs and vegetables that will eventually make their way outside. We mix potting soil with some soil from the garden—the plants' future home—and a pinch of Yule log ash, and then plant the seeds with a few magical words of encouragement:

Spring is here,
Time to grow!
Blessings on the seeds I sow!

᭡

After writing this and the accompanying ritual (on page 152), I read it over, impressed—wow, do I really *do* all that?

I try.

I would love to say that every day I rise with the sun, fill my body with organic fuel, and meander through a productive day of work that honors the Divine. The fact of the matter is that this transformation is still very much a work in progress, and far from perfect or idyllic. I forget to recycle, and I still eat processed foods. I get into head-shaking matches with my mom over religion. I've questioned my sanity when I have to go out in the cold and wet to tend to animals or gardening chores. I sometimes find myself cursing the work rather than reveling in it—and I can't count the number of times I've been so overwhelmed with the mundane aspects of a task that I neglect any attention to deity at all. This is when I take a deep breath and remind myself, *baby steps.*

A change to a spiritually infused, self-sufficient lifestyle is a big shift. It doesn't happen overnight; it's a one step, one day, one change at a time process. Changing one aspect of your life and practice, like eating seasonal, locally grown produce and honoring the elements, god, and goddess during meal preparation (and/or growth if you're growing your own) is a *huge* change that takes discipline, dedication, and time to hone. It may take a lifetime to really get it right, but that's what it's all about, isn't it?

Celestial Sway

Fern Feto Spring

THE PROMISE OF SPRINGTIME blossoms as night and day come together in a balance at the Spring Equinox on March 20, 2012. The sabbat heralds a time of growing light, as the sun grows stronger and the earth comes alive in a ripe abundance of beauty and color. The courageous passion of Aries initiates us into the future, preparing our spirits to blaze unknown trails and begun exciting new adventures. As the fire of the season propels us towards growth and change, we can tap into our inner hero/heroines, bravely facing our fears and confronting the shadows of the past.

The symbols of the Oestre/Spring Equinox sabbat: eggs, rabbits, and flowers, represent the fertility and potential available now. This is a time to brew dreams in the cauldron of possibility, drawing on the life force that arises from the earth for energy and sustenance. Our warrior selves are strong at this time, as we fight to protect our fragile new beginnings, using the power of Aries to defend against any vulnerability or weakness that may arise.

A New Moon in Aries on March 22 joins with quirky Uranus, promising an equinox season filled with surprises and unusual opportunities. This pioneering energy asks us to stretch and expand our comfort zone, taking risks that we may have avoided in the past.

Spring fever may feel particularly strong this year as we experience an internal pressure to make changes and try new directions for growth. Since Mercury is now retrograde in Aries and forming a conjunction with this New Moon, communication is emphasized at this time. We may need to work harder to express any inspirations or visionary ideas that arise now. If we patiently take the time to think things through before we try to communicate our thoughts to others, our words will have more power and energy than if we speak first and think later.

Venus and Jupiter continue to move together in the sign of Taurus throughout the month of March, accentuating the springtime abundance with a ripe, fertile and sensual energy that increases our desire for comfort and pleasure. We may even feel tempted to overindulge now, gorging on experiences that make us feel good physically. If we can find ways to seek pleasure without slipping into gluttony or greed, we will enjoy this planetary alignment more and avoid unpleasant after effects that could affect our health.

A Full Moon in Libra on April 6 exactly conjuncts (joins) the asteroid Vesta. This lunation awakens our desire to serve in a style that also reflects our individuality and truest sense of ourselves. We are challenged now to integrate the needs of others (Sun in Aries), with our desire for independence and freedom. A spring cleanse can help us gain the physical and emotional clarity that we may need to move forward with a greater sense of self-awareness and balance.

The Spring Equinox season ends with the planet Mars going direct in the sign of Virgo and roughly opposite Neptune on April 13. Mars, the god of war in Roman mythology, is ruled by Aries and this feisty planet affects our drive, energy, and passion. In Virgo, Mars has demanded that we pay careful attention to the details of our actions, perfecting and fine-tuning our energy output so that nothing is wasted. Health and physical maintenance routines have also been emphasized during this transit. The retrograde period, which lasted from January 23 to April 13, forced us to internalize and deepen these Mars in Virgo lessons, taking them to new heights.

As Mars turns direct, it forms an opposition with Neptune, the planet of surrender and letting go. We may feel a certain amount of disorientation at this time, as we are asked to simultaneously maintain a practical grounded approach to life, while also opening to the Neptunian realm of dreams, spirit, and mystery. The opposition aspect always asks us to stretch, growing beyond our known limits and metamorphosing into a new form.

New Moon in Aries

The New Moon in Aries on March 22 presents an excellent opportunity to envision plans and projects for the future. Uranus, the planet of experimentation and new experiences, people, and places, gives this lunation an added zing that can pave the way for "Aha!" moments and exciting awakenings. However, Mercury, the planet of communication, information, travel, and technology will also be retrograde at this time and forming a conjunction to both the New Moon and Uranus. Mercury slows down the action-packed momentum of the Aries New Moon cycle, making it more internalized and deliberate. Mercury's retrograde direction may also ask us to confront conflicts from the past that we thought had been resolved, so this could be a time to clear the slate and start fresh, letting bygones be bygones. You can maximize the potential of these planetary influences by gathering information and ideas for future plans and bravely dreaming up revolutionary ideas. Just wait until Mercury goes direct on April 4 (ideally wait until the Mercury retrograde shadow period has passed on April 17) to move forward.

New Moon in Aries Fire Gazing Ritual

Use the fast-moving, but introspective, energy of the Aries New Moon to gaze into the future, using fire as the doorway into the world of spirit. On the night of the New Moon (March 22 at 10:37 a.m. EDT), build a fire in your fireplace, outside, or in a cauldron or other fire safe container. Invoke Mars, Uranus, and Mercury, the guardians of this New Moon, to aid you in seeking a vision to guide your springtime new beginnings. Add a handful of mugwort to your fire to enhance your psychic sight, and/or drink mugwort tea. Gaze into the fire and notice what shapes, images, and impressions emerge. Try keeping a journal nearby to record your insights, or do this with a partner or group and take turns "reading" the fire for each other. When the fire has burned down to ash, you may want to gather some of the ash and place it in a container on your altar, asking for further insight to come to you in your dreams.

Venus in Taurus, Conjunct Jupiter

Venus in Taurus conjunct Jupiter combines Venus, the planet of love, money, beauty, and pleasure, with Jupiter, the planet of expansion, opportunity, wisdom, and growth. This union of beneficial energy takes place in Venus' home sign (Taurus), amplifying the power of this planetary configuration. Though the two planets are "officially" in aspect on March 14, the positive effects of their meeting last throughout the month of March.

Since Taurus is the sign that most appreciates pleasing the five senses—sight, sound, touch, taste, and smell—make the most of this expansive Taurean influence and plan a ritual party for your senses.

Taurus Feasting Ritual

You can plan a feast for any number of people, from a self-indulgent candlelight dinner for yourself, to a romantic meal for you and your sweetie, or, really maximize the expansive energy of Jupiter and share the bounty with a group of friends and family. The important thing is that you highlight each of the five senses with pleasant music, enticing smells, beautiful flower or table arrangements, interesting textures to touch, and most of all, delicious tastes. You may want to prepare dishes that highlight the earthy richness of Taurus—mushrooms, chocolate, and red wine all fit the theme of this planetary influence. Further honor Venus and Jupiter by dressing up for your feast and invoking the two planets before you eat, honoring their presence and thanking them for their bounty.

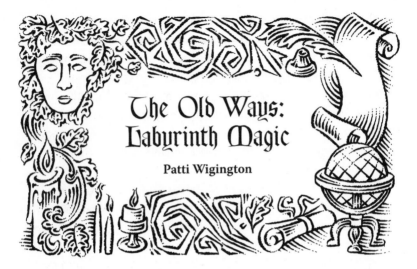

The Old Ways: Labyrinth Magic

Patti Wigington

OSTARA IS A TIME of balance, of equal parts darkness and light. The ground is still cold and hard, but at Ostara we know that life will begin anew in just a few short weeks. The nights are chilly, but the days are bright and sunny. For many of us, that feeling of balance brings a time of reflection and meditation, a season to regain our equilibrium following the long, cold months of winter.

One of the best-known symbols of balance is that of the labyrinth. Unlike a maze, which leads us in twists and turns to dead ends and false stops, a labyrinth is designed to have a beginning, a center, and an end, much like life itself. The labyrinth often becomes a magical geometric shape that lies somewhere between the mundane and the sacred. In a few Wiccan traditions, the labyrinth represents the journey of the Goddess in her return from the cold darkness of winter, on her way back to the fertile season of spring.

Labyrinths, and images of them, have been found at sites dating back thousands of years. The most typical style is the seven-circuit Cretan labyrinth, named for the legendary labyrinth of King Minos at Crete. According to Greek mythology, Daedalus built the labyrinth to hold the terrifying beast known as the Minotaur. When the hero Theseus arrived, the lovely Aradne gave him some golden thread to take with him in his quest, so he could find his way back out. While Minos' labyrinth was a maze with many choices, the word Cretan has come to represent a unicursal structure with one way in, one way out, and a very specifically designated path. A Cretan labyrinth's single path makes it easy to navigate.

In 2005, a pair of Cretan labyrinth carvings were found etched in cliff faces near Tintagel, Cornwall, England. Their origins have not yet been determined, although they may have been carved any time between the Bronze Age and the nineteenth century.

During the days of the Roman Empire, it became fashionable to work a Cretan labyrinth into floor mosaics. Often, tiles were integrated into floor designs that created a squared-off labyrinth pattern around the perimeter of a room. These designs, known as the meander pattern, later evolved into a new shape in which the labyrinth has four distinct quarters and numerous circuits. Today, in the Italian cathedral at Lucca, a version of this design can be seen as a wall carving. Visitors trace the pattern with their finger to achieve some inner peace before entering the chapel. This fourfold design with eleven circuits is best known as the Chartres or medieval labyrinth style.

During the era of the Crusades, families often built a labyrinth as a way to represent the pilgrimage to the Holy Land, and the Chartres design saw resurgence in popularity as a status symbol for the well-off. Churches often incorporated the unicursal patterns into floors in their chapels, as an earthly representation of worshippers' paths to heaven. This pattern could be walked or crawled, traveled quickly or slowly, and allowed the penitent to walk the fine line between the misery of their earthbound lives and the joys that they believed awaited them in salvation.

Later, labyrinths took on a less spiritual and far more playful meaning—wealthy landowners commissioned labyrinth gardens with high hedges as a place for romantic assignations. A number of poems describe how King Henry II fell in love with young Rosamund Clifford, despite already being married to Eleanor of Aquitaine. Henry came up with a clever plan to have both his queen and his mistress. Legend has it that he built Rosamund a lodge to live in, and then surrounded the lodge with a labyrinth garden so that Eleanor would never find her. Yet once more, we find the labyrinth as a symbol of balance, between duty and passion, fidelity and lust, and the keeping of one woman out while another was contained within.

During the reign of later kings, the simple unicursal labyrinths were replaced by complex mazes, which forced travelers to make choices and decisions, occasionally pushing them into dead ends. Today, however, the Chartres design has become popular once again, particularly among members of the metaphysical community, who have recognized the labyrinth as a wonderful meditative tool. In fact, many metaphysical events and expos feature labyrinth rooms where people can silently walk the path.

If you get the chance to walk a labyrinth, you can use this simple polarizing technique for a problem-solving meditation. As you enter the labyrinth, walk slowly and evenly. Use the approach to the center as a time to visualize a dilemma you'd like to resolve, and think about how it has been affecting you. When you reach the center, focus on solutions. If you want to ask for divine assistance from the gods of your tradition, now is the perfect time to do it. Otherwise, as you stand in the center of the labyrinth, open yourself up to possible ways of solving your problem. The center is a location of true balance—neither the path of entrance nor the way to the exit—and this, for many people, is a perfect place to find answers. Finally, as you work your way slowly out of the labyrinth, think about how things will change for you once you get your solutions in place. Consider how your life will be different when your problem has been solved.

Remember, the purpose of a labyrinth, unlike a maze, is not to force us to get lost. A labyrinth does just the opposite—it helps us find our way. Even though we may feel a bit confused because of the labyrinth's turns and winding circuits—as though we are walking between the worlds—we are always on the path to the center. Once we reach that center, we are always headed toward the exit, and the end of our journey will end with a feeling of harmony and balance.

Feasts and Treats

Susan Pesznecker

OSTARA—THE SPRING EQUINOX—is all about eggs, the font from which life springs. What better way to welcome spring than with a bountiful, eggy breakfast? Follow the old traditions: get up before sunrise and greet the equinoctial Sun, reflecting on the growing life force around you. Then hit the kitchen to cook up your Ostara repast.

Sun Babies With Apricot Preserves

Prep time: 10 minutes
Cook time: 15–20 minutes
Serves: 4

2 glass pie plates (or similar-size casserole dishes)
4 eggs
1 cup milk
1 cup flour
½ teaspoon salt
2 tablespoons butter
Apricot preserves (or other preserves of choice)
1 fresh lemon
Maple syrup

Premake the pancake batter at least 30 minutes before cooking (preferably the night): Combine eggs, milk, flour, and salt in a blender; blend until smooth. Chill.

Preheat oven to 425 degrees F. Thirty minutes before serving, put 1 tablespoon of butter in each pie plate and set the plates in the oven to heat.

When the butter is sizzling, remove the pie plates from oven. Swirl to coat with butter, then pour half of the chilled egg mixture into each plate. Put plates back into the oven. Work quickly: For maximum "puff," you want <u>cold</u> batter meeting <u>hot</u> pan meeting <u>hot</u> oven.

The pancakes should cook at least 15 minutes. Don't open the oven door during this time, as your pancakes may fall.

While the pancakes cook, spoon preserves into a serving dish. Stir in a bit of fresh lemon zest and a squeeze of lemon juice. Warm slightly in the microwave.

After 15 minutes, use your oven light to check the pancakes or open the door just a crack. They may need to cook a bit longer. When done, they should be golden brown; the centers will look done and the pancakes will have puffed up like a bowl.

Carry the finished pancakes directly from oven to table and serve there—your guests will ooh and ahh! Cut each pancake in half and serve on a warm plate. Drizzle with preserves. I also like to offer syrup for my guests who prefer that.

Egg and Sausage Tray

A tray of assorted eggs and sausages is a fun and tasty side for your Sun Babies. When I was little, my grandmother would allow me to eat as many eggs on Eostre/Ostara as I possibly could, and the eggy bounty of this breakfast honors that tradition. Sausage links and patties also evoke the promised fertility of chalice and blade, with the eggs exemplifying Ostara's life-giving theme.

Prep time: 30 minutes

Cook time: 20 minutes

Serves: 4

12 fresh eggs
Sausages links and patties—enough for four people
Salt and pepper
1 tablespoon mayonnaise

About 35 minutes before serving: Place 4 eggs in a medium saucepan. Add cold water, covering the eggs with about 1-inch of water. Place over high heat and bring to a boil. When water boils, cover the pan and remove from heat. Cover and let sit for 16 minutes, then pour off hot water and run cold water over the eggs to stop the cooking process. Set these "hard-cooked eggs" aside at room temperature.

About 30 minutes before serving: Begin cooking your sausages according to package directions. Use medium heat and turn the sausages often. As they finish, drain on paper towels, then arrange on a warmed, round platter. Set this in the oven on very, very low heat to keep warm.

About 25 minutes before serving: Crack 4 eggs into a small bowl. Add 1 tablespoon water, a dash of salt, and a sprinkle of pepper. Beat with a fork. Set aside.

About 10 minutes before serving: Heat two medium skillets—preferably nonstick—over medium heat. Melt 1 tablespoon butter in each one. Pour the beaten egg mixture into one skillet; cook until the eggs are scrambled and set, stirring occasionally. As the eggs thicken, stir in 1 tablespoon of mayonnaise. When the eggs are "set" (fluffy, with no obvious raw spots), remove these "scrambled eggs" to the warmed platter.

Crack 4 eggs into the second skillet. Allow to cook until they begin to firm up. After 2 to 3 minutes, turn carefully with a wide spatula, and cook for another 2 to 3 minutes. Remove these "over medium" eggs to the warmed platter.

Just before serving: Crack and peel the hard-cooked eggs. Cut each one in half and arrange on the warmed egg and sausage platter.

Bubblenuts

The word *bubblenuts* is a goofy family label describing a rich fruit and streusel-topped cake. Simple to make, it works with whatever fruit is on hand.

Prep time: 20 minutes
Cook time: 30–35 minutes
Serves: 6+

½ cup sugar, divided
1 teaspoon cinnamon
½ cup butter, unsalted, chilled, and divided
1¼ cups flour
1½ teaspoons baking powder
½ teaspoon salt
1 egg
½ cup milk
1 teaspoon vanilla
Fresh fruit: pitted cherries, blueberries, sliced peaches, etc.

Preheat oven to 400 degrees F. Grease a 13 × 9-inch pan. Combine ¼ cup sugar, cinnamon, and ¼ cup butter together with a pastry blender. Set aside—this is the bubblenuts' topping.

Combine flour, ¼ cup sugar, baking powder, and salt. Cut in ¼ cup butter until coarse crumbs form.

Beat egg, milk, and vanilla in a small bowl. Add to flour mixture and stir to combine.

Spread the batter in the greased pan. Arrange fruit decoratively over the entire surface—capture symbols, patterns, or numerology in your design for magickal oomph. Sprinkle with the reserved topping.

Bake 25 to 35 minutes. The center should be done, the edges browned, and the fruit bubbly.

Fruit Smoothies

Set out an array of ingredients and allow diners to mix and match. For magickal fun, arrange notecards that list the correspondences of each component.

Prep time: 15 minutes

Serves: 4

6 cups fresh fruit; washed, peeled, and chunked (strawberries, raspberries, blueberries, mango, banana, pineapple, peaches, etc.)
1 cup liquid: fruit juices, milk, yogurt, frozen sorbet
Optional spices and herbs: cinnamon, black pepper, fresh basil leaves, lemon peel, etc.
Sweeteners (sugar, honey, stevia)
1–2 cups ice

Place fruit in blender and purée. Add liquid, spices/herbs, and ice and blend until slushy.

Crafty Crafts

Ellen Dugan

Theme of the Season: Growth and new opportunities
Colors: Spring green, and pastel shades of pink, purple, blue, and yellow
Scents: Hyacinth, violet
Energy: Excitement and rebirth

Ostara/Spring Wreath for your Door

To commemorate the season of spring, make a silk floral wreath for Ostara and to celebrate the equinox! You can make this chic and stylish or over the top and cute. It's all about your own personal style, taste, and which colors and designs you like. Remember, for the best selection, you will probably want to start hitting the arts and crafts stores in late February and early March. By then the spring flowers and colored egg picks will be out. Watch for decorative ribbon with natural spring themes such as flowers, bunnies, and eggs.

Supplies
One large grapevine wreath
Glue gun or glue sticks

4–5 yards of ½-inch wide satin ribbon in yellow or purple (buying a spool is quite affordable.)

Silk flowers to add to the wreath such as lilacs, pansies, tulips, or mini-daffodils

Wire cutters

Seasonal floral picks such as eggs and butterflies

A spool of wide, seasonal decorative spring ribbon for a bow (you'll need at least three yards to make a decent larger bow)

An over-the-door wreath hanger

Instructions: To begin, lay your grapevine wreath front-side down on your work surface. Take the spool of ribbon and weave a pentagram with the ribbon through the grapevine and in the center of your wreath. (Work directly from the spool of ribbon; don't cut the ribbon until you finish weaving the star in the center.) Then knot it and adjust the ribbon star. If necessary, use a few dabs of hot glue to hold it into place. Loop a six-inch piece of the ribbon around the vine at the top of your wreath. Knot it and use that ribbon loop for a hanger. If you like, you may fasten that hanging loop with a dab of hot glue as well. Once the glue is set in a few moments, flip the wreath over to the front.

Now begin to lay out your floral pieces on the wreath. Snip the stems of the floral pieces a tad longer than you think you will need and tuck them into the wreath. (Remember, it's easier to snip a stem shorter later, than it is to be stuck with a stem that is too short to use.) Work your way around the wreath and lay out the flowers.

A trick that floral designers use is they always work with odd numbers of their main flower. So think of threes and fives. For example, if you are working with clusters of mini-daffodils and they are the main flower on your wreath, create a triangle with those flowers on your wreath.

So, if the wreath were a clock face, you would arrange the main flowers at 1, 5, and 10. That way your main floral component creates a off-side triangle. This pulls the eye around the wreath, which is actually pleasing to the eye. Then fill in with your other flowers. Once you have things where you like them, you can glue them in with the glue gun. Arrange the flowers first—glue gun them in last!

Finally, add your picks to the wreath. Again, if you are using decorative egg picks, use an odd number on your wreath. If you like, take the wide sheer seasonal ribbon and tie up a nice bow and add that as well. You do NOT have to put a bow at the center top or bottom. As a floral designer, I can tell you that the best wreaths typically have an off-center bow. I think they just look better—more artsy and personal and not so pre-made.

Once you have everything in place on your wreath, hang it either on the outside or the inside of your front door, and enjoy!

Note: If you store this wreath flat after the sabbat and keep it covered you will be able to reuse it for many years.

Cost: $15.00 and up. I recommend using coupons and sales. The large grapevine wreath was $3.99. The floral picks, sheer spring ribbon in an egg print, and floral stems cost around $10.00 but were 40 percent off. The picks were also on sale for about a buck apiece.

Time: 30 minutes to one hour

Egg Tree to Celebrate the Equinox

Decorate a tree or the shrubs in your front yard with eggs on the morning of Spring Equinox. My children were small when we started doing this, but it accidentally began a neighborhood-wide decorating trend. It's an enjoyable and clever way to take back the holiday.

Supplies
12–24 plastic, pastel-colored eggs (the kind that snap open)
Two spools of ¼-inch-wide satin ribbon your choice of the color
Transparent tape
Your chosen tree or shrubs in your front yard

Instructions: The night before the equinox, cut 10- to 12-inch lengths of the satin ribbon: one length for each egg. Then open up the plastic eggs and lay the center of the length of ribbon in the middle of the opened egg. Snap the egg closed with the ribbon inside,

and then tie the ends of the ribbon into a neat knot. (If necessary, use transparent tape to secure the ribbon to the outside of the egg.)

Gather all of the ribboned eggs together in a basket or bowl. In the morning as the sun comes up, hang the eggs on the low branches of a tree or on your shrubs in the front yard. Rearrange the eggs if necessary. However, it is cute to let the kids loose and see where they hang the eggs. Leave the eggs up as long as you wish. Don't be surprised if you start your own trend in the neighborhood.

As a variation on a theme, I have seen this done with smaller plastic eggs on topiaries and also noted colored eggs tucked into green leafy garlands draped around a front door. Be creative! See what you can conjure up for the sabbat.

Note: While clearly not natural, I use plastic eggs because they are weatherproof, affordable, and available for reuse in the future.

Cost: $5.00 and up (depending on the number of plastic eggs)

Time: 15–30 minutes

All One Family

Clea Danaan

OUR FIRST BATCH OF chickens was born near Ostara, shipped to us fresh out of the shell. The day I went to pick them up, it snowed—a heavy, wet snow that I hated driving in. With my daughter holding the peeping box on her lap in the back seat, I carefully made our way through the blinding white mess heading toward home. We spun in a circle as I turned off the main road. With a little blessing from the Goddess, I managed to not hit any other cars. I righted us and we proceeded safely home; me, my daughter, and our little pullets, a chariot of Goddesses bringing spring home to the garden.

We had already planted peas, and spinach would come next, as well as salad greens and a few brassicas like broccoli and cabbage. The snow blanketed the garden, but beneath the chill I could feel the quickening of spring. When we got everyone safely inside the house, we sat in the strange light of snow-crusted windows and held the sweet warm bodies of promise: baby chicks. One of our babies was an Easter Egger, a hen who lays green or blue eggs. We named her Tara, short for Ostara.

They didn't start laying until that summer, but just the promise of the abundance of eggs brought home the energy of the Spring Equinox for us. All my research about hen-keeping and dreaming about a simple urban homestead had now fleshed out—literally. Getting our chickens taught us about the abundance and fertility in community, too. Community is a key part of urban homesteading, or really of any venture of living on earth. We saw the wealth of community most keenly that spring, as one friend helped me when I purchased those first chicks, another lent us her dog crate to keep them in, and a third gave us a pile of scrap wood found in her crawl space out of which we built our coop. It was this last gift, the wood, that encouraged me to go ahead and pursue the dream of keeping chickens. Instead of buying an already built coop for a thousand dollars, we made our own using my friend's cast-offs and some creative engineering.

The following spring, we felt the power of Ostara again from the chickens. Now full-grown, they had been laying for eight months, but their production went down over the winter. Light sets off a chicken's laying (which is why egg factories never turn off the lights), so when the days begin to lengthen, hens produce more eggs. By the equinox, we had a fairly good supply. Though snow was forecast, we collected four eggs and knew spring was really here.

Raising chickens has attuned my family more deeply to the rhythms of the Wheel of the Year. While the garden responds to changing temperatures, the hens respond more to changing light. I feel our journey around the sun more acutely. My daughter, too, has learned more about the seasons and how they actually unfold by helping to care for our little flock of hens. She has seen for herself the magic of life: we feed and care for the hens, and they gift us with eggs. Their droppings and shells then nourish the garden, which provides them with greens and worms. The spiral continues.

Ostara is the time of year when you and your family can begin the garden, depending on your climate. To find your plant hardiness gardening zone by zip code, visit www.garden.org/zipzone. Your local cooperative extension office will also have zone information, which includes first and last average frost date, and often suggests dates for planting and other garden tasks. For instance, I live in zone 5a. My last average frost date is right around Mother's Day, the first average frost date is mid-September. I plant peas on St. Patrick's Day, and I wrap young trees' trunks to avoid winter sun scald from Thanksgiving to Easter. So on Ostara, I have peas in the ground, the hens are laying, and I get to unwrap my trees. It is a time of fertile hope and excitement.

The Spring Equinox is also a time of balance. We must be balanced in order to experience fertility and abundance. Whether you seek actual physical fertility, garden fertility, or spiritual fertility, first you need balanced nutrition, habits, and energy. A woman seeking a healthy pregnancy needs to eat a balanced diet, get good rest, and find her own center as much as possible. Balanced garden soil yields healthier plants. A balanced diet for my hens yields more nutritious eggs. Balanced energy in the home, in our hearts, and in our lives yields optimum health. This is a great time of year to examine balance in yourself.

One way to do this is through your diet. Abundant, fresh healthy food will help you make better choices for yourself and your family. Choose organic, switch to agave, honey, and stevia instead of refined sugar, and eat more fruits and vegetables. Notice the change in your overall health and well-being. You know what shifts in your diet need to happen; use the balance of day and night to enter into this dietary balance for yourself. If you do not know what dietary shifts need to happen but feel this might be an area of imbalance, seek out a skilled nutritionist to help you identify areas of change.

Another way to cultivate balance is to actually acknowledge and appreciate the balance you already feel in your life. As a parent you may be thinking—what balance?! Look at all aspects of your family life and see where you do have a sense of balance. You may find this balance in your spiritual life, your schedule, your relationship with your partner(s), your child(ren)'s education, your finances, your health, or the garden. Honor and acknowledge every little bit of balance you discover. Then ask yourself where you need more balance. Meditate on how you might create this needed balance. If appropriate, call a family meeting to discuss how to create more balance to-gether. Ways to create balance include date nights for you and your partner(s), less television viewing, more time in nature, fewer extra-curricular activities, a weekend of organizing the garage as a family, or regular family rituals.

A mother friend of mine once wondered whether balance was even possible for a parent, especially a stay-at-home, homeschooling mom who devotes all of her time to her family. I offered that perhaps balance is not ever perfect, but is more like equilibrium in nature. There is never the exact perfect "balance" between predator and prey, for instance. Instead there will be one year with lots of rain that leads to a massive insect hatching, which leads birds to hatch more babies, who grow up and eat all the insects. The supply of food goes down and thus does the bird population. This flux of growth and recession ebbs and flows over a long period, always seeking balance in its natural ways. I suspect balance in our lives is comparable. We continue to seek the best way to care for our families and ourselves, to balance work and play, love and chores, and so on. As soon as we find an answer, everything shifts—new baby, new job, new behavior from the seven-year-old—and we seek balance anew.

Rituals at this time of year can be about balance, fertility, and abundance. Examine in what ways these energies play out in your life and your family. As you plant your first seeds, notice the quick-ening green, and give thanks for spring, let yourself attune to the natural rhythms of birth and fertility. Plan a simple family circle where each person discusses what abundance he or she notices and is grateful for, and in what ways she or he is seeking greater balance. Raise the energy as a group through chant or song, then direct that energy into the areas of your lives that need more fertility or abun-dance. Let the earth help you. Feel her, poised in balance, a great goddess bursting forth all around us.

Ostara Ritual:
Cleanse, Balance, Rest

Natalie Zaman

SPRING CLEANING—THERE'S A reason we do it: to dust out the accumulated cobwebs of the winter blahs and clear the clutter built up during the long dark months of winter to make way for new life that comes with spring. We do this instinctively to restore equilibrium. It's natural to want to be balanced, but difficult to achieve when you're feeling overwhelmed by darkness, stress, and in many cases, stuff.

An essential element in achieving balance is rest—something a lot of us don't get enough of in today's demanding, fast-paced world. This ritual takes a seemingly mundane task and turns it—literally—into a magical act that will help restore balance and promote restful sleep. This isn't just for a single night or season, but to carry through the entire year, because each sabbat, though unique, carries a piece of the others inside it. This is especially needed at Ostara, as it's been deemed necessary to "spring ahead" and lose an hour!

While this ritual was written with a family or solitary practitioner in mind, larger groups can incorporate the herbal pouches and the intention behind them into their celebratory circle. Individual participants can then perform the ritual at home alone or with their families. Folks in the Southern Hemisphere will want to perform this at their Vernal Equinox

Items needed

Eight white fabric squares (for fresh starts), approximately 9 x 9*

Black ribbon or yarn (for protection)*

Equal amounts of the following herbs, enough to fill eight small pouches for each bed in your home:

- Rosebuds, to promote healing and peace, both good for avoiding nightmares
- Lavender, to refresh and cleanse
- Colt's foot, for tranquility; this herb is also known to stimulate receptors in the brain so dreams and visions are encouraged

Small quartz crystals or chips to act as a magnifier for the other elements in the mixture

Small spiral seashells to represent the water in our bodies and the path to restful sleep; the spiral shell is like a path that leads us into and out of dreams so that sleep and awakening are quiet and relaxed

Clean bedding in seasonal colors (pastels like pink, yellow, blue, green, etc.)*

Compass to determine direction

Six crystals to represent the quarters and the God and Goddess (I use quartz crystals, but you can use stones that vibrate with a specific element or deity)

Broom (the ritual kind!)

Athame or wand for circle casting

Smudge stick

Music. My favorite music for this ritual is Brother Sun, Sister Moon, a recording of acapella choral music performed by the Cambridge Singers. While the musical pieces are Christian in nature, they're universal in their power to uplift and relax. Here, again, an opportunity to bring past and present together presented itself, and I admittedly took advantage—besides, it sounds pretty.

* Whenever possible, use natural fibers such as cotton, silk, or wool—they are better next to your skin and can be returned to nature when your ritual is complete.

Note: Normally, I use candles to represent each element/direction and deities, but because this ritual requires that you leave them in place over night, open flames are neither practical nor safe. If you want to use light as a part of a ritual, battery-operated tealights work just as well, and are totally safe to use—especially if you'll be performing the ritual with children.

Preparation: Prior to the equinox/equilux, but not too far beforehand, clean and arrange your bedroom. An orderly bedroom arranged for good energy flow is one of those often-overlooked details that make a big difference in a good night's sleep. To determine the most beneficial layout for your bedroom, consult resources on feng shui (Lillian Too's *Complete Feng Shui* and Tess Whitehurst's *Magical Housekeeping* offer practical and realistic tips for room arrangement and clutter clearing.)

While cleaning up isn't part of the actual ritual, *see* your room as a peaceful sanctuary while you work. Picture the details in your mind. Wizard Oberon Zell once told me that a wizard's most important magical tool is his mind. I sincerely believe that the ability to visualize—to picture things in your head before they're a reality—is the most potent aspect of magical and ritual work, the initial catalyst that brings about change. Throughout this ritual, there are many calls to visualize. It's a good skill to develop, as it will grow creativity and help establish the connection between magical and mundane.

The night before the ritual will be performed, prepare the herbal pouches. In a large bowl, mix the herbs, crystals, and shells together. Use your hands (wash first!) to dig in and make a connection with the materials you're working with. Infuse them with your intention—to promote rest, relaxation and productive dreams.

Place an equal amount of the mixture on each fabric square. Gather the edges together to form a pouch, then tie it shut with a piece of ribbon or yarn. When you are finished, you'll have eight pouches, one for each sabbat.

Lay the pouches on a windowsill or other location where they will catch the morning light of the equinox or equilux and be impregnated with its energy.

The Ritual

On the morning of the ritual, rise with the sun (Ostara is a wonderful time to start a good habit!). Bathe, shower, and do whatever you do to get yourself prepared in the morning.

When you are ready to begin, take a moment to ground and center, taking as many deep cleansing breaths as you need to clear your mind, steady your heart rate and relax.

Welcome the deities and the elements. Using a compass, determine the location of each watchtower in your bedroom, and set a crystal to mark it. If you are performing the ritual alone, then you'll have to do all the speaking yourself, but if this is a family affair, have each person take a turn in calling the four quarters and the God and Goddess. Feel free to welcome the deities and elements in whatever way you're comfortable. My personal preference is for simplicity in acknowledging the spiritual traits of each that I hope to emulate when working with them. Call the quarters:

In the East: *Welcome air! Thank you for your presence. Bless me and my home with your understanding as I work to restore balance this day of Ostara.*

In the South: *Welcome fire! Thank you for your presence. Bless me and my home with your warmth and light as I work to restore balance this day of Ostara.*

In the West: *Welcome water! Thank you for your presence. Bless me and my home with your varying nature as I work to restore balance on this day of Ostara.*

In the North: *Welcome earth! Thank you for your presence. Bless me and my home with your solid dependability as I work to restore balance on this day of Ostara.*

Place the crystals or candles that will represent the God and Goddess in a location where they will not be disturbed (remember you will be working!) and where they can watch over the proceedings. Invoke the deities:

Welcome Lady of Spring! Thank you for your presence. Bless me and my home with your nurturing love as I work to restore balance on this Ostara day.

Welcome Vernal Lord! Thank you for your presence. Bless me and my home with your enduring strength as I work to restore balance on this Ostara day.

Dispel negativity and create sacred space. Before creating sacred space, it's important to get rid of any lingering negative or stressful energy in your room and in your bed. If you are able, open the bedroom windows. This will not only physically air out your space, but will also provide a means for energy to escape and disperse.

Strip the bed of its linen and remove the mattress from the box spring. Using the shaft of the broom, strike the mattress and the box spring three times each. With every stroke, tell the negative energy to go away. Again, I find that simple (and loud!) words are quite effective. Give a name to anything you've experienced personally that has robbed you of sleep:

Stress, get out!
Pain, get out!
Worry, get out!

Now using the broom's brush, sweep the mattress and then the box spring clockwise, visualizing any dusty, murky energy being swept away, out of the mattress, out of your room, out of your house, out of your life. See it breaking up and becoming harmless, carried away on the wind.

Finally, light a smudge stick (I like sage and cedar bundles) and using your hand or a smudge fan, smudge all sides of the mattress and box spring, as well as the room. As the smoke dissipates, imagine the room and the objects in it becoming clearer, brighter.

Once the space has been cleared, cast a circle to keep positive energy in and negativity out. If you are uncomfortable with using a wand or a blade to cast, you can do it with your finger. Stand in the middle of the room and extend your arm in front of you, pointing your index finger. Envision energy in the form of light streaming from your finger like water shooting out of a hose. Moving clockwise, "draw" a circle around you with the energy. When the circle is whole, you have transformed your room into sacred space.

The turning. Take one of the pouches and undo the ribbon or yarn. Evenly distribute the mixture over the surface of the box spring, stating your intention:

> *On this day of equal light and darkness**
> *Bless me with instructive vision or sweet oblivion*
> *Grant me the rest I need to be productive and vibrant.*

* If you are performing the ritual on the equinox, replace the word *day* in this line with the word *moment*.

Making sure that the mattress is turned so that the previously unused side is facing up, replace the mattress on the box spring keeping the strewn herbs, crystals and shells as even as possible. If you prefer, you can keep the herbs tied in their sachet and position it in the center of the box spring before replacing the mattress on top of it. Again, make a statement, your words and intentions adding another level of value to an every day task:

> *As the year turns to ever renew itself, so I renew my place of rest.*
> *Each night renew me. Each morning see me rise awakened, refreshed,*
> *Ready to face a new day full of challenges and possibilities.*

Prepare your bed for sleep with clean linens, the seasonal colors reinforcing synchronicity with the sabbat and the time.

> *Swathed in the colors of renewal,*
> *Be always a place of restoration.*

Take the remaining seven herbal sachets and tuck them into the drawer where your sheets are stored. While you don't need to repeat the complete ritual at every sabbat, take the time to turn the mattress and change the herbs, recalling the cleansing and balancing effect of Ostara. When you change the herbs, sweep the old ones up and save them to be burnt at Samhain, our new year, or at Yule (with the Yule log). You can also take them to a place of running water to release them back to nature.

Your labor done, thank each element and deity for lending their assistance to your work:

> *I thank you air for your aid and intensity. Stay with me through the rest of this day and into the night that I may carry you with me always.*

> *I thank you fire for your aid and inspiration. Stay with me through the rest of this day and into the night that I may carry you with me always.*

> *I thank you water for your aid and adaptability. Stay with me through the rest of this day and into the night that I may carry you with me always.*

> *I thank you earth for your aid and solidarity. Stay with me through the rest of this day and into the night that I may carry you with me always.*

> *I thank you Lord and Lady of Spring for your strength and love. Stay with me through the rest of this day and into the night that I may carry you with me always.*

At this point the circle can be struck (this is the time when we have "cakes and ale" breakfast style, eggs being the featured item on the menu—'tis the season!). Do not remove the candles/crystals representing the quarters and deities. Ostara is about balance: as above, so below, equal dark and light, work in the day, and repose at night.

Goodnight. When evening comes, get into bed and see yourself having a restful sleep and awaking refreshed and balanced, ready to face not only the day, but the weeks ahead as the year spins toward its next point of turning, Beltane.

Find a relaxed position. As you feel yourself drifting off, let your eyes rest on the representations of the elements and god and goddess left in their places from the ritual you performed earlier in the day (or in the direction of—don't disturb your rest to get up and look). Acknowledge and feel their presence. Know that they're not non-corporeal beings present only during ritual, but essences of life and spirit that are always with us. Again, feel free to use your own words. For me, the nursery rhyme/lullaby is a comforting means of easing into sleep and bidding goodnight to those that watch over us:

Goodnight, air, swirl and sweep.
Goodnight, fire, spark and flame.
Goodnight water, flow and seep.
Goodnight earth, feed and sustain.
Goodnight Father and Mother Spring
Thank you for the light you bring.

A word on dreams and night visions. I have found that an essential part of maintaining balance is the keeping of a dream journal. There are times when my sleep is just that—absolute oblivion. But when I am blessed with night visions, I've found that it helps to write them down. The solution to a problem, a message from the divine or from those I loved that have passed on, have all come to me in sleep.

Keep a journal and pen by your bed so that you can record your dreams upon waking; memories of these visions have a short life if they aren't promptly written down. Write out what happened as if you were reporting it before you record personal feelings and reactions (you may get insights hours, even days later). While this kind of work takes time and patience, the insights are well worth the effort. Dreams are the seeds of future deeds.

Sweet dreams, and blessed Ostara!

Notes

Beltane

Beltane: Portal of Transformation

Jhenah Telyndru

THE HOLY DAY OF Beltane was revered by the ancient Celts as a sacred bridge between the hardship of winter and the abundance of summer. Thought to exist outside of time, it is said that the veils between the worlds are thinnest at the liminal periods of Beltane and Samhain, complementary Holy Days standing opposite each other on the Wheel of the Year. For the ancient Celts, there were originally only two seasons—winter and summer—and the transition points between each season were times of great power. Marking the boundaries between the dark and light halves of the year, these Holy Days truly straddled the worlds.

These in-between periods were of great importance to the Celtic peoples, whose entire social, economic and religious lives centered around—and were dependent upon—the rhythms of the pastoral and agricultural cycles. Beltane marked the beginning of Summer, and it was a time of purification, increased activity, and abundant fertility. The livestock that had been boarded up during the long winter months were passed between two bonfires both to bless and purify them as they were set out to pasture once more. Ritual lovemaking in the fields was thought to encourage a successful growing cycle and an abundant harvest. Social and economic intercourse during the great gatherings at clan central places were marked by religious observances overseen by Druids, all of which mirrored the lush return to life literally bursting forth in the natural world all around them.

It is easy to understand the importance of the seasonal rhythms to agricultural peoples whose very survival depended upon the strength of their harvest and the well-being of their livestock. It was critical to seek the blessings of the gods and ancestors to grant increased fertility and good health, both for the land and for the tribe. Many of the Celtic celebrations that have survived the passage of time, some of which are still practiced in some form, concern the two major polar modalities of death and life—dark and light.

This fundamental reliance on the seasonal patterns is not the norm for most Neopagans today who follow paths inspired by the beliefs and traditions of the ancient Celts. However, we can still benefit spiritually by looking at the great pattern revealed by the seasonal cycle through a symbolic filter. Finding insight and relevance in its core wisdom, we can look at this primal pattern as a powerful way to guide our inner process and soul growth. From this perspective, the theme of fertility that lies at the heart of the celebrations of Beltane can be transferred to the abundance of possibilities inherent in our own lives.

The rites of fertility that centered around the fires of Beltane need not be literal. There is great power in entering into a conscious relationship with the Self, and indeed, it is from this sacred union that the spark of creativity is birthed. In Welsh Druidic tradition, this creative spark is called Awen, the inflowing stream of divine inspiration that the Irish called Imbas. Through shamanic ritual designed to pierce the boundaries between this world and the Otherworld, the ancient bards sought to obtain the gifts of Awen from the Cauldron of Ceridwen, their spiritual mother. Awen could flow forth in the form of versed prophecy, which could open the gates of consciousness by allowing information to be obtained from objects through a form of psychometry and inspire powerful songs and poetry that could influence events by shifting the hearts and minds of those who heard it.

Welsh myth and legend is filled with stories of kings and heroes journeying into the Otherworld seeking magickal cauldrons of healing, wisdom, and prophecy. The story of Ceridwen herself describes how over the course of a year and a day—a time-marking device in Celtic mythology that indicated a sacred time that is outside of time—she brewed an elixir of wisdom for her son. When the elixir was complete, it was stolen from her cauldron by Gwion, a servant boy who had been charged with keeping the fire alight. The thief tried to escape Ceridwen's wrath by using his newfound wisdom to change his shape into various animals. Yet no matter what form he took, she pursued him, changing her own shape in response to his. In the end, though Gwion tried to hide from Ceridwen in the guise of a grain of wheat lying among others on the threshing floor, she had transformed into a hungry hen who eventually devoured him. Nine months later, the servant boy was reborn from her womb as a child with a Shining Brow, the wisdom-endowed babe called Taliesin, who would become the greatest of all Welsh bards.

It is believed that this story is an encoded description of a Druidic initiation ritual, and that it represented a process through which Awen, the energy of inspiration that Celts described as a Fire in the Head, could be obtained from the vessel of the Goddess. It teaches us, too, that wisdom is something that can only be earned, and that the greatest wisdom will inspire us to embrace change—especially in the face of challenges and hardships. Awen is a deeply transformational energy, and the Shining Brow of Taliesin is a reflection that he had received the Fire Within the Head—a Celtic acknowledgment, perhaps, of the gifts of enlightenment.

Fire is an important aspect of Beltane. Indeed, the four Celtic Holy Days—the "Crossquarter" days of the eightfold Neopagan Wheel of the Year—are considered fire festivals. Welsh folk tradition speaks of gathering nine sacred woods to build the ritual fire. These woods were then kindled by rubbing together two oak staves until they sparked and set the fire lay aflame. From this sacred fire built on a hilltop, brands would be taken back into the village to re-ignite the household fires that had been extinguished on Beltane Eve—called *Calan Haf* or *Calan Mai* in Welsh—in anticipation of the renewing energies of the ritual fire that marked the passage from the dark half into the light.

In many Celtic lands, two fires were built and as the livestock were brought to their summer pastures after their long winter confinement. The animals were passed between the two as an act of purification and in hopes of increased fertility. People too, sought the blessings of the fire, and in Wales a ritual drawing of lots occurred where oatmeal cakes were broken into pieces and placed in a bag. Everyone would draw a piece, and those who pulled pieces of burned cake would have to jump three times over the sacred fire as an act of purification and to ensure fertility both for the village and for the growing crops.

The tradition of the maypole is linked to May Day celebrations across Europe and has survived to modern times as a secular dance to celebrate the spring. While the tradition itself is believed to be of Indian origin, it has taken root in Germanic and Celtic lands, where the dance of fertility may have occurred around living trees, or as in the case of some Welsh traditions, around flower garlanded birch trunks. The phallic symbolism of the pole is clear, and the interweaving of ribbons down its shaft symbolically fertilizes the earth in an act of powerful sympathetic magick. The pole becomes the World Tree, straddling the realms and creating a conduit to stream the life-bringing energies from above down to renew that which is below.

Walking Between the Worlds

Like the maypole and the World Tree, Beltane is a bridge between the worlds, and we can use this sacred time outside of time to foster a connection between the light and dark halves of the self—the higher self and the shadow. Manifesting this balanced inner partnership is, to me, the key consideration at Beltane. Without it, how can we know what needs to be released, or what spark of potential lies within us, waiting to be fanned to flame?

Here, at this threshold time, we can seek to come into Divine Union with the two halves of the Self—that which dwells unacknowledged in the land of the unconscious and that which thrives, illuminated, in the realms of consciousness. How then can we bridge these aspects of the Self, which, by their very nature, are equal and opposite to each other? We see the repetitions of this coming together over and over again in Neopagan thought and ritual; it can be literally expressed as with the Great Rite, or symbolically evoked as with the ritual union of Chalice and Blade. Yet these are but sympathetic resonances of even deeper mysteries.

From a psychospiritual perspective, the dark half of the Self can be said to be the providence of the Shadow—those experiences and memories that our psyche has deemed, for whatever reason, necessary to be filed somewhere besides the conscious mind. In my personal practice in the Avalonian tradition, we spend the dark half of the year seeking out those hidden parts of the Self in order to understand their significance and impact on our lives. We cannot rid ourselves of our Shadow side; it is irrevocably a part of us. Instead, our goal is to move energy from one end of the inner spectrum to the other, so that our gifts are nurtured while our flaws are starved.

Casting light on the inner Shadow can be painful work, but it is a crucial step along the path to wholeness. There is a saying—"that which is unconscious, controls us." If we do not know the nature of our Shadow, we cannot know in what ways it manifests itself in our lives. To come to a place of true inner-sovereignty, we must understand the source of the unconscious motivations for our beliefs and actions. We then work to bring these root causes out with us into the light of consciousness, so that we can see them for what they are and reclaim the energy that has been caught up in perpetuating patterns of limitation and negativity in our lives.

The light half of the year, on the other hand, is when we focus on birthing forth and fully actualizing the potential we found hidden in the darkness—a potential that can finally become realized now that we can see it for what it truly is. The greatest of gifts often lie at the heart of the Shadow; and like the earth itself, all seeds of growth must germinated in the darkness. At the threshold of Beltane, then, we take the gift of that once-hidden seed out into the light half with us, while leaving behind all of the fears and limitations that had committed the seed to dwell in the darkness to begin with. We harness the liminal energies of Beltane to make conscious that which was once unconscious—and in doing so, we liberate the spark which underlies and supports all acts of creation.

This spark fertilizes the new growth we seek to manifest; it is the energy that supports and empowers the work of the light half of the year. In more concrete terms, we can take the energy freed up by the insights gained about ourselves and our negative patterns and beliefs, and direct it toward choices that reinforce the person we know that we have the ability to become. As we step through the portal of Beltane, we pass through the symbolic fires of purification and embrace the fertile ground of our limitless potential. We leave behind that which has held us back, and move into a place of positive action which helps us to create the life we wish to live. What greater act of creation can there be than to set the fires of transformation alight in our souls and to use the resulting illumination to burn through any outer challenges and inner resistance that stands in the way our ultimate goal—a whole and holy self that is balanced and expressing its greatest good and highest potential. A sacred flame indeed!

Celestial Sway

Fern Feto Spring

SPRINGTIME BLOSSOMS AND EVERYWHERE we see signs of fertility and abundance. Beltane offers us an opportunity to celebrate the sensuality of life, reveling in Mother Nature's gifts. As the green earth comes alive all around us, we are reminded of our connection to the natural world and have an opportunity to tap into our "wild side." Like the Strength card of the tarot, the Beltane season is a time of learning to gracefully negotiate with our inner beast—drawing on the power and passion, while directing these untamed forces with care and respect.

Beltane 2012 takes place on a waxing Moon cycle and emphasizes the earth element, with a harmonious trine position between the Sun in Taurus, Mars in Virgo, and Pluto in Capricorn. Jupiter continues in Taurus, adding a special boost to the Beltane season. With all this earth energy, we have an opportunity to manifest in the real world. This is a great time to put effort into making money, finding new work, making home renovations, and any other practical, grounded project that we may have in mind.

Mars in Virgo and Pluto in Capricorn provide ample drive and initiative to get the job done. Our ability to focus and pay attention to details is expanded now, especially if we devote our energies toward working hard on our goals and ambitions for the future.

The Sun and Jupiter in Taurus add to our need for tangible rewards, but these planetary partners also want to be sure we enjoy ourselves on the road to success. Good food, beauty, and other creature comforts will be just as necessary now as the essentials.

Beltane culminates in a Full Moon in Scorpio on May 5, highlighting our awareness of the emotional undercurrents that shape our reality. Scorpio asks us to dig deep and unearth our hidden motivations and unconscious drives. Passion must inform our goals or they become dry and tasteless. This Full Moon amplifies the tension between Taurus and Scorpio, demanding that we integrate emotionally honesty into our need for physical security and comfort.

Venus goes retrograde in Gemini on May 15, adding a curious punctuation to the flirty potential of the Beltane season. Every planetary retrograde offers an opportunity to redo, rethink, renegotiate, revise, etc. When Venus goes retrograde, we have a chance to review our approach to love, beauty, finances, and what we value. We may need to deepen our approach to relationships, or take another look at how we approach our finances. Since this retrograde occurs in the airy, flirty, and sometimes flighty sign of Gemini, any tendencies we have to "love 'em and leave 'em," or flirt first and think later, may have heavier consequences than usual. Rethinking our approach to short-term dalliances and superficial relationships may take on greater importance during this retrograde period which lasts from May 15 to June 27 (shadow period until July 31).

The final highlight of the Beltane season is a New Moon solar eclipse in Gemini on May 20. This event amplifies the buzz of Beltane's spring fever, kicking our desire to be busy and active into high gear. The New Moon occurs at 0 degrees of Gemini and then forms a square with Neptune, the planet of dreams, illusions, and fantasy. This planetary pairing indicates there may be some struggle involved with launching new plans and ideas, but as long as we incorporate help from spirit and a healthy dose of creativity and magic into our lives, we can find interesting new ways to manifest our dreams.

Full Moon in Scorpio

Emphasizing the polarity between spirit (Scorpio) and matter (Taurus), the May 5 Full Moon encourages us to focus on integrating what is above with what is below. We may gain a greater awareness now of what is meaningful and valuable in our lives and want to take some kind of physical action to manifest our passion out in the world. Depending on where this lunation falls in your natal chart, it may be a time to meditate on how your resources, gifts, and skills are being put to use. Are you taking full advantage of your abilities and if so, who reaps the benefits of your labor? This Full Moon offers the opportunity to focus on questions such as these, though we may need to wait at least one more moon cycle before we began to harvest answers.

Venus Retrograde in Gemini

Venus retrograde in Gemini means it may be time for a makeover to take place in regards to our approach to love, beauty/fashion/art, finances and our values. During the one-and-a-half month span of this retrograde (May 15 to June 27, with the shadow period until July 31), it's time to go deeper in our approach to all things Venusian. Since Gemini is not a sign known much for its depth, we have a bit of a paradox on our hands. A sense of frustration might arise from our more shallow encounters with others, as we fail to experience the same pleasure or enjoyment that we have in the past. This can be a good time to take another look at even the most casual encounters in relationships, questioning our own motivations and analyzing others. Since Beltane energies encourage us to reach out and connect to those around us, this Venus retrograde may ask us to be more thoughtful about who we approach or welcome into our space. Yes, Venus in Gemini wants us to gather new friends and experiences, but the retrograde energies demand that we do so with caution and foresight. Ritualizing the energies of this transit can help us to maximize its possibilities.

Venus Retrograde Ritual

On the night of the Venus retrograde light a yellow candle and invoke Venus and Mercury (ruler of the sign of Gemini). Speaking aloud, talk about your current state of affairs regarding the Venusian matters of love, relating, beauty, art, money, and values. Ask Venus and Mercury for guidance during the retrograde period so that you can learn and benefit from whatever this transit has to offer. Ask to receive your answers in a clearly communicated form.

New Moon Eclipse in Gemini

The New Moon solar eclipse in Gemini takes place at 0 degrees on May 20, indicating a time of new beginnings and possibility in regard to communication, information, and social interchange. A challenging square aspect to Neptune reminds us to factor unseen factors into our plans and draw on the wisdom and magic of the universe for guidance. Planting the seeds of future plans can have a powerful effect now, as the eclipse energies open the door to change and transformation, which are amplified by the 0 degree occurring on the New Moon.

New Moon Eclipse Ritual

Draw on the magical tension created by the eclipse and Neptune squaring the New Moon and ritualize your New Moon intentions. The New Moon in Gemini opens up doors around new information and ways to communicate. On the night of the New Moon, create an altar with symbols related to Gemini (statue of Mercury, pictures of computers, phones, newspapers). Ask for the doors of communication to open for you and request that you receive any information that would be helpful to guide you on your path. Notice over the following month as you receive important news or insight from a book, website, friend, etc.

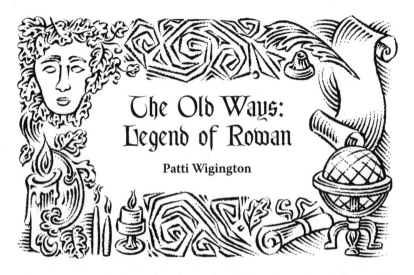

The Old Ways: Legend of Rowan

Patti Wigington

THE ROWAN TREE IS rich in legend and lore throughout the world. In fact, tales of the rowan tree appear as far back as classical Greece. The goddess of youthful beauty, Hebe, possessed a cup full of magical ambrosia. This sweet nectar was shared with the gods of Olympus, helping them stay young and beautiful, and granting them immortality. One day, Hebe's magical goblet was stolen by creatures of the underworld. The gods sent a great eagle to recover the chalice, and during the ensuing battle, drops of blood fell to the earth. From these bloody drops grew the first rowan trees.

In Norse mythology, after the first man was created from the ash tree, the first woman sprung from the rowan tree. The woman, called Embla, eventually saved Thor from being swept away in a great flood. In parts of Scandinavia, rowan was the wood of choice for making a magical staff, into which runes were carved.

In many parts of the British Isles, the rowan tree is associated with magic and witchcraft. It was believed that boughs of rowan hung over a door could keep enchantments or evil spirits from entering a home. In Scotland, protective charms and amulets carved of rowan wood were worn as a talisman against baneful magic. Interestingly, in the Highlands, custom held that only ritual objects could be made from rowan. In *Warriors and Guardians: Native Highland Trees*, Hugh Fife says that mundane tools and items could be carved from some other wood, and that people could never use "the tree's timber, bark, leaves or flowers, nor the cutting of these, except for sacred purposes."

One of those sacred purposes was that of the Beltane fire, which was lit in Scotland to keep Witches from putting a curse on the cattle. Sir James G. Frazer writes in *The Golden Bough* that branches "of rowan-tree . . . were placed over the doors of the cow-houses, and fires were kindled by every farmer and cottar (on-site farmhand)." In addition, the cattle were driven three times between a pair of brightly lit bonfires that contained rowan wood, all in an effort to keep them safe.

One popular custom was that of forming an equal-armed cross from rowan branches and tying them together with red thread. This was well known as a charm against the Fey, and could be placed in a baby's crib to protect the child or hung over a lintel to keep the Faerie folk from crossing the threshold. Some churchyards in Wales have had rowan growing in them for hundreds of years, keeping any evil spirits from entering.

Tales of the Fey, who are at their most active during the fire feasts of Beltane and Samhain, often tie in to rowan tree mythology. While many tales indicate that the magical energy of rowan kept fairies at bay, there are equally as many stories that show the Fey had quite an affinity for this red-berried tree.

From Ireland comes the tale of the Fairy Rowan Tree, which relates the story of Aine, daughter of the Mananaun, king of the sea. Aine wished to marry a poor mortal named Fergus, but her hand was sought after by Curoi, a faerie king. Her father ordered a hurling match to settle the matter, with Fergus and his tribe on one side, and Curoi and his faerie host on the other. Mananaun offered each player a handful of rowan berries to eat in order to keep them from being pulled into the faerie world, or the world of mortals.

The berries would also bestow upon them strength, and the match was won when Fergus scored a final goal.

Unbeknownst to Fergus, he had dropped one of his rowan berries, and from it grew a mighty tree. Mananaun ordered Fergus to guard it night and day, and told him he couldn't marry Aine until he found someone to stand watch for him. Fergus sent a messenger to Crom Dubh, a giant, offering him land in exchange for guarding the rowan tree, and Crom Dubh was happy to take his place. Fergus and Aine were reunited, and Crom Dubh still guards the tree to this day.

Another Irish faerie story comes from County Sligo, in which a group of faeries known as the Sidhe planted a giant rowan as a guardian between the faerie realm and the land of men. Folklorist J. F. Campbell tells in his *Popular Tales of the Western Highlands* of the habit of Scottish and Irish faeries of planting rowan trees in a ring outside of stone circles. Protected by the stones and the trees, which kept mortals and other outsiders away, the Fey could dance and celebrate to their hearts' content at Beltane.

During the fertility festival of Beltane, the Fey are believed to be highly active. Some magical traditions hold that if you wish to contact the Fey, this is the season when the veil between our lands and theirs is the thinnest. Most faerie legends say that the best way to find the Fey was to locate a hidden entrance to their world—often, this was a secret cave, a well-concealed spring, or beneath the roots of a large tree. Some people believe that if you lie beneath a rowan tree at Beltane, once you fall asleep, you'll be able to travel into the faerie realm.

In many magical traditions, Beltane is the best time to harvest gifts from the rowan tree if you're going to be using it for a magical purpose. The berries are toxic, so shouldn't be eaten, but at Beltane they're typically blooming with a bright red, vibrant hue. Pick a few and allow them to dry, and then string them to form a garland. Hang it above your doorway to prevent the Fey from causing mischief in your home.

Called mountain ash in North America, the wood of the rowan is a strong, sturdy wood that can be cut and carved for a variety of uses. Take a long straight branch of rowan and strip the bark from it to make a staff or walking stick. Engrave it with protective runes and inscriptions to provide some magical self-defense. You can also cut a small piece of rowan and carry it in your pocket or on a thong around your neck as a talisman to keep away negative magic. Finally, try using rowan for a wand or a dowsing rod. If you're lucky enough to find a rowan tree near you at Beltane, be sure to leave an offering beside it—and if your tradition requires it, ask for permission—before you cut any pieces off.

When Beltane arrives, it means the fertility of spring has arrived, so why not take some time to get outside and find a rowan tree? Who knows what sort of magic you might discover!

For Further Reading:

Popular Tales of the West Highlands, Vol. 1, 1890. Translated by John F. Campbell. Ithaca, New York: Cornell University Library, 2009.

Fife, Hugh. *Warriors, Kings, and Secret Guardians: Native Highland Trees.* Glendaruel, Argyll, Scotland: Argyll Publishing, 1994.

Frazer, Sir James George. *The Golden Bough*, 1890.

Green, Dr. Miranda. *The World of the Druids*, London: Thames and Hudson, 1997.

Feasts and Treats

Susan Pesznecker

BELTANE CELEBRATES FERTILITY AND welcomes the new life bursting forth from Mother Gaia. This Beltane meal features fresh, light foods that leave you feeling nourished but not weighed down; you'll be ready for your Beltane celebrations, whatever they may be!

Gaia's Fresh Flower Salad

Eating this salad is like dining on a fresh spring flower patch. If you have an organic yard, you might step outside and search for goodies like miner's lettuce, blood sorrel, pea sprouts, garlic shoots, fiddleheads, or early dandelion greens—all of which make gorgeous, additions to your salad.

Prep time: 30 minutes
Cook time: (Dressing must be made in advance)
Serves: 4+

¾ cup seasoned rice vinegar
¼ cup vegetable oil
3–4 peeled and sliced garlic cloves
¼ cup pine nuts
¼ cup sunflower seeds

4 cups assorted organic baby greens, wild greens (see above), and
spinach, washed and patted dry

Other salad veggies: cherry or grape tomatoes, scallions, shredded
carrot, cucumber, mushrooms, sweet onions, sweet peppers, etc.

Fresh flower mixture: your choice of rose petals; viola tricolor
(Johnny Jump-Up) blossoms (shades of purple and white); young
dandelion flowers (yellow); nasturtium blossoms (orange, red,
gold); chive blossoms (lavender-pink) and leaves (cut finely with
scissors); calendula petals (yellow, gold, orange, and burnt red)

Optional: croutons; cooked and peeled shrimp, chilled

Several hours before the meal, prepare the dressing by shaking
together the vinegar, oil, and garlic cloves. Place in refrigerator to
"marinate." This makes a light, slightly sweet and salty vinaigrette
that is nicely flavored with garlic.

An hour or more before serving, roast the pine nuts and sunflower seeds by toasting in a dry skillet over medium heat for about
5 minutes. Stir often and watch carefully. The pine nuts will change
color slightly and develop a rich flavor. Cool to room temperature.

Just before serving, toss the greens and veggies together in a large
bowl. (A clear glass bowl is ideal for this salad.) Top with the flowers,
then with the pine nuts, sunflower seeds, and croutons, if desired. If
you're offering shrimp, arrange them on a nice plate on the side.

Serve the salad and dressing separately so your diners can dress
their own portions.

Note: As the dressing is used, add new vinegar and oil to restore
the original volume and proportions. The garlic cloves will last for
months before they need replacing.

Herbalicious Bread

This tasty side adds a bit of "heft" to your supper, while paying homage to seasonal herbs.

Prep time: 15 minutes

Cook time: 5 minutes

Serves: 4+

1 loaf French bread, sliced

1 cup real mayonnaise

1 cup Parmesan cheese, grated (preferably fresh)

¼ cup sweet onion, chopped

¼ cup green onion, chopped

¼ cup fresh herbs of your choice: chives, thyme, rosemary (use only a dash of this), parsley

1 tablespoon milk

Toast the bread slices lightly under the broiler, turning once—this should take just a few minutes. (Watch carefully so they don't burn!)

Combine the mayonnaise, cheese, onions, herbs, and milk. Stir until smooth.

Just before serving, spread a layer of cheese mixture on each bread slice. Put slices on a cookie sheet and toast under the broiler until browned and bubbly—about 4 to 5 minutes.

Passionate Peanut Butter Pie

This pie is the perfect ending to the Beltane meal: light and rich all at once, it'll sweeten your evening's passions!

Prep time: 20 minutes

Serves: 8

10 ounces full-fat cream cheese, room temperature

⅔ cup creamy peanut butter (for best results, do <u>not</u> use "natural" peanut butter)

¾ cup powdered (confectioner's) sugar

⅓ cup milk

9-inch graham cracker crust (or vanilla wafer or chocolate crusts)

1 8-ounce container Cool Whip*

Chocolate bar

Chocolate syrup

Using a mixer, combine the cream cheese, peanut butter, and powdered sugar until blended. Cream until the mixture is light and fluffy (1 to 2 minutes).

Slowly add the milk, beating to a smooth consistency. Spoon into pie crust and top with the entire container of Cool Whip. Freeze for at least two hours to help it "set." Once the pie has set, you can allow it to freeze and serve it frozen. Or, move it to the refrigerator 2 to 3 hours before serving and allow to thaw. It's delicious either way!

To serve: Cut into wedges and garnish with chocolate shavings (use a potato peeler) and a drizzle of chocolate syrup.

*Instead of Cool Whip, you may use a heavy cream that is stabilized with gelatin. Start with ½ cup chilled heavy cream. Stir ½ teaspoon plain (unflavored) gelatin into 1 tablespoon hot water and stir to dissolve, then cool to room temperature. Whip the chilled cream in a chilled bowl; when it begins to form soft peaks, add the cooled gelatin and stir in ¼ teaspoon vanilla and 1 to 2 tablespoons sugar. Continue beating until the cream forms soft peaks.

Strawberry Lemonade

Prep time: 20 minutes (plus cooling and freezing time)
Cook time: 10 minutes
Serves: 6+

2 pints fresh strawberries (reserve a handful of small, perfect berries; leave stems on)
1 cup white sugar
6–8 fresh lemons (reserve ½ lemon; cut into thin slices)

At least four hours in advance, wash and stem the berries. Puree and pour them into ice cube trays and freeze solid.

Combine sugar, 1½ cup water, and 1 tablespoon grated fresh lemon peel in a medium saucepan. Bring to a boil, stirring to dissolve sugar. Cool slightly. Then juice enough lemons to yield 1½ cups juice. Add to the sugar syrup. Refrigerate and chill very well.

To serve, place strawberry cubes in a glass and pour the lemonade over. Garnish with a lemon slice and a whole strawberry.

Extra zip: For an adult twist, pour an ounce of limoncello liqueur into each glass before adding the lemonade.

Crafty Crafts

Ellen Dugan

Theme of the Season: Unity and partnership
Colors: Green, white, rose pink,
Scents: Lilac, peony, and thyme
Energy: Romance, lust, and joy

May Day Flower Cone

This Beltane craft is fun to make, but more fun to give away! These flower cones are traditionally left as a surprise on a front door as a way to welcome the sabbat and the spring. Plus it's an enchanting way to tell someone you are thinking of them.

Supplies

8-inch square of decorative heavy-duty paper (scrapbook paper) in a solid pastel or a floral motif
Double-stick tape
Hole punch
1 spool of ½-inch satin ribbon, your choice of color
A zipper-type plastic sandwich bag
A damp paper towel

Fresh spring flowers and blooming herbs from the garden—or an inexpensive cash-and-carry type of mixed bouquet of spring flowers from the florist

Instructions: Roll the piece of decorative paper into a cone shape, and use double-stick tape to seal it together. (Tape the outer flap of the cone.) Punch two holes on opposite sides of the open part of the cone. Tie the ends of the ribbon through each of the holes to make a handle. Gather your flowers and herbs from the garden and arrange them, or split up and rearrange your purchased flowers. These cones are small, so you could probably make several of these with one purchased bouquet.

Strip off any foliage/leaves from the lower part of the flower stems. Eyeball the length of the flowers by holding it up to the paper cone, so they are not too tall or too short *before* you give them a final

cut. After you have calculated the correct length, snip off the longer stems to make the flower stems in the bunch mostly the same length.

Next, wrap the stems with a damp (not dripping) paper towel. Tuck the paper towel–wrapped stems inside of a plastic lunch bag and zip it closed as far as you can without mashing the flower stems. Take 12 inches of ribbon and tie a pretty bow around the top of the plastic bag to secure it. Slip the flower stems and bag down inside of the cone so the flowers show prettily out of the top of the cone.

For variations on the theme, you could make these cones very small and fill them with diminutive flowers from your backyard such as violets, pansies, and lilys of the valley straight from your own witchy garden. Or you can make a flower cone entirely filled with romantic and fragrant herbs such as lavender, lilac blossoms, rosebuds, peonies, and mint. For children, you could fill the cone with small chocolate candies, clementines, or lollipops.

If you like, attach a note that says "Happy Beltane" and sign it. You could also add a quick note explaining all of the magickal meanings of the blossoms you have chosen for your friend.

Finally, for the tricky part … Hang the cone on the front door doorknob. Ring the bell and run!

Time: 30 minutes or less

Cost: Under $10.00. If you are a scrapbooker and have a garden, chances are you have everything you need at home.

Kitchen Witch's Pot of Culinary/Magickal Herbs

May is the perfect time to start a big pot of culinary herbs for your own kitchen witchery and culinary wizardry. Container herb gardens work very well in small areas like a sunny patio, porch, or deck. They can be grown right outside your kitchen door for easy access when it is time to conjure up a little something tasty in the kitchen.

Supplies

Large pot with saucer or container with drainage hole in bottom

A handful or two of small rocks to assist with drainage

Quality potting soil

A large spoon or garden trowel

Fresh herbs in small pots, ready to plant (thyme, rosemary, basil, oregano, curly leaf parsley, and Italian parsley have worked for me)

A nice sunny spot that receives at least 6 hours of direct sunlight.

Watering can and water to keep your plants watered throughout the growing season

Instructions: Toss the small rocks or pebbles in the bottom of the pot. Make sure the rocks do NOT completely cover up the drainage hole. Next, dump in potting soil to fill about three quarters of the pot.

Now remove your herbs from their little packages and add them to your container. Take your time to arrange the plants as you desire.

Put the thyme close to the edge of the pot so it can spill over, and put the rosemary and the basil in the center or back as they will grow tall.

Add the rest of the potting mix slowly until the roots are completely covered and you are two inches from the top of the container. Gently, but firmly, pat the soil down and water the herbs well. Water the herbs every other day (and at least once a day in high summer). Let the herbs settle in their new home for a week or so before you begin gathering from them. Nourish the herbs with a slow-release fertilizer every other month and they will produce for you until frost. (Your parsley may stop producing in the summer heat but will come back as soon as things cool off.)

Magickal qualities of the suggested kitchen herbs:

Basil: Love and wealth

Oregano: Love, protection, and cheer

Parsley: Fertility and repeller of bad luck

Rosemary: Health, protection, and purification

Thyme: Healing, fosterer of restful sleep, and courage

A charm to bless the pot of herbs:

Hold your hands out over your newly planted container of herbs. Send some of your own loving energy into the plants and bless them with this charm:

By the powers of earth, air, fire, and water,
Bless these good green herbs with health, magick, and laughter.
This Garden Witch's charm is cheerfully spun,
For the good of all and bringing harm to none.

Happy herb gardening!

Cost: $20.00 and up, depending on container size and how many plants you buy

Time: 30 minutes to one hour

All One Family

Clea Danaan

CELEBRATE THE HOLIDAY OF bright fire by honoring passion. Each of us has our own passions: writing, gymnastics, singing, gardening, football, sign language... What are yours? What passions excite each of your family members? For this holiday, craft a passion staff and call on Brighid, the Goddess of poetry, fire, and smithcraft, as you share a bit of your special joy with your family.

A passion staff is something like a talking stick used in Native American circles. It looks just like a miniature maypole. This is a craft that can be as elaborate or as simple as you like. Help the youngest members of your family with gluing and such, but try to let them do as much as they can, as this is their staff. To make one you need a stick or a dowel, about a half inch in diameter and from one foot to six feet long—whatever feels right. You will also need ribbons as long as the stick in any colors you like. Red, white, and the colors of the flowers blooming in your area on Beltane are traditional. You might also use team or school colors, colors of the sea or another magical spot, favorite colors, or magical correspondences. Attach the ribbons (at least three, but up to a dozen) to the top of the stick with a rubber band, glue, or yarn so that they hang down freely. You can leave it at that, or decorate the staff further by gluing gems, sequins, feathers, beads, or whatever you have handy to the tip of the mini-pole. While crafting the staff, each person should think about his or her passion and send that energy into the passion staff.

When your staffs are complete, stand in a circle and share what you have made and what it means to you. This could be part of a full Beltane ritual, with a cast circle and calling of the directions and such, or it could simply be time to share. You will know what style suits your family. You might invite friends to participate or have this be a family-building practice. If you are having family troubles, you could try having a therapist or priestess guide you through the sharing.

American and European cultures, and perhaps human nature, seem to fear passion. Sharing what fills us with pride, joy, and excitement can be overwhelming. We can feel vulnerable and shy. When others share their passions, we might automatically try to tone down the high energy by belittling or ignoring. Or we might deal with our discomfort by making sexual jokes about staffs and passion—these are related but not the same thing and obviously not appropriate for young children. If this fear of passion applies to you or your family, let this exercise be a practice in opening to passion in yourself and each other. Notice your inclination to shut down. Let it be there, and then make a different choice about how to interact with the bright fire in yourself and others. Our passions ignite the world, and as we as a species and as souls evolve, we will learn to fan the flames of our and others' passions with joy and reverence.

Even if you do not create a full ritual around your passion staffs, at least light a candle in the middle of your circle. This brings a sense of the sacred to your work, and one's passions are sacred. A simple ritual might be to light a candle (red would be perfect but not necessary), call on Brighid, who is associated with Beltane and with fire, or on the Lady of the Flowers and the Lord of the Dance, and cast a circle by simply holding hands, raising them, and dropping them.

Now each person in turn holds up their passion staff and shares what makes them happy. What did you think about while making your staff? How are you able to follow your passion at this time in life? Would you like more time to devote to your passion? This sharing will, of course, differ depending on age. Preschoolers will talk about what they love: cats, the beach, visiting Aunt Bess. Older children will share their growing passions and favorite things, maybe just one activity or maybe a whole list. Teens are defining themselves and homing in on their passions as they get closer to "growing up" and "being" something. This might even be a stressful discussion for them if they feel any ambivalence or pressure regarding their interests. Let any age of child share whatever he or she wishes to share without judging, editing, or baiting. As a parent, that can be surprisingly difficult. We want our children to be happy and successful, and we can project onto them our own feelings about talents without noticing we're doing it. This Beltane circle is a time for them to share whatever and however they choose.

For adults, we might also feel conflicted about our passions. Jobs, self-esteem, and fear can get in the way of what we really love. The best way for us to encourage talents, interests, and passions in our children is for us to follow our own loves. Our children learn how to find balance by watching us. When it is your turn, hold up your stick and speak or sing or chant what you love. Let emotion come. Share with your family if you would like more time to devote to your passion, or share the joy you feel having found balance in your life around family, work, and passion. Sometimes these intersect; sometimes balance is hard to find. There is no wrong or right in your circle—just share where you are, how you feel about it, and if you wish to take any steps to change an aspect of your life.

When you have finished your ritual, give your passion staffs a place of honor. Poke the free end in the garden or hang them on the wall or line them along the hearth. Young children can play with them while older family members will want to look at them and feel the power of their passions in life. Then later, when the children have gone to bed, share the more grown-up aspects of passions with your lover(s) and let the fires of Beltane fuel your love.

Beltane Ritual: Between the Worlds

Jhenah Telyndru

AT BELTANE, A JOYFUL celebration of fertility and regeneration, we can harness the spark of creation to birth ourselves anew. Weaving together the wisdom that lies in the realm of the unconscious and the insight that dwells in the light of consciousness, we kindle the spark of Awen—the inflowing spirit of the Divine that empowers us to change and impels us to growth. Standing between the worlds at Beltane, when the veils are thinned and we have increased clarity to look at both the Light and Shadow aspects of the self, we can use this time of great fertility to plant the seeds for a ripe harvest of the soul as we enter into the light half of the year.

The following is set up as a solitary ritual because it focuses on coming into a creative relationship with the Self. However, it can be adapted for as a group of individuals seeking a powerful inner relationship with themselves with the support of their community.

Ritual Supplies
Red altar cloth
Prepared maypole (details follow)
A quartz crystal to act as the Stone of Intention
Mistletoe herb for burning to represent the Realm of Sky

Incense charcoal in sand-filled vessel, with handle (as on small cauldron) or on trivet

Green growing plant to represent the Realm of Land

Water-filled cauldron to represent the Realm of Sea

A red candle, with the symbol of the three rays of Awen /|\ carved into the wax (seven-day pull-out candles work really well for this purpose, but a regular taper or votive candle will do)

Beltane incense blend (a blend of hawthorn, cowslip, and rowan will set a good energetic tone, but use what feels right to you)

A silver branch (apple branch with nine silver bells affixed) or rattle

Offerings of food or libation to leave for the ancestors

Seasonal flowers to decorate the altar

Images or symbols of divinities with whom you have a relationship

Matches or a lighter

Ritual Preparation

In the days before Beltane, take time to meditate on your ritual focus. Think about the person you would be if your greatest gifts and desires were made manifest. What would your life be like if nothing stood in the way of you becoming the person you most feel called to be? I am not talking about acquiring material possessions or societal measures of accomplishment, but about fully expressing the wholeness of the inner Self. Are you confident, manifesting your dreams, living in right action, engaging in right-livelihood? Do you love the person you are? Are you actively nurturing the person you know that you can be?

Coming into a fruitful relationship with the Self may be your most difficult relationship ever, yet it is the key to our wholeness. Knowing the fullness of our potential (as well as the limitations we have accepted because of our fears) helps us chart the course of our unfolding and allows us to map every necessary step on the journey to authenticity. What will you concentrate on manifesting during the light half of the year? To what end will you direct your creative energies? What do you wish to see birthed as a result of entering into—and maintaining—a positive and conscious relationship with the Self?

When you have narrowed this down, spend time at your altar visualizing this goal and its future impact on your life and your spiritual path. For at least three consecutive nights before your working, charge the quartz crystal (or another stone that holds significance for you) with these energies, transforming it into the Stone of Intention.

Creating the Maypole

Creating a personal maypole is a powerful ritual focus and is especially useful for solitaries and those for whom constructing a full-sized maypole to dance around is not possible or practical. We will be using a personal maypole to channel the creative energies of Awen in support of the inner balance we seek to manifest during the light half of the year. If you are doing this ritual as a group working, each person should create their own individual maypoles.

You will need:
Straight oak branch (approximately ½-inch thick) or dowel (easily purchased at a craft store) at least 1 foot high
Small cauldron or flowerpot
Modeling clay
2 pieces of ribbon (one red, one white) twice the length of the branch
Potting soil or earth
Quartz crystal or other stone of your choosing

Gather your supplies on your altar and assemble the pieces with clear intention and focus. Securely tie the red and white ribbons to the top of the oak branch or dowel. Press the modeling clay into the bottom of your cauldron, creating a layer several inches thick. Insert the unadorned end of your branch into the clay so that it stands upright in the vessel. Holding the ribbons out of the way, fill the cauldron with soil up to its rim, packing it around the base of the branch so that it is firmly supported and upright.

Once your maypole is securely erect in the soil, drape the red ribbon over the edge of the left side of the cauldron and the white ribbon on the right side. This will create the symbol of the Awen, a

Druidic symbol for Divine Inspiration—the creative force that will empower your endeavors. If possible, create your personal maypole ahead of time to keep the ritual work focused on its intention.

Setting Up the Altar

Beltane is a fire festival celebration of fertility and rebirth, and your altar should reflect this in ways that are meaningful to you. A red altar cloth is appropriate, as are decorations of flowers traditionally associated with Beltane, such as hawthorn and rowan.

Place your maypole in the center of the altar with the ribbons in the Awen position. Place the red candle representing the energies of Awen at a safe distance to the right the maypole, so that it will not interfere with the ribbons when you are weaving. Lay your charged quartz crystal directly in front of the maypole. Place the filled offering dish for the ancestors on the left side of the altar and a small bowl containing your incense blend to the right of the maypole.

Since this ritual is inspired by Celtic tradition, we will work with the energies of Land, Sea, and Sky, rather than the four elements Neopagans often use. Place the cauldron filled with water on the left side of the altar to represent the Realm of Sea. The plant should be placed in the center of the altar directly behind the maypole to represent the Realm of Land. The vessel containing the lit charcoal and a small dish filled with mistletoe should be placed on the right side of the altar, representating the Realm of Sky. (Note: Mistletoe can be poisonous if consumed in large quantities. If concerned, use dried oak blossoms.)

A Ritual Between the Worlds

Cleansing and Centering

Take some time to assess your personal energy and connect with those places where you are holding negativity and stress. Breathe these energies out and down into the earth, visualizing them sinking deep into ground and being absorbed into the planet. Use your breath once more to envision streams of vibrant green energies rising up from the planet to fill your aura with the life force of the earth. These energies both cleanse and center you, leaving you grounded, renewed, and ready for the working to come.

Connecting with Intention

Place some of your Beltane incense blend on the lit charcoal disk, adding more periodically as the ritual progresses. Keep the goals of this working clear in your mind, and pour any last energies into the Stone of Intention already charged and waiting on your altar.

Marking Sacred Space

Taking the silver branch or a rattle, walk a circle sun-wise around your working space as you shake it slowly and deliberately nine times, marking a boundary between this world and the Otherworld. When done, sing or speak the Portal Chant three times:

It is a Day that is not a day
At a Time that is not a time
In a Place that is not a place
Between the Worlds am I.

Evoking the Three Realms

Pick up the water-filled cauldron, and with your breath and intention, connect with the Realm of Sea. When you feel immersed in this watery energy, lower the cauldron toward the ground and say:

I stand nurtured in the deep reflective energies of the Realm of Sea, resting place of the honored dead, our blessed ancestors, and those awaiting the gifts of rebirth. Bless my strivings with the elixir of the Cauldron of Wisdom, and may these sacred waters overflow the inner chalice of my soul. So may it be.

Return the cauldron to the altar. Pick up the plant, and with your breath and intention, connect with the Realm of Land. When you feel immersed in this earthy energy, extend the plant in front of you. Say:

I stand centered in the life-sustaining energies of the Realm of Land, in-dwelling essence of the spirit of nature and vitalistic force which empowers the sacred landscape. Bless my strivings with the energies of the Ancient Pathways, and may these lines of power revitalize the inner landscape of my soul. So may it be.

Return the plant to the altar. Place some mistletoe on the lit charcoal and as the tendrils of smoke rise carefully pick up the vessel by the trivet, and with your breath and intention connect with the Realm of Sky. When you feel immersed in this airy energy, carefully raise the smoldering vessel above you and say:

I stand reaching toward the illuminating energies of the Realm of Sky, eternal cosmic tapestry weaving the primal pattern of all existence. Bless my striving with the clarity of far-reaching Sight, and may the breath of the Divine reawaken my consciousness to its connection to Source found deep within my soul. So may it be.

Return the burning incense to the altar.

Blessing the Stone of Intention

Immerse the stone in the waters of the cauldron (Realm of Sea), saying:

I ask that the energies of the Realm of Sea empower and bless the changes I seek to manifest during the light half of the year. Standing at this time between the Worlds, may I know true transformation on the emotional plane, and accomplish healing of the wounds of the past.

Lay your stone on the soil of the plant (Realm of Land), saying:

I ask that the energies of the Realm of Land empower and bless the changes I seek to manifest during the light half of the year. Standing at this time between the Worlds, may I know true transformation on the physical plane, and become centered in the blessings of the now.

Pass your stone through the smoke of the mistletoe incense (Realm of Sky), saying:

I ask that the energies of the Realm of Sky empower and bless the changes I seek to manifest during the light half of the year. Standing at this time between the Worlds, may I know true transformation on the mental plane, and obtain release from the worries for the future.

Return the blessed and empowered stone to its place on the altar.

Calling Forth the Awen

Clear your mind and center the red Awen candle on the altar in front of you; focusing on the symbol of the Three Rays carved into the candle which here represent the three aspects of the self that come together in the act of co-creation.

Begin to chant the word "Awen," drawing out the vowels to make the sounds "*Aaaaa—oooooh—eeeen*" ("eeeen" rhymes with "when," not "wean"). You may begin slowly, and as the energy builds you may find yourself chanting faster and faster. Stay as focused and intent as possible as you chant, and when you feel the energy has built to its peak, light the candle. Chant the word "Awen" three more times and use the flame as a focus to hold all of the energies you have built.

Weaving Intention

Literally and symbolically, you have kindled the Beltane fire, and it stands between the worlds filled with the fertile energies of all possibility. Pick up the Stone of Intention and hold it in front of the Awen candle. With your breath and your focused will, fill the stone with the creative energies you have raised through chant and intention. As the stone becomes charged, envision the energies of Awen being directed to empower your intention to manifest your sovereign Self.

When the crystal is completely charged, bury it in the soil directly in front of the central branch of your maypole. Hold the white ribbon in your right hand and say:

I call upon the energies of the Upper World, dwelling place of the Sacred Divine and storehouse of all Knowledge. I call forth the essence of my conscious self, and seek to connect with the high peaks of the mind. May all that I need to pull down from the realm of the Higher Self be revealed, and directed to birth my Sovereign Self.

Hold the red ribbon in your left hand and say:

I call upon the energies of the Lower World, dwelling place of the Blessed Ancestors and archive of all Wisdom. I call forth the essence of my unconscious self, and seek to connect with the deep well of the emotions. May all that I need to bring forth from the realm of the Shadow be revealed, and directed to birth my Sovereign Self.

Connect your intention with the maypole's central shaft and say:

I call upon the energies of the Middle World, dwelling place of all who live, and the realm of abundant manifestation. I call forth the essence of my integrated self, and seek to connect with the vitalistic bridge of the body, where that which is above and that which is below can come together and take form.

Visualize the three-rayed symbol of the Awen overlaying the maypole and its outstretched white and red ribbons. Connect your intention with this energy of creativity and Divine inspiration. When you are ready, weave the red and white ribbons around the maypole, alternately passing them one at a time from right hand to left hand in front of the pole, and from left hand to right hand behind the pole.

Weave the ribbons slowly and deliberately, willing the energies of creation emanating from Source to travel down through the Realms as the ribbons—the colors of the Celtic Otherworld—wind their way down the pole. As the energies descend, envision them entering and empowering the crystal buried at the base of the pole, imbuing your intention with the sacred energies of creation.

As you weave you can chant or recite the following, three times:

Creative spark of Awen flow
Through Sky, and Land, and Sea
From Source Above, to birth Below
Channeled through the World Tree

When you have woven the energies down to the bottom of the maypole, ground the energies by tying off the ribbons so the weaving remains affixed to the central branch. Visualize that the essence of your intentions have grounded themselves into the crystal "seed" you planted—empowering and sustaining it through the light half of the year. Spend time in the energy you have built and focused, meditating on your work and visualizing your intention being made manifest.

An Offering for the Ancestors

Take up the plate or cup that has been sitting on the altar filled with a food offering or libation for the ancestors. Charge the offering with some of the energies you have built in gratitude for their guidance and support. Bless the gift with the energies of the Three Realms by sprinkling it with some water from the cauldron, adding to it some soil from the plant, and passing it through the mistletoe smoke. After the ritual, leave the offering outdoors or on a windowsill overnight.

Releasing and Honoring the Three Realms

After completing your meditations, pick up the water-filled cauldron representing the Realm of Sea. Extend it toward the ground and say:

I give thanks to the deep reflective energies of the realm of Sea, resting place of the honored dead, our blessed ancestors and those awaiting the gifts of rebirth. May I ever know the blessings of the elixir of the Cauldron of Wisdom, and may these sacred waters continue to overflow the inner chalice of my soul. So may it be.

Return the cauldron to its place on the altar. Pick up the plant representing the Realm of Land. Extend it out in front of you and say:

I give thanks to the life-sustaining energies of the realm of Land, in-dwelling essence of the spirit of nature and vitalistic force which empowers the sacred landscape. May I ever know the blessings of the Ancient Pathways, and may these lines of power continue to revitalize the inner landscape of my soul. So may it be.

Return the plant to its place on the altar. Place some mistletoe on the lit charcoal and carefully pick up the vessel by its handle or by the trivet. Raise it above your head and say:

I give thanks to the illuminating energies of the Realm of Sky, eternal cosmic tapestry weaving the primal pattern of all existence. May I ever know the blessings of the clarity of far-reaching Sight, and may the breath of the Divine continue to reawaken my consciousness to its connection to Source found deep within my soul. So may it be.

Return the incense vessel the altar.

Opening the Sacred Space

Once again, hold the silver branch or rattle in your hand. Walk the perimeter of the circle moon-wise as you shake the branch nine times, visualizing the remaining energies of the working being absorbed and grounded into the earth. Feel the boundaries between the worlds fading, and shift your consciousness back to the here and now. If you are not feeling grounded and centered, place both hands flat on the ground and discharge any remaining ritual energies into the planet until you feel balanced and clear.

Keeping the Spark Alight

Once a candle has been lit with a sacred flame, its spirit can remain in the wick of a candle even after it has been extinguished. To preserve the energies of Awen in your candle, smother the flame of the candle with a candle snuffer or a spoon while envisioning the Divine Spark becoming concentrated in the burnt wick. Use this candle for meditating on the work you have set into motion or at anytime you can use the blessings of Awen in your life. When you light it anew, it will still hold the essence of this working and the energies of Awen.

Keep your personal maypole on your altar until Lughnasadh/ Gwyl Awst as a reminder of what you seek to manifest during the light half. Then, at Lughnasadh, time of the First Harvest, reflect on how far you have come in manifesting your intention and what yet needs to be done, and bury the ribbons to bring your work into full fruit. Always remember: obtaining spiritual Sovereignty is an ongoing process and each turn of the Cycle gives us the opportunity to further create the person we were born to be. Awen!

Notes

Litha

Midsummer: Otherworldy Magic

Bronwynn Forrest Torgerson

MIDSUMMER HAS A UNIQUE mystique, an aura of mystery and otherworldliness. On Summer Solstice, the sun prepares to die. The Fey are all about. Magic grows underfoot. Love is in the air. The energy is thick and seductive, as sweet as honeysuckle on the vine.

Midsummer has always been dear to my heart. Even as a child, I felt the energy of the day draw near and sensed that magic was afoot. To go play in the woods nearby might mean that something unseen might call my name from a grove of trees. Fairy lights might appear as patches of sunlight that were somehow thicker than the surrounding air. Anything could happen.

Midsummer or Litha, celebrated near Summer Solstice, marks the zenith of the sun's power in the summer sky. After the sun's height of glory on June 20, the longest day of 2012, the sun begins to wane. For a scant handful of moments each day thereafter, we gradually gain more cooling, healing rest, and repose of night. The year wheel turns slowly, but inexorably toward Winter Solstice when we'll welcome the sun back, gaining once more light from darkness.

To ancient people, a decline in the vitality of any living thing, be it a fruit fallen from the tree or a deer felled by an arrow in the field, signified death. It is not a far stretch then, to understand why the sun, annually surrendering its intensity and fire to darkness and to cold, was seen to go through cycles of death and rebirth as well.

In the United States, Canada, and some other countries, Summer Solstice is regarded as the start of summer. For people living in Ireland, the United Kingdom, China, and Japan, Summer Solstice is regarded as Midsummer. An Irish summer begins on May 1 and ends on July 31. East Asian calendars refer to Summer Solstice as "the extreme of summer," not just the beginning.

The sacredness of Midsummer comes from myths of the Dying God, the Sun who loses his life at Midsummer and is born again at Midwinter. These themes of dying and rebirth among ancient peoples were sometimes literal as well as metaphorical. Among the early Celts was the practice of the Seven Year King, wherein a hero was chosen for his youth, vigor, and valor and ritually married to a priestess symbolizing the queen of the land. At the end of seven years, before the start of his middle-aged physical decline, the sacred king was sacrificed at Midsummer and his blood and bones given back to the land. He had always known that thus was his fate. His seven-year reign was based on numerology, three being the number of heaven, meeting the number four of earth.

Sun gods were not exempt from death either. In the Egyptian pantheon, the Sun god Ra was the only God to suffer decline. Stories tell that he withdrew from the world of man for a while, then with the aid of the goddess Hathor, was renewed. A Polynesian god of a similar name, Raiatea, married the daughter of the earth, Tu-Papa, and dwelt half a year underground with her. Another Egyptian solar deity, Osiris, became the lord of the underworld after being slain by his brother Set. His physical form was resurrected by the love of his wife, the goddess Isis who bore his son Horus, the falcon-headed sky god.

The list goes on, with the cycle of splendor and love, disappearance, and loss. Some scholars of Christian lore state that it is no accident that Jesus as a sacrificed god figure was assigned a birth date near Midwinter, and wonder if the crucifixion didn't take place closer to Midsummer.

Let us consider the brighter Midsummer's themes of fairies, magic, and marriage. As day and night stand poised in perfect balance to one another, the doors between the worlds swing open wide and fairy folk just might pay us a call.

Wherever our ancestors roamed, they encountered the indigenous spirits. Ireland has its sacred springs, thought to be the home of water sprites and guarded to this day. In Iceland, roads are diverted around fairy mounds, lest the Fey be disturbed by vehicular intrusion into their domain and become offended. In America, there are spirit woods. At California's Muir Woods, it is not uncommon to catch a glimpse of dryadic faces peering through the bark of redwood trees. If your eyes are honored with such a sight, do not think to capture it on film, for your batteries will go dead in an instant.

The stories one hears at Midsummer are strange and filled with things not easily explained. Hartzell, a stoic friend of mine, shared this late-June tale. Through life circumstances not of his making, he and his family had been forced to give up their home and move into a tinier place. They forfeited much that they owned, mourning the memories attached to each thing. Hartzell wondered if they would ever have anything like that again. Then came Midsummer morn. An unfamiliar woman kept staring at him on the bus, then she got off at his stop. As Hartzell walked toward the drugstore to buy his morning paper, he heard her footsteps behind him. He stopped, thinking perhaps she was lost and wanted to ask for directions.

The stranger gazed into his face, with all knowing eyes, and said softly, "You asked for a word of promise last week. I am here to tell you that all will soon be well. All you gave up will return to you seven-fold." She laid a slender hand on his arm and the tingle of energy made his head spin. Hartzell nodded and blinked back tears, unable to speak. He reached for the drugstore door, to hold it open for her, only to turn and find that the woman had vanished. The following dawn, a friend called him up on the phone. Money that Hartzell had loaned out and forgotten could be repaid now, if he would just go stand outside his door and wait for his pal's arrival.

Hartzell's wife, who is Catholic, is convinced that God sent an angel their way. Hartzell believes he met a fairy maiden. Perhaps they are one and the same thing. The blessings have continued to flow.

As for myself, one Midsummer night I sat with Brenda, a dear Midwestern friend, out in her leafy back yard. My flight the next day would take me back to the desert, and I was soaking up the last bit of sweetness from her wonderful trees, hot coffee, and good conversation. I wished aloud for one thing I really missed in the desert. "If only there were fireflies," I sighed, "But they don't come out here until much later in the year..."

Suddenly Brenda sprang forward in her lawn chair and pointed. "What on earth is that about?!" she exclaimed, seeing one low tree branch that without any wind, had begun to whip around in dizzy circles. We watched for several minutes as its leaves continued their merry twirling dance. Then out of the darkness a tiny light twinkled. Small wings flew by and she gasped, "Oh my gosh, that's a firefly!" The insect gave quite a show, looping all around the yard, flitting up over our heads. Finally it winked out of sight.

My friend turned to me astonished and said, "Obviously some-one heard you. They sent you just one firefly, but one is all it takes..."

Although as with Hartzell, the Fey may offer up a boon or a bit of magic, one should never take it for granted that every dweller in Fey is kindly disposed toward humans and at our beck and call. Hardly! That notion is as preposterous as the thought of accosting someone you've never lain eyes on, demanding that they do you a favor, and expecting the results to be good. Fairies, like humans, can be capricious and have their own unique personalities. William Shakespeare wasn't far amiss when he wrote of the Midsummer high jinks of Puck, Titania, and Oberon, who made mirthful may-hem of the lives of mere mortals.

A relationship with the Fey takes some cultivating, just as one between two humans. You must first find a meeting place to invite their company. Explore the parks in your community or pay more attention to the trees in your own backyard. If one small place stands out, devote some time to it on a regular basis. Sit by a particular tree and have lunch. Put your hand on its bark and express appreciation for its strength or shelter, or just the simple beauty of the day. Pour a bit of bottled water at its base or bury a crystal or a silver coin there. Prove yourself worthy of knowing.

If you are an apartment dweller and have a remotely green thumb, grow a small collection of herbs and flowers in pots, remembering that mint attracts the Fey. Likewise, when space is cramped, you still can buy a cut flower and place it in a special vase, stating that you are sharing its beauty with the spirits of your home. I guarantee that you will feel a warm-hearted presence. These things establish a positive and respectful rapport. As in any friendship, make sure you know each other before requesting aid. If help is given, be grateful and return the gesture in a manner you feel will be best received.

Midsummer is also green magic time. For centuries, woodlands and garden have been scoured on solstice day to stock one's magical pantry. My experience with far memory revolved around this activity. In my early twenties, an old mage named Cecil with pale blue eyes and silver locks led a roomful of parapsychology students in an exercise in hypnotic regression. In a soft voice, he counted us down to the first day of school, then to a safe time of our choosing before this birth. His tape recorder was turned on in order to capture any interesting developments in the session. One by one, we were asked where we were and what we were doing.

When Cecil's attention turned to me, a child's voice answered his question. "I am in the woods," I said. What was I doing, he asked. "I am gathering herbs for my mother," I told him, "and there are fires on the hill."

"Is your village under invasion?" he asked, startled. He tells me I shook my head, then repeated "It is Midsummer. There are fires on the hill." My tone, when he played back the tape, was matter-of-fact and a bit peeved at having to explain a custom that everyone ought to know was common place. The fires of Midsummer mirrored the searing sun, and holy herbs strewn into those same fires spoke both of consecration and consumption, as all that once grew green and tall must fall and seed the earth again.

It is my firm belief that although our lineage may differ from life to life and our DNA change accordingly, our soul remembers every place our other, older journeys have ever taken us.

Herbs gathered just after the dew has dried or at midnight on Midsummer are said to be most potent. Rosemary, lavender, parsley, mint, St. John's wort, and dandelion are staples for magical pantries, while vervain, mullein, wormwood, and mistletoe cut, dried, and hung in one's household will protect from all manner of harm. Before you gather, please ask permission both of the plant and of the Fey, who may dwell nearby. Never take the last stalk of any green being.

Midsummer's moon beams down with romance. In June the hives are full of honey, which in ancient times was fermented and made into mead, a kind of honey wine. June being the month of marriage, our "honeymoons" today are a romantic reminder of an earlier time, when couples would sweeten the dishes they cooked and shared together with honey for a month, in honor of their new-found love. Bees can be cultivated, but they remain wild. Midsummer is that "wild magic" time of year.

It is said that if an unmarried maid fasts all day on Midsummer but sets a table for two and leaves her door open, at midnight either the true form of her future mate or his spirit will come and feast with her. Irish maids melt lead into water and try to discern clues in the shapes. In Spain, girls do the same thing with eggs. In Poland, girls fashion a wreath of wild flowers, place a candle in the middle, and set it adrift on the river, foretelling their future by watching the wreath's fate.

And so at Midsummer, all the world is enchanted. Magical beings watch our comings and goings and sometimes step a wee bit closer. Magic springs up from the fertile earth itself. The Sun gives up its life and yet returns. Fires on the hills and in our hearts are relit with the flame of love.

I leave you with this simple petition to the unseen realms:

Midsummer's light is burning bright,
Each leaf a fairy bower.
Preserve this night, we in your sight
When dark becomes the hour.

Blessed be.

Celestial Sway

Fern Feto Spring

AT THE SUMMER SOLSTICE, the Sun reaches a peak, climaxing in an energetic display of power and potency as the Goddess and God dance together in a passionate union out of which new life is formed. At this magical time, anything is possible and opportunities for growth and expansion are in abundance. Communal gatherings are emphasized as we share our blessings and creativity with those around us. Litha offers us the opportunity to be recognized for our gifts and abilities, basking in the golden glow of the sun's light.

The New Moon in Gemini on June 19 sets the stage for Summer Solstice 2012. The buzzing, energizing aliveness of Gemini introduces us to new ideas, opening our minds to different ways of viewing the world and experiencing reality. This Gemini influence is stimulating and invigorating, a perfect backdrop for solstice energy. At this time, we can learn about the world from a completely fresh perspective, reconnecting with our youthful selves and setting intentions for the future. Our questioning mind is on high alert now, as we listen with interest to what is being communicated in our immediate environments. This is a time to cultivate openness, letting go of judgment and rigidity and allowing ourselves to gather incoming messages and ideas from others.

Venus, which has been retrograde since May 15, goes direct on June 27 in Gemini, and will soon form an energizing sextile to Uranus. The planet of love is now fully prepared to forge new territory in love and romance, breaking down barriers from the past and welcoming the future with open arms. Venus direct in Gemini opens us to new information about relationships, helping us to rapidly absorb a variety of diverse perspectives and experiences. The powerful energy of the Litha sabbat only adds to Venus' fresh start now, awakening a hopefulness and innocence in love that welcomes the sexiness of summertime with open arms.

The Gemini theme continues with Jupiter, the planet of expansion and opportunity, which entered the sign of the Twins on June 11. Jupiter in Gemini brings an expansion of ideas and information. Our minds become far more active during this year-long transit as we try to learn as much as we can about what is happening around us. This is a time to develop new concepts, educate ourselves, and communicate as much as possible. All forms of writing, speaking, listening, and learning are emphasized and supported during Jupiter's movement through the sign of Gemini. At this time, our opportunities and good fortune will come through our ability to mindfully cultivate Gemini's qualities in our lives.

Jupiter forms a square to Neptune on June 25, amplifying our ability to expand our consciousness and our connection with other realms and spiritual realities. Though the square aspect may bring some confusion and misunderstandings (especially at first), this powerful energy can also help us move beyond our limiting beliefs and open to new ways of being.

A Full Moon in Capricorn on July 3 conjuncts Pluto, the planet of the underworld and squares Uranus, planet of surprise and innovation. The ongoing square of Pluto and Uranus, which lasts for much of 2012, is emphasized under this Full Moon, bringing the lessons of this planetary configuration into bold relief. Collectively, we will be asked to make great changes and begin to take steps to restructure the foundations in our lives that we have come to depend on. The split between our private "at home" selves versus our need for recognition and achievement will also feel particularly pronounced at this Full Moon as we feel a powerful call to create new structures and forms for the future. It will be important to strike a balance now between our internal needs, emotions, and relationships with others and our external work or "calling." Though the tension created by this Full Moon may be intense, if we can find productive ways to channel it, much can be accomplished.

Venus Direct in Gemini

Venus, the planet of love and beauty, goes direct in Gemini on June 27 while entering into a creative sextile aspect to quirky Uranus. This planetary configuration promises some spicy solstice love magic. Opportunities for new and exciting encounters with others could manifest suddenly and in surprising ways. Existing relationships may undergo a revival at this time as a breath of fresh summer air infuses new life into old habits and patterns. Use this energizing Venusian power to wake up your love life and form new relationships.

Venus Direct Ritual

Because Gemini thrives on words, communication, and information exchange, invoke Venus in Gemini by verbalizing and writing your wishes for love. Ritually write a love letter to the Goddess of love. You can do this in the more traditional way with pen and paper, or write her a letter on the sand at the beach, make a "picture letter" with images, or create a song or poem. Venus is the goddess of the arts, so try and engage your creativity to express your love of love. You can thank the goddess for all the love blessings she has brought you in the past and also ask for blessings to come in the future. You may also want to write a letter to the next lover who will come into your life. Write down all the things you love about this person and your relationship as if they already exist in your life.

New Moon in Gemini

The Gemini New Moon awakens our curiosity, ability to learn, and our interest in new ideas and information. Our openness to others ideas and concepts is heightened at this time and we will have an opportunity to exercise our brains and process thoughts with renewed strength and energy under this lunation. The energy of Summer Solstice brings a unique power to this New Moon, ensuring that the information that comes at this time may be particularly important or impactful in our lives. Maximize your receptivity to the New Moon with a ritual.

New Moon in Gemini Solstice Ritual

Decorate your solstice altar with symbols related to air: birds, athame/swords, words, ideas, thoughts, information. Call on Mercury, Gemini's ruling planet, to join you at your ritual and light a yellow candle in honor of Mercury and Gemini. Ask that your ears, both inner and outer, be open to what you need to hear. Use your athame or other sacred knife to cut away anything that is preventing you from being an open channel to listen to whatever communication you most need at this time. In ritual space, began to write whatever comes into your mind on paper or in a computer. This process of "automatic writing," can help you to gather information from spirit that your conscious mind might block. Keep writing until you feel complete and when you are ready, read over what you have written, assessing what messages might be helpful for you in your life.

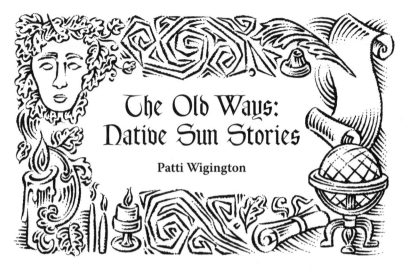

The Old Ways: Native Sun Stories

Patti Wigington

LITHA IS THE TIME of the Summer Solstice, and for many of us, it's a time to sit back and enjoy that powerful sun energy. This is the time of the year when the gardens are blooming, the days are long and warm, and we can get outdoors and enjoy ourselves. Perhaps it's a trip to the beach, an afternoon in the pool, or just a lazy day at the park that makes this time of year so worthwhile.

The Summer Solstice has been observed for ages by people around the globe, but few cultures have such a wide variety of tales and legends about the sun as the Native American tribes of North America. After all, for tribal peoples, the sun was more than just an excuse to play outdoors. It was a life force, a light-giving spirit in the heavens, and one that was worthy of being honored. Because this life energy was so important, many Native American tribes have stories that detailed the quest by man and beast alike for a source of light and warmth.

Grandmother Spider and the Sun (Cherokee)

The Cherokee people of the Southeastern United States have a tale that involves the search for the sun. Like many Native American stories, animals are integral to the legend. This story begins when there was no light at all, and everything was dark. In fact, it was so dark that people couldn't go anywhere because they couldn't see. Parents didn't know what their children looked like, no one had ever seen a flower bloom, and people were always bumping into each other and falling down in the darkness.

Finally, the animals decided to help out by bringing light to mankind. Woodpecker, who was very clever and had flown great distances, knew that on the other side of the world, there was light. He suggested that perhaps someone should go get some light and bring it back.

Possum, who had a lovely bushy tale, volunteered to go get the light. He said, "I can hide the light inside my tail, and no one will ever know I've taken it." But the sun burned all the fur from his tail, and Possum came scampering home with no light at all.

Buzzard decided that he had a better idea, so he flew up into the sky to the far side of the world. He plucked off a bit of the sun and put it on his head, amongst his feathers, and began to fly home. But the sun burned his feathers off, and by the time he got back, Buzzard was bald, and he too had no light to share. The animals were fresh out of ideas.

Finally Grandmother Spider, who was very old and very wise, said she would try to bring home some light. Grandmother Spider took a ball of clay and shaped it into a bowl, and then she began rolling it toward the sun with her legs. As she rolled the bowl closer, she left a fine strand of thread behind her. When she finally arrived at the light, she gently placed the sun in her clay bowl. Grandmother Spider used her silken web to find her way home, traveling from east to west, and as she moved, the sun's rays went with her and illuminated the earth for all to see.

The Sun and Earth Make the First People (Hopi)

Among the Hopi of the Southwest, the Sun plays an important role in creation legends. Tawa was the Sun God, and he controlled all of the magic and power up above, while Spider Woman, the Goddess of Earth, controlled everything on the land below. There were no people or animals, because Spider Woman and Tawa had not yet made them.

Tawa came up with ideas for beautiful things to create—fish, bear, birds—and Spider Woman used the clay of the earth to make these creatures. However, they just lay there and did not move. It was not until Tawa and Spider Woman joined their magic together that the creatures had Spirit, which allowed them to live and breathe.

Tawa said to Spider Woman, "Now, let's make a pair of beings that look like you and me, so that they can live with the animals we have made." Spider Woman took up her magical clay, and formed the first man and the first woman, and she and Tawa gave them life as well. Tawa promised to give the man and woman light so that they could see, and Spider Woman promised that the man and woman and their descendants could live off the land. As the people multiplied, Spider Woman divided them into groups and gave them names, such as the Hopi, the Zuni, and the Paiute, and this is how the sun and the earth worked together to create the first tribes.

Raven Steals the Light (Inuit)

In some Native American cultures, the sun is not a primary figure of legend, but instead plays a secondary role, despite the importance of daylight and warmth. In Alaska—where sunlight is in short supply for part of the year—the Inuit have a tale in which Raven, the trickster, steals the sunlight. The people lived in perpetual darkness, but Raven—like the Cherokee's Woodpecker—had traveled far and seen much and knew that there was light on the other side of the world. The people thought it would be wonderful to have some light to see by, so after much cajoling and persuasion, Raven finally agreed to go get the sun.

When he finally got to the village in which the light was, Raven found that the chieftain kept the sun in a box. Raven was able to trick the chief's little grandson into playing with the ball of light, and stole it away from him. He flew back to the Inuit people, the sun trailing behind him on a string, like a balloon. When he delivered the sun, there was daylight and brightness everywhere. However, Raven warned the people that because he had only stolen a single ball of light, it would have to rest every six months. This is why there is six months of light, and six months of darkness. The people were still grateful, because it was more than they had before.

Although these tales are old ones, many Native Americans still take time to honor the sun at the time of the summer solstice. Take a few minutes out of your Litha celebrations, and remember to give thanks for all the marvelous gifts the sun has given us!

For Further Reading:

Bruchac, Joseph, and Michael Caduto. *Native American Stories*, 1991.

Hazen-Hammond, Susan. *Spider Woman's Web: Traditional Native American Tales About Women's Power*, 1999.

Mitchell, Judy. *Handbook of Native American Mythology*, 2004.

Spense, Lewis. *Native American Myths*, 1999.

Feasts and Treats

Susan Pesznecker

At Midsummer, the Sun's power is at it peak and life bursts from the earth. Our Midsummer vegetarian luncheon honors the sun and features herbs, berries, and new greens typical of late spring and early summer.

Veggie and Cheese Quesadillas

At the center of your sunny lunch is an orb-like quesadilla, brimming with golden cheeses and vegetables.

Prep time: 15 minutes
Cook time: 15 minutes
Serves: 6+

Vegetable oil
Small (6–8 inch) flour quesadillas
Cheddar cheese, grated
Sweet onion, sliced thin
Red, orange, and/or yellow sweet pepper, julienned
1 yellow zucchini; peeled, seeded, and julienned
1 carrot, julienned or grated
8 mushrooms, sliced

Black olives, sliced
Refried red beans
Salsa
Salt, pepper, and red pepper flakes
Avocado wedges (optional)

Oil a large skillet very lightly—use a cast iron skillet if you have one. Place the pan over medium heat.

Lay a flour tortilla in the skillet. Spread a layer of grated cheese on the tortilla then add your choice of vegetables and refried beans. Spread small dollops of salsa over the vegetable mixture. Season with slat, pepper, and a few red pepper flakes. Top with more cheese and a second flour tortilla.

Cook for several minutes—until the tortilla browns and the cheese begins to melt. Use a pancake turner to flip the quesadilla, and brown the other side.

To serve, cut into fourths and arrange on a dinner plate like a big round sun. Offer avocado and additional salsa if desired.

Hint: If preparing several of these for a group, place the finished quesadillas on a cookie sheet in a barely warm oven. You can hold them like this for 30 minutes or so while cooking a large batch.

Crunchy Quinoa Salad

With its emphasis on round seeds and grains, sunflowers, lemons, and golden carrots, this salad pays homage to the life-giving Midsummer sun, while its greens give a nod to the sustaining fecund earth. My friend Jonathan first shared this salad with me; it's a vegan dish but so delicious that even your most devotedly carnivorous friends will ask for seconds.

Prep time: 15 minutes
Cook time: 25–45 minutes
Serves: 6

1 cup quinoa, rinsed well
1¾ cups water

6 tablespoons sunflower oil (use corn oil if sunflower not available)

2 tablespoons apple cider vinegar

1 tablespoon lemon juice

½ teaspoon tamari (or soy sauce)

1½ teaspoons black pepper

¼ pound carrots, grated (2 or 3 good-sized carrots)

¼ cup sesame seeds, lightly toasted

¼ cup sunflower seeds

3–4 stalks green onion, sliced (use white and green parts)

¼ bunch parsley, coarsely chopped

Fresh baby spinach

Fresh mixed baby greens

Salt (optional)

Cook quinoa until water is absorbed (about 25 to 45 minutes). Stir several times during cooking process. After quinoa is cooked, remove from heat and cool slightly, stirring every few minutes to speed cooling.

While quinoa is cooling, make dressing by combining the oil, vinegar, lemon juice, tamari, and black pepper. Either shake the mixture in a lidded jar or use an immersion blender to create a smooth emulsion.

Mix cooled quinoa with dressing to coat well. Add the rest of the ingredients and mix thoroughly. Taste, and add a bit of salt if you feel it's needed. Serve chilled or at room temperature on a bed of spinach and mixed baby greens.

This salad keeps for several days, but the texture is best when served within 24 hours of preparation.

Strawberry Shortcake

Round biscuits, summer-sweet berries, and a fluff of cream create a decadent finish to your solstice meal.

Prep time: 15 minutes

Cook time: 10–15 minutes

Serves: 6+

A favorite biscuit mix (or your favorite biscuit recipe)

2–3 tablespoons unsalted butter, melted

5 tablespoons sugar, divided

2 pints fresh strawberries

1 cup heavy cream (well-chilled)

¼ teaspoon vanilla extract

A mixing bowl and beaters (refrigerated for at least a half-hour)

Rinse strawberries quickly and pat dry. Remove green hulls. Cut or slice each berry into halves or thirds. Sprinkle 2 tablespoons sugar over the berries and stir well. Set aside so that the berries have time to become juicy.

Make one recipe of biscuit dough according to package instructions. (You may make biscuits from scratch, if you wish.) While stirring up the biscuit dough, add in the melted butter and 1 tablespoon sugar. Mix well.

Roll the dough out ½ to ¾ inch thick. Use a round biscuit cutter (or a drinking glass) to cut circles. Pour about ½ tablespoon heavy cream into a custard cup; dipping one finger in the cream, moisten the top of each biscuit just a little with the cream, then sprinkle each biscuit with sugar.

Bake according to package instructions. Cool on wire racks. When completely cooled, cover loosely with a tea towel and store at room temperature.

Just before serving, pour the chilled cream into the chilled bowl. Beat at medium-high speed until it thickens—about 1 to 2 minutes. Stir in ¼ teaspoon vanilla and 1 to 2 tablespoons sugar. Beat for about 10 seconds, then taste. If not sweet enough, add a bit more sugar. Continue beating until the cream forms soft peaks. (Do not overbeat: overbeaten heavy cream turns to butter!)

Split biscuits; top with berries, the other biscuit half, and a big, generous dollop of whipped cream. For extra decadence, spoon vanilla ice cream between the biscuits.

Fresh Herbal Sun Teas

Dazzle family and friends with an assortment of sparkling iced teas: capture midsummer energy by brewing the teas under the sun.

Prep time: 24 hours (start early!)

Serves: Makes one quart

2–4 tablespoons fresh herbs (mint, raspberry leaves, lemon balm, thyme, chamomile, etc.), coarsely chopped

Spices: cinnamon stick, whole cloves, black peppercorns, whole cardamom, whole allspice, citrus peel, etc., crushed slightly in a mortar and pestle

1 cup sugar

Lemon, sliced

Sugar

In a quart Mason jar, combine herbs and spices. Fill jar with cold water and set outdoors in direct sun for at least 8 and up to 24 hours.

Make simple syrup by boiling 1 cup sugar and 1 cup water until dissolved. Chill.

Strain tea into cold glasses. Sweeten to taste with simple syrup and garnish with lemon slices.

Crafty Crafts

Ellen Dugan

Theme of the Season: Growth and tides of change
Colors: Green, white, and beachy tones (sand, aqua, and ivory)
Scents: Rose, rosemary, and lavender
Energy: Enchantment and connection

Stone Herb Markers for the Magickal Garden

Smooth, large rounded stones make gorgeous and earthy plant markers. This is an easy craft and is suitable for older children as long as they are supervised.

Paint these stones in a clever way and add the names of your favorite herbs for one-of-a-kind garden markers. Your magickal garden will be the talk of the town this Midsummer!

Supplies

Smooth round beach or cobblestones, 4 to 6 inches wide
Acrylic paint: ivory and dark green
2 paintbrushes—one ½-inch wide and one fine brush for lettering
A paint pen in dark green (if you prefer to write out the letters)
Pencil
Waterproof sealer

A foam disposable brush
A paper-covered work surface

Instructions: With the pencil, lightly draw an oval on the stone. Using a wide brush, paint inside of the oval with the ivory paint. Let it dry completely on the paper-covered work surface. If you do this project outdoors on a warm summer day, the paint will dry quickly. Repeat with a second coat of the ivory paint for good coverage. Let the second coat dry as well.

With the pencil, in the center of the ivory oval, lightly write the name of the herb or plant. If you do not like the way the letters look, wipe off the pencil mark with a damp paper towel and try again.

With a thin paintbrush and green paint (or a dark green paint pen), carefully paint the name of the herb onto the stone.

Next, using the green paint and a bit of green mixed with the ivory for light green, paint a simple decorative border of leaves and vines around the oval edges. Don't worry about perfection, just make simple leaf shapes and vines. Have fun with it and don't stress over the artwork. Simple is usually best. Let all of this dry completely.

After the entire garden marker is thoroughly dry, you can use the foam brush to add a coating of clear waterproof sealer to the stones to make them even more weatherproof. Allow this to dry as well. (Refer to manufacturer's directions for drying times.)

Fun Variations: Here are a few additional thoughts for variations on the theme. Write the words *Magick* or *Faerie Garden*, *Witch's Garden*, or even *Enchanted Garden* on the stones. Or use even larger smooth stones and write out magickal messages such as *As I will it, So shall it be.* Or, using the paint pen, you can write your favorite gardening quotes.

You can even use four larger smooth stones to mark your quarters if you like. Think of writing *East*, *South*, *West*, and *North*, and then decorating (or painting) these with the themes and the colors of each magickal element—yellow for east/air, red for south/fire, blue for west/water and green for north/earth.

Finally, when you go to look for the rocks, hit the landscaping section of the local home-improvement store. They do sell bags of cobblestones. Also some arts and crafts stores sell them by the small bag. Or try a business that specializes in landscaping stone. They typically sell by the pound. Several six- to eight-inch smooth cobblestones would be fairly affordable purchased that way.

Of course, if you live in an area that has natural smooth stones, go on a rock hunt and pick them up for free!

Cost: $10.00 to $20.00 and up for the larger projects

Time: 1 to 2 hours, but note longer drying times if the weather is humid.

Seashell Wreath for Midsummer

I love seashell crafts for the summer months, as they are fun, textural, and different. The subdued and natural colors of the shells are softly soothing and cheerful no matter where you happen to live. Seashell wreaths are so gorgeous and appealing because of their textures. Don't worry about every shell being perfect. Besides, you want it to look natural and handmade, not slick and commercialized, whether you find your shells at a local beach or pick up a bag of them in the arts and crafts store. This is a natural and enchanting summertime project.

Supplies

Eight 6-inch grapevine wreaths
Spanish (*Sphagnum*) moss
Assorted seashells, starfish, and sand dollars
Tiny pieces of driftwood, and rounded stones
Low temperature glue gun
Glue sticks
Floral wire or chenille stems to create a hanger
Sheer 2-inch-wide ribbon in ocean blue or off white (if desired for a
   soft bow for the shell wreath)

Instructions: Before getting to the creative part of this project, you need to make a hanger (because it's more difficult to do after the wreath is decorated). Simply cut a length of floral wire or use one chenille stem and wrap it around the wreath and twist the ends together to create a loop.

Now the fun begins!

Using the hot glue gun, cover the wreath with the Spanish moss. To begin the design, place the largest shells or starfish first. Also, remember that rule of threes when it comes to wreath design. Make off-kilter triangles around the wreath with the largest shells. (For example if the wreath were a clock face, you could place a large shell at 2, 7, and 11.) Hot-glue the large shells firmly in place.

Then fill in around the largest shells with the medium-size shells and stones, gluing those items in place as you go.

Finally, glue in the smallest shells/driftwood twigs, etc., making sure to leave some of the moss exposed.

Allow the glue to set and pick off any glue strings.

If desired, tie a soft bow around the wreath and allow the streamers to hang down. If necessary glue the bow in place with a dab of the hot glue. (That sheer ribbon will be soft and loose and informal). Hang it up and enjoy.

Cost: $15.00 dollars and up (If you live by the water, you may be able to use gathered shells and not purchase any shells at all; if so the cost of the wreath would go down dramatically.)

Time: 30 minutes to an hour

Note: If you are gathering shells on the beach, be sure they are "critter free." Collect only empty shells.

Variations: Here are a few more ideas spun off the seashell wreath project. You could do the same shell wreath design on a much smaller scale and create candle rings for ocean-scented pillar candles. That would be gorgeous for a Midsummer altar and gathering. Or, decorate a wooden picture frame or even cover a wooden box in shells and beach stones. See what you are inspired to create now that you have the basics under your belt.

All One Family

Clea Danaan

MIDSUMMER HONORS THE FULLNESS of life, as the garden has shifted into warm season vegetables and daily the fruits of our labors grow plumper and more ripe. Depending on where you live, the chill of spring has passed, but the deep heat has yet to set in. It is the same energy we feel when in the thick of a project, full of ideas, optimistic, and energized. I associate this feeling with late childhood and mid-adulthood, when ideally we feel sure of our path and the world around us.

At this time, the spring vegetables like greens and peas are just about to tire from the heat, so my family eats salad every day. The juices from lettuce are cooling and energizing and help us to digest our meals. In a few weeks, when the days just begin imperceptibly to shorten, I will harvest the garlic and focus more on peppers, tomatoes, eggplant, and summer squash in my cooking. These fruits speak of warm summer nights and ripeness, but we have not yet reached this peak of summer heat. At Midsummer, the longest day, we are still in the bright joy of summer, when days feel long and full and happy.

Use this time of year to eat more fruits and vegetables. Honor the gifts of the mother and prepare lightly cooked meals of color and flavor. Grill or lightly steam fresh vegetables from the garden or farmers' market. If you have one, spend time in the garden soaking in the abundance offered. Bring young children into the garden with a magnifying lens to look for bugs and inspect plant leaves close up. Notice the variety of leaves: corn is long and grassy; squash and melon have fat, scratchy leaves; and tomato leaves are fuzzy and moist. This teaches children to honor nature on her own terms through their natural curiosity and love of learning. Older children and teens will enjoy time to themselves in the garden; send them out with a basket and invite them to plan your meals based on what they find. They will learn now how to live in synch with the seasons and develop their own agency through simple activities like harvesting, planning, and cooking.

This is the best time of year to visit farmers' markets. Don't forget your reusable canvas bags! My four-year-old beamed with pride as she made her very first purchase at a market; she couldn't bring herself to actually hand the farmer the four dollars for two beautiful bunches of chard, so she shyly set the money on the table and brought me the chard with a huge grin on her face. She said, "I think this is called rainbow chard!" She was trying to make a joke since the stalks were so colorful—but she was right! It was rainbow chard. She marveled at the name and ate lots with butter at dinner.

Take time to eat your meals slowly and with reverence for the miracles of fresh food. Give thanks. Eckhart von Hochheim, a German theologian and mystic commonly known as Meister Eckhart, said that if you only ever say one prayer, let it be "Thank you!" Let us teach our children to give thanks all year, not just in the fall.

Midsummer is about light and the power of the sun. This closest star makes life on earth possible. All plants and animals derive energy from the sun: plants directly and animals through plants. Even deep-sea creatures living off hydrogen sulfide from hydrothermal vents consume energy that was once part of the sun and is now nestled deep in the core of the earth. On Midsummer, discuss with your children the power of the sun and its role in our lives. Light candles and marvel at how this flame is the energy of the sun captured in stasis, released when we light the candle. Reflect on the role of light in your life.

Each of us carries this light deep within ourselves as well, both literally because we are all made of stardust, and metaphorically as spiritual beings. You know those moments when you see your own children's light shining so brightly it brings tears to your eyes? This is the time to share that vision with them. It will embarrass and delight them. You will never be able to fully convey the depth of your love for their light, but by honoring each other's light as a family, you fan the fires and help that light to grow. Every parent most wishes one thing for his or her child: to see that child's inner light expressed most fully. As you sit around your Midsummer fire (or candles), share with each other the light you see in each family member. Let this lead to a discussion of how that light might be expressed more fully. This discussion will depend on the ages of your children, of course. But all ages of children like to talk about what they want to be when they "grow up." All children enjoy talking about their interests and having them be taken seriously by the adults in their life. When you honor this discussion, you honor your child and the work she is here on earth to do. In doing so, you honor your own light.

Take time for yourself, as well, to explore the idea of your light. What do you see as your purpose on earth? How are you expressing that purpose? In what ways do you wish you could do more, or do things differently? Are there small or large steps you can take right now to make that happen? Maybe you can take a few classes online or go back to school. Maybe you can pull out those paints and practice your art again. Or perhaps you want to volunteer for a cause you love—bring the kids along and learn as a family. How can your family, who loves and supports you, help you express your light? Write out your thoughts in a journal and discuss them with your partner and, as appropriate, your family. We are here in this life for such a short time. Let your purpose shine.

As fiery sun energy abounds, Midsummer is a very masculine time of year. In many traditions the sun is masculine and is associated with the God. This is a great time, therefore, to honor the men in your life. Call in the Green Man or the Horned God, dance around the fire, and give thanks to the fathers and sons in your life. We are raising a generation of men who will be able to truly embody healthy masculinity. The men's movement has laid down the foundations for this transformation, and now our sons can grow up to be strong *and* sensitive, embodied *and* intellectual (as can women). Adult men, too, are learning on a cultural and individual level what it means to be healthy men. The same is true of the masculine within women. Take time now to honor the God in us all, as the bright sun burns at full strength.

Find, Claim & Name Your Magical Tool

Bronwynn Forrest Torgerson

I DRAW ON MY long slender tiger's eye ring and recite my own daily charm:

Stone and Crystal guard me well, where I work and where I dwell.

I am putting on my power. The name of this ring is Balance, and it wraps my right middle finger like a sheath of primal silk. Tiger's eye will serve as my anchor in this world on this day and help keep me focused on the work ahead in a calm, clear-headed manner.

Forestal, a ring set with diamond-shaped green amber, connects me to the woodlands of the world at times I seek the aid of dryadic spirits in my quest. The Blue Jay–colored labradorite stone, christened Felicity, brings joy and lightening of spirit my way.

When Majesty, the big oval carnelian ring, comes out of that onyx box, stand clear. Carnelian is the stone of courage and solar power. Carnelian enables one to step up to the plate and take an unflinching stance. The lips are empowered to speak what must be said and heard by those who need to heed them.

The custom of naming enchanted objects is rooted in ancient lore. King Arthur reached for the otherworldly sword Excalibur, a gift, some say, from the Lady of the Lake. The Norse goddess Freya bartered with four dwarven brothers for her magickal necklace Brisingamen. Thor wields his hammer Mjollner and smashes giant obstacles in his path.

The system I use to attract, acquire, and christen my tools of power will work equally well for powerful pendants, altar tools, or ritual implements. There is no better time than Midsummer, when the doors between realms open wide and unseen helpers with all-seeing eyes may know just where to find the thing you seek.

How then, once it has arrived, should we practitioners of magick call an object to us and bless, name, and dedicate it to our purpose? First, determine within yourself what you are looking for. Create its image in your mind. Think how it might feel in your hand, its weight and its warmth. What attributes should it have to make it singularly yours?

Go to the garden or grove where you have felt Fey power and feel welcome. Call to the appropriate elemental spirits of that place, and ask for their aid. Describe in great detail the thing that you are seeking. Be honest about how much you are willing to pay, as many of us have heard the old taboo about haggling over a magical tool.

If it is a special athame or boline you are seeking, call to the energy dragons and to the keepers of the fiery forge whose energies have worked through the hands of those who crafted your blade. You may also wish to invoke a deity associated with blades or metal craft, such as Greco-Roman Athena, Welsh Govannon the smith god, or Lugh of the Celts. Ask that a powerful blade, suited just to your purpose, find its way to your hand and that the steel sing in your grasp.

If you long for an altar bell, speak to the merfolk whose voices are said to awaken wondrous delight. Siren songs, like the peel of a bell, reverberate on the air. You might wish to also address such gods and goddesses as Ganesh of the Hindus, Huehuecoyotl the Aztec goddess (who was said to wear golden bells as adornment on her cheeks), or a deity associated with merriment and mirth such as Greco-Roman Baubo. Ask that the sound of summoning, that of a special bell, ring out soon in your life.

This method works equally well for chalices, wands, pentacles, scrying mirrors, and ritual jewelry. Just figure out which element your object has the most affinity with, and call to those spirit guardians and gods most appropriate.

Always end your request for aid in finding the object with this phrase:

I am open to this ___ finding me in a most unusual way.

The object of your desire might show up at a yard sale or on eBay. It may come to you in trade for something else, or appear to you at a place in the wild. For the longest time, I had searched for a wand. Then one day in a canyon where streams gurgled past glacial boulders, a piece of driftwood swept into my hand. I blessed it and adorned it with garnet, topaz and peridot. It nestled into my hand and whispered, "I am Elkimer."

❧

Let us fast forward to the time that your magickal token has arrived. It is magnificent, and you need to consecrate it to your art. If done well, this will take a full lunation to accomplish. Be patient and consider how long you waited to receive this coveted thing.

First, if it would not damage the object, leach it clean by burying it in a shallow dish of earth during a night of the Dark Moon phase. (You may safeguard your talisman from damage or decay by placing it in a plastic sandwich bag, then covering it with dirt.) Then chant:

Out of the womb of the Mother you came. Rest with Her, then receive your name.

If you work with runes, you may wish to trace the rune Perthro (ᛈ) which symbolizes the cup lowered into the dark well of Wyrd, into the air. After the following day, unearth the object, shake the dirt off, and set it aside to receive its next purification.

At the New Moon, light your best incense. I prefer a stick of frankincense and myrrh, but a sandalwood cone or smoldering sage or sweet grass works equally well. Pass the object through the smoke, saying:

Dream and vision, I called to you. Gift of the gods, be born anew.

Trace the rune Berkana (ᛒ), herald of new beginnings, in the air.

The moon swells silver, full and round, and sails the midnight skies. Depending upon the nature of your magickal object, either immerse it in a wash of spring water (bottled water will do) into which you have sprinkled a few grains of sea salt and a pinch of the herb mugwort, or place the object on a flat surface and sprinkle the blessed water in a circle around it. As you do this, chant:

All doors are now sealed from your journeys past. Creature of magick, thou art thrice blessed at last.

Trace the rune Laguz (ᛚ) over your tool, signifying that it has traveled down the stream of chance; prior destinations are now lost in the distance, and it has washed ashore in your hands.

Now you are ready for the naming of your tool. Light your altar candle and invoke the deities of your pantheon or Path. Take your artifact in your left hand, the receptive one and trace the rune of signals and communication, Ansuz (ᚨ), over it with your right, or sending hand.

Speak to the talisman, telling it in your own words of your search for it and of its importance in your future magickal workings. Raise it to your lips and bestow a gentle kiss upon it, making it officially yours. In some traditions, practitioners may anoint the new tool with a bit of saliva or sweat, or drop of blood. This is a solemn gesture of binding the thing to you alone, and is purely optional.

Next ask, *What shall I call you?*

Listen for an intuitive answer in your mind. If none is given at this time, state that you are willing to wait until such time as the object reveals its name to you. One will come. Enjoy this gift of the gods and care for it accordingly.

What is it you need now? Picture that tool in your mind. Imagine a golden threat connecting that thing and you. Envision one end of the thread as tied around your wrist, the other attached to the tool you seek. Give an imaginary tug on the string, to awaken the token to the fact that there is a good new magickal home waiting for it, with you. Let the way be cleared between you and may it be with you soon. Blessed be.

Notes

Lammas

The Feast of First Loaves

Kenny Klein

One Lughnasadh many years ago, I entered a small occult bookshop in New York's East Village to check out a lecture on Wicca. The lecture was presented by a Wiccan tradition called Blue Star. The High Priestess spoke about the Wheel of the Year and explained the holiday of Lughnasadh. Then they gathered everyone into the back courtyard of the shop and performed a ritual, one that—though I have done a thousand rituals since—I vividly remember to this day. I was hooked, and delighted when I was invited to further rituals at their covenstead in Brooklyn. My visits there became a commitment, and in time I was initiated into the Blue Star Wiccan tradition.

I came to learn that Lughnasadh was the perfect time for this to have happened for me. It is the time of the harvest, celebrated by giving the first harvested loaves back to the Gods, and of a tradition named "Calling The Pagans Home," in which we send our energies into the world to gather to us all people who may be looking for the Craft, but have not yet found it.

Wicca is the European Pagan tradition, and some current traditions of Wicca, gleaned from centuries-old sources, come from the 1950s and earlier. Some people call these the Old Guard traditions.

Others are more current and less adherent to hierarchy and structure. Blue Star is an Old Guard Wiccan tradition, based in hierarchy and a consistent teaching style that includes oral teaching and experience-based learning.

While most Old Guard Wiccan traditions work with a specific moon Goddess (like Diana) and a specific antlered god (like Cernunnos or Pan), we work a little more broadly, with many European goddesses and gods. We feel that the Goddess or God (or pantheon, which is a group of dieties from a specific region) draws a seeker to their worship, often by drawing you to a group or tradition that works with that god or goddess. If it happens the right way, it can be a very deep, powerful, and sometimes taxing connection.

In Blue Star we do not create a new ritual each time we meet, as some more modern Pagan groups might do. We use a standardized ritual format that is consistent each time. We believe that in using the same words and actions for each sabbat and esbat (moon circle), we encourage the conscious mind to "turn off" in the familiarity of the ritual, and the unconscious mind to come to the fore, creating a trance state or a state of communion with the gods and goddesses. We also feel that within the consistency of words and actions there are many layers of meaning and magic, which one could not explore if one changes the wording each time one performs a ritual.

Of course, this type of traditional Wicca is not for everyone. Some people need constant change for spiritual stimulation. Others do not work well in a group or within a hierarchy, which are important elements of learning and practicing traditional Wicca. But for those who, like me, are drawn to this type of worship, a coven using a traditional Wiccan format and traditional hierarchy feels like "home." It is also a great place to gain a very deep knowledge of the secrets and mysteries of Wicca.

The only part of the Blue Star ritual that does change each time is the "work of the circle," the portion of the ritual that is specific to the time of the year or the phase of the moon. On full moons, we draw down a goddess, and raise power (draw energy into the circle for some purpose like healing or doing magic); on new moons we draw a god, and usually do a class; and on each sabbat there is work based on the time of the year. At Lughnasadh we will invoke a God and a goddess related to the harvest and the sun, and we will "call the Pagans home."

Lughnasadh

August 1, Lughnasadh (LOO-na-sah), might be the most down-played and overlooked of the eight Pagan sabbats. There's no dramatic shift in the weather; while Imbolc brings the snows of February and Samhain engulfs us in the chill of late Autumn, Lughnasadh is still just as warm and summer-y as Litha or even as the weeks leading up to Mabon. There are also no well-known holidays that correspond. Unlike Yule, with its traditions preserved in Christmas, Imbolc with its ties to Groundhog's Day, or Samhain with its Hallowe'en vestiges, most of us did not grow up celebrating August 1 for any special reason. It can be a subtle holiday, perhaps observed by many Pagans simply because the founders of our Neopagan traditions (Gerald Gardner, Doreen Valiente, Alex and Maxine Sanders) happened to put it on our calendar. But Lughnasadh has as rich a history as any of our seasonal holidays, carries its own beautiful traditions, and tokens the start of the harvest that will bring food to our table and drink to our merriment.

Lughnasadh is celebrated on August 1, but it has something in common with the other sabbats that form the "X" portion of the Wheel of the Year. While the "cross" portion of the Wheel, the solstices and equinoxes, all have names in Saxon English (Yule, Oestara, Litha, and Lammas, the last one replaced on the modern Wheel by the Welsh holiday Mabon, and all falling near the 21st or 22nd of their months), the "X" holidays all have names in Gaelic: Samhain, Imbolc, Beltain, and Lughnasadh. While we Pagans have fixed the dates of these (November 1, February 2, May 1, and August 1) traditionally they were celebrated as "movable feasts," holidays that would begin according to some sign from nature. Samhain was celebrated whenever the harvest ended, Imbolc whenever the salmon returned to the streams, Beltain when the first white flowering trees got their bloom, and this holiday, Lughnasadh, was celebrated on the very first day that berries and grains were ready to be harvested. That could have been as late as August 12 in Europe, and there are references to "old Lughnasadh" on that date.

Drink, Boys, Drink!

Because the harvest will result in food and drink, Lughnasadh is a feast day and a day for drinking. In England it is the custom for workers to quit work early on the first day of the harvest, and go to a pub (a bar, as we Yanks call it). There they ask passersby if they'll buy the group a round of drinks. If the passerby agrees, the group will "halloo a largess" for them, meaning they'll drink in their honor as a blessing. The landowners welcome this blessing, and will buy a round to receive it.

There are many songs that are sung today in rural England that reflect this tradition. One goes like this:

Here's a health unto the master, he's the founder of our feast
We hope to God with all our hearts his soul is ever at rest
Here's hoping that he prospers, whatever he takes in hand
For we are all his servants and we are at his command

So drink, boys, drink, and see that you do not spill
For if you do you shall drink two, for that is our master's will.
(Traditional)

Games and songs that are even more obviously Pagan holdovers are also used to celebrate on this day. In one part of England, a game is played where each pubgoer places a rack of antlers on his head and balances a pint of ale on the rack, singing this song:

Oh so swiftly runs the hare
And so cunning runs the fox
Who would think that this little lamb

> *Would grow to a noble ox?*
> *To lay among the briars*
> *And run among the thorns*
> *And die the death that his father did with his*
> *Large pair of horns*
> (Traditional)

If the person spills any of the pint while singing, he must drink whatever is left in his glass and then go through the ordeal once again. You can imagine that there are some tipsy revelers at this sort of event.

The Name Game

The sabbat we celebrate on August 1 bears two different names (as many of our holidays do) because the same day was observed in two different cultures. Lammas, the name in Saxon English, is formed by squishing together the words *Loaf* and *Mass*, making *Loaf-Mass*, shortened by use to Lammas. This name seems to come from a Christian observance of the day, related to Saint Catherine's Day (which was originally set in early August and later moved to November 25). On Lammas people would bake loaves made from the first sheaves of barley and leave them on the steps of the church. The poor could then gather them up.

But the name by which the Irish call the day, Lughnasadh, comes from the Celtic God Lugh, who is said to have created the feast to honor his foster mother, Tailtiu. The town of Teltown in County Meath, Ireland, was named for her, and is said to be the place where Lughnasadh was first celebrated.

Lugh, God of the Sun

Lugh is a God known by many epitaphs: Lugh of the Long Arm, Lugh of Many Skills, and Lugh of the Magic Spear are just a few. As Lugh of the Long Arm, his name probably refers to the rays of the sun, which reach from the heavens to the Earth. (The Welsh God

Llew is known by a similar name, Llew of the Steady Hand. He became a sun God by killing the wren of winter.)

According to Irish myth, Lugh wanted to join the Tuatha dé Danann, the "People of the Goddess Dana." But he could not enter the hall of the Tuatha unless he had a skill with which to serve the king. Lugh explained that he was a wright (a maker of carts and wheels) but was told the Tuatha had a wright. Lugh then said he was a smith (a maker of swords), but the Tuatha had one of these, too. He offered his services as a champion, a swordsman, a harpist, a hero, a poet, a sorcerer, and a craftsman, but each of these roles was taken. Lugh then asked if any man there possessed all of these abilities; he was allowed to join the Tuatha De Danann as Lugh of Many Skills ("Skilled in Many Arts").

Lugh was also said to have a magic spear, which when loosed would fly by itself and kill all of his enemies.

Each of these myths reflects Lugh's role as a god of agriculture and the harvest: as Lugh of the Long Arm, Lugh is a sun god; in August the sun shines brightly, making the grain to grow tall and strong. But Autumn is just around the corner now; the sun god will begin to wane as the harvest progresses, facing his own death in the winter. Lugh's long arm will cause the growth that will feed us, but we recognize his sacrifice in the harvest and in the dying sun. As God of Many Skills, Lugh has all of the talents needed for growing, harvesting, and preparing food and drink. And his magic spear represents the scythe blade that will cut down the fields of grain (represented by lines of standing enemy soldiers).

Lughnasadh: Life and Death

Lughnasadh is the first of three harvest festivals, the starting point from which we will reach the great harvest festival at Mabon, and the end of the harvest at Samhain. While August is still teeming with life in the green trees, growing grain, and still-young animals of the field and forest, it is the beginning of a time when we consider death. In fact, in one myth of Lugh, that god had to enter the

241

underworld to fight Bres, the God of Death. This represents the life-giving harvest resulting from the death of the grain.

We Pagans see that sustaining life is a struggle between the forces of life and the forces of death. To eat, we must kill the grain in the fields and the animals of the forest or pasture. Lugh the Sun God represents the solar energy and the growing crops that give life. However, he must also negotiate the dark forces of the underworld, land of death, where the harvested crops and the hunted or slaughtered animals will go to be reborn as the sun is reborn at Yule. During our celebration of Lugh's feast, we recognize that the warm, vital sun in the late Summer sky is waning, and will die as winter approaches. We begin the killing of grain, and we commemorate the spirits we are taking by making loaves that will nourish us through the dead of Winter. In the Lughnasadh feast, we offer the first of these loaves to our Gods.

Celestial Sway

Fern Feto Spring

LAMMAS FINDS US IN the heart of the summertime, basking in the warmth of the sun and reveling in the first early harvests of the year. Lammas is known as the "wake" or "feast" of Lugh the Sun King. Traditionally, the king who dies on the Summer Solstice is now honored and mourned at his wake on Lammas. As the Sun King sails away across the sea, he journeys toward the land of the dead, or the "Isle of Apples," and takes with him our hopes and fears for the fall harvest season.

This then is a time of celebration, but also a reflective period, when we cull and clear away whatever will make our final harvest stronger and more bountiful. Lammas 2012 features a powerful Full Moon in Aquarius, which forms an energizing sextile aspect to Uranus, the trickster planet. These two complementary energies bring a special zing to the sabbat, encouraging us to innovate and experiment. The first harvests that arrive during this Lammas may bring a few surprises, but will also likely move us forward in exciting new directions.

Mercury has been retrograde in the sign of Leo since July 14, so we may need to carefully consider how we are communicating during Lammas. This is a time to review old creative projects and assess how we are presenting ourselves to the world. Do we take up to much space or not enough? As a sabbat related to a Sun deity, Lammas calls us to focus on issues of identity and self-hood. The Mercury retrograde cycle takes this introspective process even deeper, calling us to look closely at our relationship to ourselves.

Mercury goes direct in Leo on August 8, allowing us to begin to move forward with Leo-related themes in our lives: creativity, self-expression, celebration and romance. Our confidence in ourselves begins to return and we are able to communicate and connect with others more easily as Mercury slowly picks up speed, moving out of its retrograde "shadow" period by August 23.

Venus, planet of love and resources, moves into Cancer the day before Mercury goes direct—August 7. These simultaneous planetary shifts indicate an energetic seasonal change that shapes the Lammas season, bringing a greater desire to connect with loved ones, particularly old friends and family members. Venus in Cancer loves to nest and thrives on cultivating a welcoming home to entertain guests. This Lammas may be a particularly good one to have a dinner party for friends and family, featuring the first "fruits" (and vegetables) of the harvest. Since the sign of Cancer also values memories from the past, this Lammas is an excellent time for remembrance and recognition of traditions from past Lammas celebrations.

Mars, the planet of passion, action, and excitement is in Libra through most of the month of August and forms a conjunction to Saturn, planet of patience and perseverance on August 15. Both planets then form a sextile to the Sun and the New Moon in Leo on August 17. This cosmic configuration may teach us lessons around expressing our anger with diplomacy and care. We will need to work hard at this time to not let feelings of aggression boil beneath the surface and come out in more passive-aggressive forms. But there is also the potential for great creativity and artistic expression at this time if hard work and patience are cultivated.

The Lammas New Moon in Leo presents us with many opportunities to cultivate love and romance. This is a time to woo our beloved, creatively planning experiences that will open their hearts and bring them joy. The playful energy of this New Moon is supported by Saturn's stable hand, so our efforts to instill more fun into our love connections can lead to more substantial benefits down the road.

Lammas Full Moon in Aquarius

The Lammas Full Moon in Aquarius brings our attention to the harvests we hope to reap and share with friends and community. The bold light of the Moon shines on us as we are made aware of the unique gifts we have to share with others. A Leo Sun reminds us to play and have fun with life, even as we prepare and strategize for the future. Our hopes and fears may seem particularly obvious now, as we stretch to accommodate and provide for our community.

Full Moon Ritual

This is the perfect Full Moon to ritually celebrate with friends and community. Plan a gathering and ask everyone to bring one thing that they have created to share with the group. This could be food, art, a story, a picture of children or grandchildren, or a house. Ritually invoke Lugh the sun king and ask him to share his light and warmth with you. Have everyone at the gathering share their creation and what it represents to them. You may also want to ask people to talk about how their creation also serves the community or larger group. Gather all the creative works and place them in the center on an altar and dance or sing to charge them up—setting an intention that each person's creative energy help to support the greater community.

Mars in Libra

Mars in Libra has a paradoxical feeling that calls for adjustment and reconciliation. The fiery nature of Mars is muted in this air sign and efforts to express our more "wild" sides may feel repressed, particularly when the Saturn conjunction takes place on August 15. This is the time to cultivate energies of the peaceful warrior, while staying alert for any signs of passive aggression that we may direct toward others or that others may send our way. Mars in Libra asks us to take action around issues of justice, balance, and equality.

Mars in Libra Ritual

Choose a situation in your life that feels somehow out of balance, unjust, or unfair. What would it take to bring more equality or harmony to this situation? Draw, write, paint, gather, or photograph symbols or objects that represent the peace, harmony, and balance you hope to bring to this situation. Place these symbols or their representations on an altar you have created to celebrate the Lammas season and light a white candle on Lammas Eve. Ask Lugh to help you harvest the justice you want in your life.

Venus in Cancer

As Venus transits through the watery and mysterious sign of Cancer, we will feel called to nurture and feed our inner world, paying attention to our dreams and intuitions. We also may experience a greater desire to take care of and support our loved ones at this time. Activities like cooking, nesting in our homes and cultivation of our imagination will help us to maximize this Venusian energy.

Venus in Cancer Ritual

Prepare a magical feast for friends and family using ingredients that symbolize qualities you want to cultivate in your own life and support in others' lives. Try a fish stew to help invoke the watery powers of dreams and imagination, or use roses or other flowers to bring love. As you prepare your meal, focus on the qualities you'd like to inspire and let them infuse your cooking with Cancer's unique healing powers.

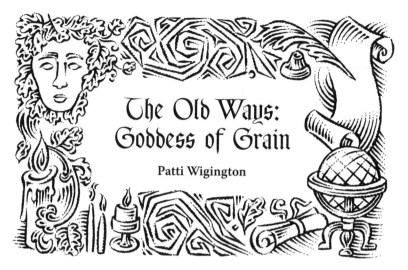

The Old Ways: Goddess of Grain

Patti Wigington

FOR THE ANCIENT ROMANS, late summer was a time to honor Ceres, the goddess of the grain harvest. She was known as a benevolent agricultural goddess who watched over the fields and farms, and the season that is today called Lammas was her domain. Like her Greek counterpart, Demeter, Ceres is associated with the shortening days and the coming darkness of the cold winter months.

The tale of Ceres and her daughter, Proserpina, parallels that of Demeter and Persephone. In the Roman version it is Pluto, rather than Hades, who steals the girl away. When her mother searches for her, she finds that Proserpina has eaten six seeds from a pomegranate. Because these represent the food of the dead and the underworld, Proserpina is doomed to spend half of each year with Pluto in the darkness. When the autumn harvest arrives each year, Ceres must bid farewell to her daughter for six months. Much of Ceres' mythology is tied to that of Demeter; in fact, very few verifiable legends of Ceres do not correspond with the Greek tales of Demeter.

Ceres was the basis of a Roman cult that held rites in a temple on the Aventine hill. She was primarily honored by the class of Romans who were associated with agricultural work—farmers, grain merchants, bread bakers, and other members of plebian society.

This was quite fitting; according to legend, Ceres is credited with discovering how to plant and harvest grain such as corn and spelt, which was crucial to the survival of Roman people. In fact, Pliny the Elder wrote that according to the Twelve Tables—the source of all of Rome's laws—that any crime that had a negative impact on the harvest could be punished with a sentence of death in Ceres' name.

Interestingly, Ceres is tied not only to the harvest of grain but to death and the underworld itself. Barbette Stanley Spaeth says in *The Roman Goddess Ceres* that a curse tablet unearthed in Capua, Italy, includes a tribute to Ceres Ultrix, the Avenger. Virgil cites Ceres as part of a trinity, along with Liber and Libera, two other agricultural deities honored by the residents of the Aventine. Because of her status as a goddess of earth and the underworld, plebian families sometimes made offerings to her following the death of a loved one, in order to purify their homes following a funeral.

Worship of Ceres has been documented in ancient Rome as far back as 700 BCE. Her spring festival, the Cerialia, fell in April, and involved ritual designed to protect the year's crops. Come the reaping season, more celebrations were held in her honor, and she was offered the first fruits of the harvest. Cato the Elder recommended sacrificing a sow to Ceres before the harvest actually begins, as a gesture of appreciation. He wrote, "Before you will gather in the harvest, it is proper for the sow to be offered in this way. Offer to Ceres using a female pig … before you store away these crops; spelt, wheat, barley, beans, [and] rapeseed." Later, he tells worshippers to give Ceres the sow's entrails and some wine to conclude the ritual.

Very little is known about the proper worship of Ceres, but at some point during the turbulent history of the Roman Empire, she was consulted during times of great upheaval. She was called on particularly in the event of famine, which was a regular occurrence. By around 150 BCE, an annual fast called the Ieiunium Cereris was held in her honor each fall. At this time, the women of Rome would conclude their fast with an offering to honor Ceres in her role as patroness of grains, in hopes of an abundant harvest.

Folklorist Sir James George Frazer says in *The Golden Bough* that there has been a global phenomenon of the honoring of the spirit of the grain, much as Ceres was honored by her followers in ancient Rome. In some cultures, the harvest is celebrated with a corn mother, a doll representative of the grain goddess. While grain may seem small and insignificant to us in today's society, for the Romans, it was a staple crop that kept millions of people alive each year. The far outposts of the Roman Empire were relied upon to export grain to the major cities, including Rome itself, which had hundreds of thousands of mouths to feed. Although Ceres began as a goddess of the working classes, later on rulers knew the importance of paying her homage. Julius Caesar, at one point, issued a silver denarius (coin) with his own face stamped on one side, and the face of Ceres on the other—both a tribute to her power and a way of pleasing the plebian ranks.

The word *cereal*, used today, comes from Ceres' name and pays tribute to her status as a goddess of edible grains. Without her gift of the harvest each year, fields would remain barren. Today, we can honor Ceres with our Lammas celebrations. By marking the early grain harvest, we can pay tribute to her by threshing grain and baking bread. Here are some ways to celebrate Ceres today:

• Make an offering before you pick your fall garden crops. You don't need to sacrifice a sow as Cato recommends; instead, offer a large vegetable such as a pumpkin or squash.

• Bake a loaf of bread, and incorporate it into a ritual celebrating the spirit of the grain harvest.

• Conclude a short ritual fast with prayers, songs, and offerings in honor of Ceres at the beginning of the harvest season.

• Construct a corn mother out of husks, and place her in a position of honor to watch over your home in the fall.

• At Lammas, when you begin preparing your rituals and celebrations, be sure to take a moment to thank Ceres and pay her tribute for watching over the crops in the fields, and for the abundance of the harvest season.

Feasts and Treats

Susan Pesznecker

LUGHNASADH IS SUMMER AT its peak! The harvest rolls in and everything around us glorifies earth's bounty and the sun's life-giving power. This summer dinner features magick spun from seasonal fish, vegetables, grains, and fruits.

Grilled Curry-Cured Salmon with Otto's Salmon Sauce

The Celtic traditions view the salmon as the bringer of wisdom, and this recipe came from my father, a very wise man. The salmon cures in a dry rub, taking on delicious flavors and deep color. A tart, crispy, crunchy garnish plays against the mellow fish, while a scrumptious sauce adds decadence.

Prep time: 30 minutes (plus curing time)
Cook time: 15 minutes
Serves: 6+

Wild salmon fillets with skin (allow ⅓ to ½ lb. per person)
2 tablespoons sugar
1 tablespoon salt
1 tablespoon curry powder
1 tablespoon dry mustard

1 cucumber, peeled, seeded, and sliced
1 sweet onion, peeled and thinly sliced
⅓ cup seasoned rice vinegar
½ teaspoon black pepper
1 cup butter
1 clove garlic, crushed
4 tablespoons soy sauce
2 tablespoons prepared mustard
4 tablespoons ketchup
1 teaspoon prepared horseradish
Juice of ½ lemon
¼ cup fresh basil

Rinse the salmon and pat dry. Place in a glass baking dish. Combine sugar, salt, curry, and mustard. Pat the mixture evenly over the flesh side of the salmon. Cover with plastic wrap and refrigerate 1 to 4 hours.

While salmon cures, prepare the garnish. Combine cucumber, onion, vinegar, and pepper in a medium bowl. Stir well, cover, and refrigerate, stirring occasionally.

Next, prepare the salmon sauce. In a small saucepan over low heat, melt butter. Stir in garlic, soy sauce, mustard, ketchup, horseradish, and lemon juice. Heat until blended and warm. Do not boil—the mixture will separate. If this happens, use a blender or immersion blender to emulsify the sauce.

About 30 minutes before serving, rinse the salmon thoroughly to remove the salty cure. Pat dry. Place the fillets skin side up on heavy-duty aluminum foil. Preheat a gas grill or light charcoal for a charcoal grill. (For flavor, I prefer charcoal.)

Grill the salmon on a covered grill for 12 to 15 minutes (alternative: bake in a 425 degree F oven on a rimmed baking sheet), until salmon is still moist and opaque but not "raw" in the middle. With a thin pancake turner, remove the fish to a serving plate—the skin will remain behind, stuck to the foil.

Add chopped basil to the cucumber mixture; stir well, drain briefly, and spoon around the salmon for garnish.

Serve the warm salmon sauce along side.

Crispy Rice

Lughnasadh is a harvest holiday and traditionally a harvest celebrating grain. In this dish, we choose rice as the focus grain and cook it into a crispy, buttery, sun-like orb that makes a gorgeous accompaniment to the salmon.

Prep time: 10 minutes

Cook time: 15 minutes (early step) + 30 minutes (just before serving)

Serves: 6+

6 cups water
2 cups long-grained white rice
1 teaspoon salt
Nonstick cooking spray
2 tablespoons unsalted butter, solid
2 tablespoons unsalted butter, melted
Thin shreds of green onion

Several hours before serving the meal, boil water, add rice and salt, and cook for 13 to 15 minutes or until just tender. (All of the water will <u>not</u> be absorbed!)

Pour the rice into a colander and rinse with cold water until the rice is completely cool. Allow the rice to drain completely, stirring it every few minutes. Set aside at room temperature.

About 35 to 40 minutes before the meal, spray a heavy skillet (cast iron is ideal) very lightly with nonstick cooking spray. Heat the pan over medium heat for about 5 minutes. Add 2 tablespoons butter. When pan is hot and butter sizzles, swirl the pan to coat. Spoon in the cooled rice, packing it down to form a cake and smoothing the top. Drizzle the melted butter over the top. Stretch a couple of paper towels or a kitchen towel over the rice and cover the pan tightly. (Be especially careful if you are using a gas cooktop!)

Cook over medium heat for 20 to 25 minutes. Use a kitchen knife to "peek" under one edge of the rice cake—a golden crust should be forming. When it has, the rice cake is ready.

Use the knife to loosen the edge of the rice cake; invert the cake onto a large platter. It will have a crusty, crunchy, golden surface. Garnish with green onion shreds.

Bountiful Blackberry Cream Pie

A crumbly crust, creamy center, tart glaze, and bursting fresh berries… What could be better? Blackberries are sacred to both Lugh and Brigit—a powerful way to honor summer's bounty.

Prep time: 20 minutes (plus chilling time)
Serves: 6+

8 ounces cream cheese, at room temperature
3 tablespoons sugar
1 teaspoon vanilla
1 cup heavy cream, chilled
Pie shell (either graham or pre-baked pastry)
½ cup sugar
2 tablespoons cornstarch
¼ cup water
3 pints fresh blackberries, rinsed and drained

In a large bowl, combine cream cheese, 3 tablespoons sugar, and vanilla, beating until fluffy. Add cream and beat (using a mixer) until thick and smooth. Pour into the pie shell and chill for several hours.

In a medium saucepan, stir together ½ cup sugar and cornstarch. Add ¼ cup water and 1 pint blackberries. Cook, stirring constantly, over medium heat until mixture thickens and *just barely* comes to a boil. Remove from heat.

Force blackberry mixture through a strainer to remove seeds. Cool the resulting mixture. Spread cooled mixture over chilled cream pie base. Chill at least 6 hours before serving.

To serve: Arrange remaining blackberries in concentric "solar" circles on pie.

Peach Fuzzie

This icy drink makes a delicious, cooling counterpart to your meal, and the rosy color mimics the summer sun.

Prep time: 5 minutes

Serves: 4–6

2 small or 1 large ripe peach, stoned and sliced (leave skin on)
1 6-ounce can frozen lemonade or limeade concentrate
6 ounces vodka
8–10 ice cubes

Combine ingredients in blender and blend until ice is crushed and mixture is slushy. Serve immediately in chilled glasses.

Crafty Crafts

Ellen Dugan

Theme of the Season: Goal-setting and creativity
Colors: Gold, yellow, green, and golden brown
Scents: Orange, rose geranium, and sage
Energy: Relaxation and reflection

Decorated Grapevine Candle Rings

This is an enjoyable project for a coven to do together for the sabbat. If everyone brings a bit of supplies, you can all share and help each other. After you are finished, use the decorated pillar candles for your Lughnasadh/Lammas observances.

Supplies

5-inch mini-grapevine wreath
Low-temperature glue gun
Glue sticks
Silk miniature sunflowers, yellow daisies, or yellow flowers (or dried heads of yellow yarrow, stalks of wheat, and purple statice)
Silk miniature blackbirds or silk butterflies
½-inch-wide satin ribbon (your choice of color)
A pillar candle in off-white or golden yellow

Instructions: To begin, make sure that the miniature wreath will fit around the base of a standard sized pillar candle. Then set the wreath flat on your work surface and lay out the flowers or dried botanicals around the ring. In essence, you are creating a miniature wreath. Now begin to lay out your floral pieces on the wreath. Snip the stems of the floral pieces a tad longer than you think you will need and tuck them into the wreath. (Remember, it's easier to snip a stem again, than to be stuck with a stem that will be too short to use.) Work your way around the wreath and lay out the flowers. You may choose to completely cover up the grapevine with floral material or leave some of the grapevine showing.

Once you have it all arranged to your liking, attach the floral pieces with a glue gun. When that is set, tie a nice multi-looped bow with the satin ribbon, and attach the bow to the candle ring. (You may also choose to wrap the ribbon all around it and in between the flowers.)

Finally position the butterflies or silk birds and glue those in. Now slip the ring around the base of your pillar candle and enjoy!

Cost: $10.00 to 15.00

Time: 30 minutes

Herbal Door Spray for the First Harvest

In honor of the August Wort moon (*wort* being the old Anglo-Saxon word for "herb") and at a time of year when the herb garden is bursting with its bounty, try crafting this herbal spray for your own home. An herbal spray brings a touch of nature's magick right to your very door.

The spray will look like a shaggy and rustic Witch's broom when you are finished. (How very appropriate!) Plus, it will smell terrific as it dries!

Supplies

Assorted long-stemmed herbs and grasses from the garden. Suggested plants: boxwood, Artemesia, Russian sage, rose hips, lav-

ender, rosemary, basil, hydrangea blossoms from the bush, ornamental grasses, cockscomb, marigolds, culinary sage, and roses from the garden.

Floral wire

Wire cutter

Scissors

Sheer ribbon in metallic gold

Instructions: Gather the long, leafy, and twiggy plant material into a bundle and tie together on one end with floral wire. It will look sort of like a shaggy broom. Wrap the wire around the stems and leave 4 or 5 inches of plant material above the wire. (The longest part and the plant stems and blooms will be below the wire.)

Insert the stems of the flowers and or berries under the floral wire and then wrap the wire *again* around those new stems, several times, to fasten them in place. Twist the wire toward the back of the spray and snip the wire about six inches long.

Make sure that the wire is securely closed and toward the back of the spray. Make a hanging loop out of the extra six inches of the floral wire. Tie a loose informal bow around the wire to hide it. Allow the streamers to dangle down.

Finally, hang the spray with the bow to the front, and the stem (short) end up.

Note: If you want to put a little more witchiness in your craft, you could choose the herbs with intention. Consider lavender for protection, Artemesia for the Moon Goddess, rose hips for healing, hydrangea blossoms for hex-breaking, rose blossoms for love, cockscomb for energy and protection, marigolds to keep negativity at bay, basil to promote loving emotions between two people, sage for wisdom, and rosemary for purification. Cast a careful eye around your garden and see what you are inspired to harvest for this bewitching herbal spray.

Cost: under $10.00

Time: 30 minutes to one hour

Shimmery Leaf Outdoor Candleholders

These terra cotta pots shimmer and shine with vibrant metallic colors. Perfect for making outdoor candleholders for an enchanted summer night. These would be just the thing to hold citronella candles or medium-sized pillar candles. Imagine these sitting outside on a table on your patio or deck in the evening.

Supplies

Leaves from a tree in your yard (choose interesting leaf shapes)

A heavy book to press the leaves flat (if necessary)

2 medium-sized terra cotta flowerpots and saucers

An outdoor work area covered with paper

Gold spray paint

Burgundy or deep purple spray paint

Rubber cement
Gold metallic paint pen

Instructions

1. Choose leaves (like maple leaves) with interesting shapes that will fit on the side of the terra cotta pots. To flatten curved leaves, place them under a heavy book until they become flat.

2. Wash the pot and saucer. Allow it to dry. (In direct sunlight, this won't take too long.) After the pot is dry, turn the pot upside down on your paper covered work surface and spray two light and even coats of gold spray paint over the pots and the saucers. Let the paint dry. (Note: You will want to paint both the outer and the inner sides of the saucer, as they will show. So after the saucers are dry, flip them over and paint the opposite side. Again, let all of the paint dry completely.)

3. Brush rubber cement on one side of the leaves. Let it dry. Brush on a second coat and let it dry to a tacky, but not wet stage. Position leaves on the pot to make a pattern. Or, position them randomly, whichever way appeals to you most.

4. Spray a light (misty) coat of the desired accent color over the whole terra cotta pot(s). Mist a bit of the accent color over the saucers too. Let this paint dry.

5. After the saucers are dry, you may care to embellish the edges of the outer saucer with a paint pen. You could draw spirals and stars, vines, or tiny leaves. Allow this final accent to dry as well.

6. Peel off the leaves. Rub any remaining rubber cement from the pot gently with your fingers.

Cost: $20.00

Time: 2 to 4 hours (including drying times). Drying times will vary significantly depending on humidity when you are outside spray-painting the pots.

All One Family

Clea Danaan

AT LAMMAS, THE SMALLEST zucchinis and tomatoes call to us and suddenly it's fresh Italian food for dinner every night. The weeds sink underground just a bit as the high heat of August bakes the earth. Green apples the size of my daughter's fist hang from the tree, a promise of cooler days to come. The corn has seed heads, but not yet ears or tassels. The garden is a bounty and a promise all at once.

Lammas is the fullness of harvest when there is still much more to come. Energetically we feel this at mid-life, or when beginning the last half of a project, or when we soak in the raised energy of a ritual circle before we release the power and close the ceremony. This energy can charge us and fill us up, or it can be overwhelming and draining if the body is not prepared for it. As a family, and especially as a mother, we have to take care to not overdo it. If you have ever been exhausted after a day of lying in the sun by the pool, you know what I mean. The high energy, high heat, and long days call to us to push ourselves until we drop; over time this can lead to burnout. Even the simple energy of the hot sun all day can drain us.

Many cultures with hot summers balance the intensity of the season with a siesta, a midday nap. When your children are young, the family nap can be a great way to recharge everyone's batteries. While the youngest ones sleep, establish a quiet time for older children and adults for at least an hour. Everyone can lie down and shut their eyes, read, meditate, or play quietly by themselves in their rooms. Television is not quiet time, nor is playing games on the computer. The idea is to give everyone's body and mind a rest. With a very intense, high-energy child, I always scoffed at the idea of "making" her have quiet time once she stopped taking naps. I found, though, that a part of her welcomed it, and once the afternoon downtime became routine, she didn't resist it.

Parents and grandparents deserve the same downtime. When the crickets still and the birds hide from the heat of the day, put up your feet. Read a magazine. Let your eyes close. Stare out the window. In order to be strong, healthy adults (who raise strong, healthy children), we must balance going and doing with stillness. This is the way of all energy: yin and yang, day and night, summer and winter, activity and rest.

While I can struggle with insomnia at any time, I realized that my difficulty falling asleep hits the worst right about Lammas. One reason for this, I finally figured out, is the heat and intensity of long summer days. Where I live, July and August mean temperatures 90 degrees or hotter every day. Though I drink plenty of water to stay hydrated, I sweat out too many minerals, and by bedtime my mind and body can't settle. I feel jittery and restless. Upping my B vitamins and other minerals, especially magnesium, really helps. If you have trouble settling or struggle with increased anxiety at this time of year, talk to your natural health practitioner about a good vitamin regimen for you and your children.

When your energy is balanced by taking care of your physical body, even in the intensity of the Lammas sun, you are better able to take advantage of the energy of the season. Neither you nor the kids are too crabby to enjoy the pool, sprinkler, or beach. Travel is more fun. The mess of kids at home is less overwhelming—and the whole family has more energy to pitch in and help around the house. This is a great time of year to get organized, since family energy is focused at home. In a month or so, we will go back to school (even for homeschooling families, the energy will shift) and the start of holiday planning, but for now kids are home from camp and school and most vacations. Consider a family meeting to discuss what needs to be done at home before the energy of autumn rolls in. In our house this means getting the garden ready for fall, cleaning out the garage, and cleaning the house for late-summer guests. While the rhythm of your family will differ from ours, the same late-summer energy exists. Consider how it might apply best for your family.

One way to get organized and prepare for fall is to have a yard or garage sale. Pagan families can add a little twist on this popular summer ritual, either secretly or more obviously if you feel comfortable doing so. Gather in one place your items to sell, and the night before the sale do a family blessing ritual upon your items to release them and send them toward the highest good of whomever purchases them. Honor that these energies have served you well and you are now ready to let them go. As you smudge or sprinkle salt or water upon your garage-sale goodies, know that releasing them will free up new energy in your home and life. You might tell each other stories of these items and discuss why you want to pass them back to the world at large. Some garage-sale items will be harder to let go of, like baby clothes when you are done having babies. Others will have taught you about frivolous purchases, like toys that were never played with or expensive shoes you rarely wore. When you open your family circle, honor that your family is still strong even as you release past energies. On the day of the sale, burn incense off to one side to create an air of calm and respect. Watch as your old energy is transformed into new financial energy:

One thing becomes another, in the Mother, in the Mother.

Discuss as a family how this money will be used: fun, groceries, savings, or in whatever way serves your current needs best.

When your old energies are cleared out, plan a family grounding ritual. Bake bread or cookies together for your ritual, mixing in something fresh from the garden like herbs, zucchini, or garlic. Sit in circle together and share stories of home and family. What are you grateful for at this time? How does your home—the physical and emotional space—serve you? In what ways can you renew your commitment to the family and your home? Even young children can participate in this discussion, offering sweet and sometimes surprising comments on the home and family. Then share your homemade baked goods and some fresh herbs and let yourself come home.

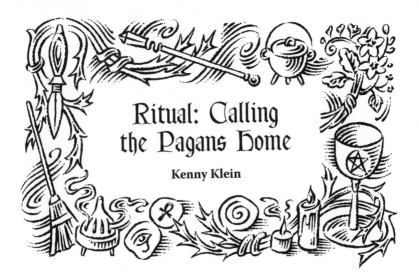

Ritual: Calling the Pagans Home

Kenny Klein

IN THE BLUE STAR coven, Lughnasadh is a big deal. It is the start of the harvest, so it is important to us to feast heartily, drink a bit, and show our faith that the gods will give us more food and drink (through the harvested grain) when our cupboards are empty. We also do a special magic termed "Calling The Pagans Home."

Lughnasadh is the harvest, the time of gathering in, so we ask the gods to allow anyone looking for the Pagan path to find their way to our communities. We know that finding the Pagan community, a responsible group, and Pagan friends can be daunting. So we do "harvest magic" at Lughnasadh to help those seeking us. We do not call them to our own coven or tradition; your or my coven or tradition might not be right for everyone. We simply call them to the Pagan community, where they can explore for themselves. (It's my experience that a few always seem to end up at my own doorstep.)

Lughnasadh Myth

We spoke of the Irish god Lugh in the opening Lughnasadh piece, but you may not know that the Welsh have a similar god, Llew Llaw Gyffes (translated as The Lion with the Steady Hand; a similar title to the Irish Lugh of the Long Arm). This Llew, whose story is told in an ancient Welsh saga called *The Mabinogion* (easily available on the Internet, or in print form), is a sun god much like his Irish counterpart. His mother, the celestial goddess Arianrod, curses Llew three times: he cannot have a name unless she names him, he cannot bear a sword unless she arms him, and he cannot marry a mortal woman. With the aid of his uncle, Llew tricks Arianrod into naming him (he earns his name by killing a wren, the bird of winter, proving that he is the true sun god who will make the crops grow); into arming him (with a blade he will use for the harvest); and into allowing him to marry the flower goddess Blodeuwedd (BLUD-weth). Llew's skill at killing the wren, wielding a blade, and his skill as a husband are comparable to the Irish Lugh's command of all skills.

As the harvest ends and winter approaches, Blodeuwedd falls in love with Gronw, the antlered god of the underworld. A battle ensues between Gronw and Llew Llaw Gyffes (like the battle in Lugh's mythology between Lugh and the underworld god Bres; this is also seen in the familiar Cornish tale of Sir Gawain and the Green Knight). After Llew spends the winter as a wounded eagle, he returns to slay Gronw so that summer may return.

Early in my study of Wicca, I was drawn to these Welsh gods. So in our Blue Star Lughnasadh ritual, we will use Llew Llaw Gyffes and Blodeuwedd as our God and Goddess pair. It would be a good idea to read the Fourth Branch of the Mabinogion, in print or on the Internet, while preparing for the ritual. You may also substitute a similar sun God and grain Goddess, such as Apollo and Ceres, Orpheus and Pomona, or Ra and Hathor.

Ritual Supplies You Will Need

A round altar

A broom

A wand, an athame, a chalice, and a pentacle

Incense, a red candle, a bowl of water, a dish of salt

A bell and a candle snuffer

Three candles

Ale

Cakes made of oats, salt, and honey or sugar. (If you wish to use store-bought cakes, bran muffins come closest to traditional cakes).

If you are working as a group (however small), and do not have these members, you should designate a **Priestess, Priest,** and **Handmaiden**. In an informal or eclectic group, gender may not matter in these designations. The Handmaiden may take the place of the youngest female in sweeping (we'll get to that in a moment).

Preparing for Ritual

This ritual may be done indoors or outdoors, and as it is still summer, should be done in the afternoon (the time of the south, associated with summer). In Blue Star, we often work either robed or skyclad, but you may also work in loose, comfortable clothes.

We use a round altar at the center of the circle, which connects us to the Wheel of the Year and the cyclic nature of life. Three candles stand in the altar's center, representing the Goddess we will call, the God we will call, and the union of the two.

On the outside edge of the altar are tools and symbols of each of the four elements: in the east portion of the altar, we place the athame, used by the **Priest**, and incense; in the south, the wand used by the **Priestess** and a red candle; in the west, a chalice of ale and a bowl of water; and in the north, the pentacle and a dish of salt.

When the altar stands ready, we gather around it. The **Priest** stands on the east edge of the altar, before the incense and athame. The **Priestess** stands opposite him in the west, before the chalice and the water bowl. The other attendees may stand anywhere in the circle formed around the altar. When all is ready, the candle in the center of the altar (representing the union of Goddess and God) is lit. This is the signal that the ritual is starting.

We sing a song together at each meeting to begin ritual with music and joy. Because Lughnasadh is the first harvest festival, we sing the traditional song "John Barleycorn." Many recordings of this song are available, and most Pagans know some version of the song. (My version can be heard on www.kennyklein.net/circlesongs.html.)

Joining of Salt And Water

After singing "John Barleycorn," the first act of the ritual is blessing the water and salt. The **Priestess** holds up the water, saying:

> *Spirits of water, children of the west*
> *I cast out from thee fear, depression and ill will*

At each of these words, she casts out a drop of water with her athame. Now she places the tip of the athame in the water:

> *Spirits of water, children of the west,*
> *I bless you with love, happiness and pleasure.*
> *In the names of Llew and Blodeuwedd, so mote it be.*

Priestess lifts the salt dish and sets the tip of her athame inside:

> *Spirits of earth, children of the north,*
> *I ask for your strength, wisdom and firmness*
> *In building this temple before the Gods*
> *In the names of Llew and Blodeuwedd, so mote it be.*

The **Priestess** uses her athame to take salt from the salt dish and place it into the water bowl, symbolizing the union of male and female. She stirs the mixture three times, saying:

> *Salt joins to water*
> *As man joins to woman.*
> *As we all join within the circle.*

Sweeping the Circle

In Blue Star rituals, the youngest female has the honor of sweeping the circle. While some traditions believe that sweeping the circle represents cleansing the space, we believe that the broom represents the union of male and female (the phallic ash handle and the yonic broom corn shape), and that this fertile energy will be used by the Priestess to "birth" the magical circle. The youngest female has the greatest potential to create life. Whether she is too young to bear children, or an adult who is simply the youngest woman there, she carries within herself the most regenerative energy.

She begins by presenting the broom to the east, then sweeping three times around the circle deosil (clockwise). While she sweeps around the outside of the circle, the group sings the "Sweeping Song."

Corn of golden broom
Tied beneath the moon
Ashen handle, oak seed charm
Dance in magic, ward off harm
Weave the circle well, weave the enchantment well
Sweep the circle well, sweep the circle well

By the scycle shorn
By the maiden born
Tread the floor and thread the air
By the spell craft that you bear
Weave the circle well, weave the enchantment well
Sweep the circle well, sweep the circle well
(Kenny Klein)

When she is finished, she presents the broom to the east, replaces it, and steps back into the circle.

Casting the Circle

The **Priestess** casts the Circle with the wand (or sword or athame). As she walks around the outside of the Circle three times, the **Priestess** says this incantation, one couplet per lap:

Cast the Circle three times round
Once for seed beneath the ground

A second time the Circle tread
For sun and rain cloud overhead

Cast the Circle, go times three
With wooden wand grown from the tree

Censing and Asperging

The **Priestess** (or anyone she appoints) takes the incense around the outside of the circle, saying: *With sweet air and sacred fire do we bless the sacred temple.* Then the water dish is taken around the circle, saying: *Where this water falls, let no sadness remain.*

Inviting the Elements

All **attendees** face East. The **Priestess** or **Priest** says:

> *Spirits of the East / Hear my voice*
> *Spirits of East / Your children call*
> *Spirits of East / Join us in this circle / Join us in this rite.*
> *Spirits of East / You are welcomed*
> *Spirits of East / You are remembered*
> *Spirits of East / You are here.*

When done, a member of the circle rings the bell. This is repeated in the South, the West, and the North, with members facing that direction, and the bell rung each time. The **Priestess** or **Priest** then returns to the East to complete the circle, saying, "The Circle is cast."

Inviting Llew and Blodeuwedd

Lighting the candle at the center of the altar representing the Goddess, the **Priestess** says:

> *Blodeuwedd, bright flower,*
> *lovely owl of the night*
> *Your children call.*
> *Join us in this circle, join us in this rite.*

The bell is rung three times.

The **Priest** then lights the candle for the God, saying:

> *Llew Llaw Gyffes, bright Sun,*
> *Eagle in flight.*
> *Your children call.*
> *Join us in this circle, join us in this rite.*

The bell is rung twice.

Invocation

At each sabbat, we invoke the goddess and god we are calling. This is a difficult skill that takes a long time to master. If you are not trained in invocation, I recommend you do not try it, but find a good Priestess or Priest to teach you. Here, the Priestess and the Priest will recite a piece that characterizes the deities we have called into the circle:

Priestess:

I am the flower of the heath
I am the moon in the summer night
I am the owl of the winter forest
Wings spread in deathly flight
I am the ripening of the seed
Springing from the bounty of summer blue
I am the stalk in the winter field
When flowers wilt and the earth stands mute
And with my feathered mantle
I drape the earth in peaceful snow
So as you drink of the summer barley
Spare a thought for winter's cold

Priest:

I am Llew, the unnamed
I am Llew, the wren-killer
I am Llew, armed with spear and scythe
I am Llew, green shoe maker
Do not seek to harm me on sea or strand
In feasting hall, or green heather'ed land
On my mount, or as I stand
For the flight of eagles I command!
And though I die I will live again
In the sun, the sky, and the growing grain

Calling the Pagans Home

All members of the circle face outside the altar area, and hold hands. Begin with eyes closed, and visualize the many people in your town or city, in your state or province, in your country, who feel a yearning for the mysteries and traditions of our Pagan ways, but have not been able to find like-minded individuals. Imagine these people stumbling on the right person, the right group, the right website, and suddenly feeling they have come "home."

Now the **Priestess** and **Priest** begin to chant the word "home," and each member of the group takes up the chant. Chant for some time, and if you are inclined, move around the circle with hands held, slowly at first, and then more briskly and energetically.

When this has gone on for what seems like a good long time, slow down and bring the chant lower, and then slowly end.

Priestess: *May all who seek the Craft find its true way, and find teachers and friends who best suit them. In the names of Llew Llaw Gyffes and Blodeuwedd, so mote it be!*

All: *"So mote it be!"*

Cakes and Ale

The **Priest** joins the **Priestess** at the west portion of the altar, holding his athame. The Priestess holds the chalice of ale, and the Priest positions his athame over the chalice with the tip just over the liquid.

Priest: *Be it known that a man is not greater than a woman!*
Priestess: *Nor is a woman greater than a man!*

Priest: *For what one lacks*
Priestess: *The other can give*

Priest: *As the athame is to the male*
Priestess: *So is the chalice to the female*

Both: *And when they are joined they become one*
For there is no greater magic in the world
Than that of love.

The **Priest** lowers the athame into the liquid, and holds it there as the last line is spoken. The **Handmaiden** holds up the plate of cakes, and the **Priest** holds his athame over these, saying:

For the seeds that bore them
For the sun, the wind and the rain that nurtured them
For those who harvested, and those who baked
We give thanks.

All drink from the chalice and eat cakes. When all are done, the **Priestess** holds the chalice aloft, and says:

For the gift of the harvest
For the gift of ale
For the gift of fellowship
we give thanks

She then drinks all that is left in the chalice.

Ending the Circle

Now the **Priestess** (west) and **Priest** (east) return to their sides of the altar. The Priest holds his athame over the center candles, and the Priestess takes up the snuffer and holds it over these.

Priest:
Llew Llaw Gyffes, God of the sun
Eagle of the rocky crags
We thank you for joining us in this circle.
Though we extinguish your candle,
You live on in our hearts
Blessed be

All: *Blessed be!*

Priestess:
Blodeuwedd, Maiden of flowers
Blodeuwedd, winter owl
We thank you for joining us in this circle.

Though we extinguish your candle,
You live on in our hearts
Blessed be.

All: *Blessed be!*

Priestess (or participant) walks to the east. All in the circle face east and raise their hand in a salute:

Spirits of east
We thank you for joining us in this circle and in this rite
Now as you depart for your lovely realms
We bid you hail and farewell

All: *Hail and farewell.*

Repeat in the south, west, and north, returning to the east and bowing.

Priestess or participant walks widdershins around the circle with an athame, saying:

We cast this circle back into the earth
Until we need to call upon its energies again
Pagans all.

All: (in unison)
Merry we have met
Merry we have been
Merry may we part
And merry meet again

The circle is ended. **All participants** hug, kiss and feel good. A feast should follow, with all products of the harvest: grains, fruit, vegetables, brandy, ale, and cider. Before eating, participants should bless the feast by saying:

We thanks the Gods for the fruits of the harvest. Blessed be!

Notes

Mabon

Summer's End

Dallas Jennifer Cobb

MABON MARKS THE TEMPORARY balance of light and dark. It's a time of duality—beginnings and endings, sorrow and joy, feasting and storing.

Bare feet slip into socks, wooly sweaters wrap close. We draw into ourselves, and inside our homes. No longer gardening and swimming, we curl up with books, stoke the fire, and take stock before winter. Mabon feasts draw us nearer to family and friends.

Also called *Alban Elfed*, *Winter Finding*, and *Autumn Equinox*, Mabon takes its name from the Celtic god Mabon, son of Modron, who was stolen from his mother and rescued by King Arthur. Mabon, "the Great Son," is considered a minor sun god, and commonly known as "the power in darkness."

At Mabon, the Goddess passes from Mother to Crone, and the God prepares for death and subsequent rebirth. At second harvest, we store and enjoy the fruits of sun and soil. The root cellar is filled with autumn colors: orange, red and burgundy. We feel bountiful, in balance, but know when the wheel of the year turns, it moves us toward scarcity, winter and metaphorical death. Facing mortality, we celebrate earthly abundance.

Deities invoked at Mabon include mother goddesses Demeter and Modron, wine deities Dionysus and Bacchus, and gods Mabon,

Thoth, and the Green Man. Common magical symbols are dried leaves, seedpods, grapes and wine, grains, vines, and gourds. Feast foods often include cornbread, squash soup, wine or cider, and roasted root vegetables. Traditional herbs and flowers include calendula, dahlias and chrysanthemums; sage, thyme, and rosemary. Mabon animals are hunters—dogs, wolves, and birds of prey.

Mabon symbols and colors are like the magical quality of light, representing the power that's held in darkness: umber-yellow soybeans await the swift blade of harvest; golden jewels of cow corn harden; sun glowing orange low in the sky, rust and burgundy painted leaves, brown fields speckled with ripe orange pumpkins.

Magically, Mabon is a time for creating balance, honoring duality, and knowing your own power in darkness. Deeply feel both joy and sorrow. Absorb breathtaking beauty while simultaneously mourning the passing of summer. Walk in the woods, releasing what you don't need to the ground to decompose with the leaves.

It is also a time for preparing for the darkness—spread compost on the garden, apply mulch to protect tender plants, and gather seed heads to ensure renewal. Your personal magic includes the contemplation of what you must protect, compost, or seed within yourself, to grow in the seasons to come.

So air your blankets, duvets, and comforters, and inspect them for holes. Try snowsuits and boots on the children, and pass on what doesn't fit. Like children, we all outgrow things, and Mabon is a time to let go of what longer fits who you have grown to be. What do you need to repair, discard, replace or let go of?

As you sort and mend manually, dually engage in the inner work of soul, for here you will find your "power in darkness"

❧

For many years, in the city, I was part of Reclaiming Tradition circle. When I moved to a rural village on the shores of Lake Ontario, my magic changed. I lost my circle and ritual community, added a partner, a daughter, and many new friends, and these changes shaped my magical practice. Synthesizing the Reclaiming/Goddess tradition with Kitchen Witch, ecofeminist and traditional agricultural traditions I am both nature-oriented and magical, practicing simplified rituals open to non-pagan participants. In community I honor all that's good in my life. And that means lots of food, friends, and kids.

I hold "self" sacred, a magical center point deeply connected to my environment. I am a Witch at heart, and practice witchy parenting, magical friendships, and sacred community building. I believe, and teach, that we are all part of a divine and wise ecosystem, whether or not we identify as pagans. I advocate stewardship of the land, animal protection, wilderness and nature preservation, and a deep spiritual and emotional bond to the land. I abide by the seasons, observe the cycles of the Earth, Sun and Moon, and honor the cycles of self. At the center of my belief is the practice of "observing how I feel."

Rituals are powerful teaching tools that engage and enchant people without being overtly Pagan, magical, or witchy. Most people like rituals and celebrations, and use them to make sense of change and transition, mark time on the wheel of the year, and the stages of life.

Rituals help us talk and work through things symbolically, things that might otherwise go unsaid—how difficult situations and people can be, how challenging and engaging life is. Everyone experiences these things, young and old, urban and rural, Christian and Pagan, so rituals can help us to connect across our differences, as we celebrate and enjoy life in the midst of its diverging energies.

I live in a rural community that is strongly Christian, but even more deeply agricultural. We connect to a strong community through our shared reverence for the Earth and her cycles, and as parents.

Because the creation of community is more important to me than the bold declaration *I am Pagan*, I facilitate rituals that enliven people, leaving them feeling empowered and aware. I don't want to say or do anything that might evoke fear or uncertainty. And, because I am a parent, I facilitate child-friendly rituals that are loosely organized and flexible. All the elements of a formal ritual are included, like creating sacred space, opening a circle, calling for protection and so on, but it's very informal.

The Power of Darkness

Mabon is deeply sacred to me, filled with delicious dreams and frequent déjà vu. I feel the power in the lurking darkness, magical and seductive. The scent in the air stirs me, I keep sniffing, sniffing, eager to recognize exactly what it is and why it stimulates such deep, magical feelings.

Mabon is also the time in which my family bids goodbye to beach season, the sultry days of sun, sand, and swimming. Because wind, water, sun and sand are all present on the beach, it feels like one of the most powerful and sacred spaces around, a place where all the elements intersect.

At Mabon I invite family and friends to gather on the beach, on the shores of Lake Ontario, purposefully bringing the fifth element, Spirit, to the mix. I advertise it as "an Autumn Equinox celebration" and urge people to share in one last swim.

Ritually, it is a time to communally express sadness and uncertainty for the end of summer, metaphorically the imminent death of the God. It is also a time to celebrate the fruits of the harvest, and acknowledge the need to store some of the abundance away, as metaphorically the Goddess ages from Mother to Crone.

On Mabon, I gather with family, friends and acquaintances on a beach facing due west. The west, where the sun slips silently into oblivion, is ideal because it is symbolically connected to Autumn, the earth, balance, and grounding.

I am a "wing and a prayer" sort of person and believe that rituals should be fluid, flexible, and changing. Influenced by weather, who is present, and even their moods, I tend to decide in the moment what, and how much, is appropriate. While I spend time in advance contemplating the major themes of the sabbat and deciding what symbols and actions to use in the ritual, when I am facilitating a ritual, I shape my ideas of what the ritual might generally feel like, but I prefer to travel light. No tools or sacred items, just food, food, and food.

Because the beach is in a relatively secluded area, we treat it like a pilgrimage. Children are gathered after school. Cars are loaded with people and preparations, and we excitedly drive the short distance toward the beach. It's a mile-long walk in, so everyone carries something—food and drink, towels and warm clothes, sand shovels and buckets. As we walk, we talk quietly to the children, reminding them that today is Mabon, and the seasons are shifting.

"Today we say 'goodbye' to summer and to the once warm water we've swum in almost daily for the past few months." We recount our glorious days spent playing in the sun.

Arriving at the beach, we climb over the dunes, and are greeted by the rich warmth of late afternoon sun.

Facing west, the beach is a two-mile-long, open expanse of sparkling sand. Few people come here in nonpeak season, so it feels safe and private. Because it's visually open, people are easily spotted, and most simply steer clear. There is lots of space here for everyone.

We spread blankets and table clothes, pull toys out for the kids to dig and build with. It is a time for easy conversation, a long walk on the beach, or laying in the late afternoon sun. There's luxury in the warm orange sun, and reverential enjoyment of this magnificent beach. Oh, we are all so lucky to live here.

As the sun begins to descend, towels and warm clothes are pulled out and organized in small piles. Mothers call their children.

"Let's take a last swim," we all say. For most kids, skinny-dipping is fun, but for teens and tweenies their nakedness, and yours, can be a frightening experience. So we stick to bathing suits.

Reminding the kids that the water is "awfully cold now," we stand at the shoreline facing west. We dip toes in and feel the thrill of cold. Hairs on arms stand up. We remind the kids that the days will now grow shorter, the nights longer. It is time to say goodbye to summer.

For safety, there are a few rules: "No splashing" and "Anyone with chattering teeth or blue lips needs to get out now." It's important not to get chilled.

Wading quickly into the cold water, I breathe deeply, my heart pounds. I am alive with bodily sensations. Half submerged in water, half exposed to air and sun, I'm balanced between the elements, between the seasons.

I gaze lovingly at the fiery orange sun that slides toward the horizon. Soon darkness will come, and warmth will seep away. I bid farewell, my heart aching. I know the sun god will metaphorically die, rebirth will come later. Like Modron, I feel the anguish of losing Mabon. Anguish peaks as I look at my daughter, knowing how quickly children grow out into the world. But I can't stop time, so I take a deep breath and plunge into the chilling water. I feel cleansed when my crown chakra is submerged, so I dive deep. There's power in the dark, cold water.

I surface gasping, feeling electrified. Ritualistically I cleanse myself, rubbing arms, legs, torso, and head. Skin contracts, pores close—my body is readying for the winter.

Before chill sets in, we herd the children out of the water, vigorously rubbing everyone dry with a rough towel before snuggling into warm clothes. While people dress, I move quietly down the beach and draw a giant spiral on the sand. They're easier to draw than labyrinths. You start by drawing a gigantic circle in the sand, and just before closing the circle, angling in about eighteen inches to begin another concentric circle. Do this repeatedly to form a spiral. Leave a small area of about 3 feet in diameter at the center for sacred objects.

Natural objects help to teach reverence and connectedness. For Mabon I choose snail fossils. Littering the beach, the millions of years old remnants of the great inland sea are beautiful spirals solidified in limestone. They're finite reminders that energy cannot be destroyed, only changed and transformed.

Gathering together, we join hands, bringing safety into our circle.

"We stand in balance," I say, "Mabon, when light and dark are equal. We've enjoyed an abundant summer, but winter's scarcity may lay ahead. Today, we walk the spiraling inner journey of Mabon, to find the power in darkness. When you're ready, go quietly, spiral inward, into yourselves, into autumn. Each step focuses intention and raises magical power. As you walk, cast off what you no longer need. Let go of what doesn't work, release what you don't want, be done with what hurts you.

"At the center, contemplate all you have released. Allow for a seasonal exchange of energy. What ends with summer? What begins with autumn? What will fill the empty spaces? What new activities, habits, routines, ways or thoughts will you cultivate? What relationships will you mend or build? What do you welcome?

"When you know, pick a small symbol of the seasonal exchange of energy from the center. Take it with you while spiraling slowly out, back to your life, changed and ready for the season ahead. That symbol is a reminder of the changes you undertake to create balance in your life. Place it on your altar, or in a special place.

"Gather here after, and wait until everyone has spiraled in and out."

We walk the spiral, circling inward as though to the hearth of the house, cycling further around the wheel of life. Some people chant, or whisper, some instinctively move their arms as if throwing something to the ground. Many of the children have their eyes fixed on the ground, reveling in following the spiral path.

We each choose a talisman, a touchstone, to carry into autumn, the spiral shape a reminder to circle deep within to find power in darkness, and to curl close to hearth, family and self.

Later, we face the setting sun, calling farewell to summer deities, to warmth, water, sand and surf, farewell to the sun. Circling, we hold hands to close the circle, ground magical energy, and pull people back to the group.

"Moving inside, we take comfort in family, friends, home, and hearth. Let's celebrate with a feast. In the cooling air, let's warm one another."

Much later, we pack up sleepy kids, heft our burdens, and turn north for the long, dark walk away from summer.

Celestial Sway

Fern Feto Spring

LIGHT AND DARK REST in a perfect balance as the Sun moves into the sign of the scales on the Fall Equinox. Libra's season introduces a time of harvest and preparation as we gather and store away what we will need to sustain us through the long cold months ahead. At the Fall Equinox, there is a pause in time, when we can simultaneously look back toward the bright light of summer and forward to the dark winter approaching. Standing at the crossroads, we can meditate on our lives, grateful for what we have reaped thus far.

The Fall Equinox of 2012 arrives under a waxing Moon, with three planets in Libra. Balance, harmony, justice and relationships are front and center now, as we seek to learn the lessons of the seventh sign of the zodiac. Saturn, which has been traveling through Libra since the middle of 2010, is poised to transition into Scorpio at the beginning of October. The last weeks of Saturn's transit through Libra gain particularly intensity, amplified by the Fall Equinox and a Full Moon, which triggers the ongoing Pluto and Uranus square.

Pluto, newly direct on September 18, steps into a prominent role as Saturn gets ready to move into Pluto's home sign of Scorpio and the Full Moon triggers the ongoing Uranus/Pluto square. Our awareness of the subtle energies that make up the life force will be particularly heightened as we come into contact with our deepest values during this time.

Venus brings us her gifts in the sign of Leo, which she moved into on September 6. Pampering, generosity, fun, and romance are front and center stage as this "good-time girl" planetary energy lights up the sky. Venus moves into an exciting, but challenging, square relationship with Mars on September 27, creating a steamy heat in the galaxy and plenty of opportunities for a spicy equinox sabbat. Whether you are fighting or making up, you'll likely be engaged in some kind of intimate exchange as these two cosmic lovers dance in their ancient mating/war two-step.

The Full Moon in Aries on September 29 only adds to this intense planetary light show, as the Moon forms a conjunction to revolutionary Uranus. If that's not enough, the Sun, Moon, and Uranus also form a dynamic square to powerful Pluto, guardian of the underworld and initiator of change. More than ever before, we are now asked to spend time looking at the crossroads of our lives: public/private, self/other, romance/family/work/home.

Stretching to encompass the complexity of our humanity, we can reach for the stars, but we will need to embrace the changes that go along with growth. Collectively, this is a time when we feel ready to courageously move forward into the future, but we also may feel challenged by the structures of the past. Keeping up our "social graces" (Libra), may be particularly difficult now, but Saturn's last days in this sign remind us that peace and justice must not be sacrificed as the cost of "progress."

Jupiter, the planet of growth and expansion, goes retrograde in the sign of Gemini on October 4. We are asked to reflect on what opportunities we might want to develop during the six-month retrograde period of this planet. Gemini themes such as communication, information exchange, transportation, and education are particularly highlighted during this time.

Saturn's movement into the deep, dark depths of Scorpio occurs on October 5. Our lessons around structure and commitment take on a watery hue now, as we learn about the mysteries of life and death and the power of transformation from the sign of the Scorpion. Saturn will move through Scorpio for the next two and a half years, teaching all those who have planets in this sign about the gifts that come through hard work, patience, and persistence.

Pluto Direct in Capricorn

Pluto goes direct in Capricorn on September 18, amplifying the structures and foundations we are ready to renew in our lives. Any plans we have made for deep and lasting change will need action now to make them become a reality. However, we may need to first "clutter-clear" our emotional baggage or our physical spaces to move forward into the future. Use the following ritual to maximize the power of the Pluto direct transition.

Pluto Direct Ritual

On the Dark Moon on September 15, choose a foundational area of your life that is in need of renewal: health, relationships, work, home, or family. Imagine what it might look like if this area of your life felt empowered, transformed, and renewed. Pick three symbols that represent this area of your life and bury them underground. On the night of the Pluto direct (September 18), dig these symbols up and place them on your altar. Ritually cleanse and purify them, welcoming their transformation and rebirth.

Full Moon in Aries

The Full Moon in Aries on September 29 lights up the night with a bang as it forms a powerful conjunction to Uranus and squares Pluto. Emotionally, there may be a desire to experience freedom at all costs and we may do whatever it takes to get rid of the chains that bind us. The Sun in Libra serves as a reminder to factor our relationships with others into our plans, otherwise we may find ourselves without the benefit of friends and family as we journey along our path. This Moon can be a minefield as we try to balance the many varied needs and responsibilities of our lives, but if we take steps to try and harness the potent energy of this Mabon Full Moon, we may be able to infuse our lives with a new sense of meaning and purpose.

Full Moon in Aries Ritual

On the day of the Full Moon, spend one part of the day engaged in an activity alone that gives you a sense of freedom. Then, spend time with a close friend, partner, or family member engaged in an activity that makes you feel connected and close to them. Notice how you feel during each activity—is it more fun, easier, or less complicated to do the alone-time activity or the activity with another? What is the right balance of alone time and together time in your life? Think of one action you might take in your life to bring more balance and write this down. Place the paper on your alter and burn a red candle to activate and empower this action.

Venus in Leo

The gratitude and abundance of the harvest season is heightened when Venus moves into Leo on September 6, introducing a period of romanticism, drama, luxury, and play in our relationships with others, as well as in our spending habits. Make the most of this Venus transit through Leo by honoring the planet of love and beauty with a special day designed just for you.

Spend some quiet time meditating on what luxury means to you. On the day Venus enters Leo (or sometime before Venus moves into Virgo on October 3), plan a "Venus in Leo" day that is all about indulging yourself. Plan a special meal, beauty treat to a spa or other activity that helps you to celebrate yourself and feel pampered and valued. You may want to ritualize this activity by creating a special Venus in Leo altar and placing items on it that reflect your experience of this passionate sign.

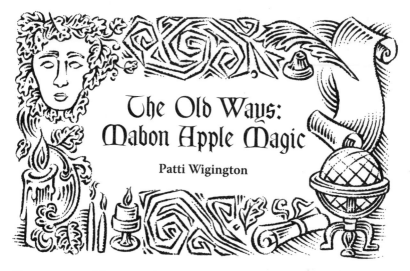

The Old Ways: Mabon Apple Magic

Patti Wigington

BY THE TIME MABON rolls around, the orchards are in full bloom, and apples are everywhere. These all-purpose fruits find their ways into pies, stews, sauces and snack trays during the fall months, and have a long history. In addition to their use as a food item, however, apples are also well known as a tool of divination and magic.

Apples have been used for centuries in divining matters of the heart. There are a number of English and European folk customs that survive to this day, all of which can help with questions of love and romance. This may go back to the days of the ancient Greeks, when the apple was known as a divine symbol of Aphrodite, the goddess of love. In fact, Christopher Faraone says in *Ancient Greek Love Magic* that a man who wished to propose might toss an apple at his beloved. If she caught it, she had accepted his offer of marriage, but if she ignored it and allowed it to fall, he was rejected. Apples were associated with love, lust, and everything in between.

Because of their association with love, apples were also closely tied to beauty. In fact, the entire Trojan War began because of a slight involving an apple. When Peleus and Thetis were married, they forgot to invite Eris, the goddess of discord, to the party. She strode in and tossed a golden apple on the gift table, saying, "Let this be given to she who has the most beauty." Zeus chose Paris, a prince of Troy, to select who should receive the apple. Hera, Athena, and Aphrodite all wanted the apple, and Paris gave it to Aphrodite when she promised him the love of Helen of Sparta, wife of King Menalaeus. Pretty soon, everything was in turmoil because of a quarrel over a Discordian apple.

In some parts of Scotland, girls knew that apples could foretell the identity of their future husbands. By peeling the apple and letting the peel fall to the ground, hopeful young romantics could learn the first initial of the man they would someday marry. In other areas, if a girl had multiple suitors, she could use the seeds to figure out who would be the lucky man. Each apple seed was assigned the name of a potential lover, and then the moist seeds were stuck to the girl's cheek. As the seeds dried and dropped off, so did the chance of each young man. The last seed on her cheek represented her true love.

In some cases, apple divination is a matter of a simple "yes" or "no." A popular method is to ask the apple a question and twist the stem. For each twist, call out either "yes" or "no." Whichever one is said on the final twist, when the stem is released, is the answer to the question. Another technique is to remove the stem first, and then use it to poke at the apple while saying "yes" or "no." When the stem finally punctures the skin of the apple, you have your answer.

Many customs came over from the British Isles with emigrants to the New World, and are still followed today in rural Appalachia and the Ozark mountains. Mountain girls know that if you cut an apple into nine even wedges and eat the pieces at midnight, when you get to the last piece, throw it over your shoulder and look in a mirror. The face of your future love should appear in the mirror behind you.

The magic of apples was not strictly limited to love divination. Apples were also known as a divine symbol of youthfulness, as well as a path to the worlds other than our own. In Celtic myth cycles, an apple branch bearing grown fruit, flowers, and unopened buds was a magical key to the underworld. The legend of the hero Cormac's visit to the Land of Promise tells of three magical golden apples that dangled invitingly from a silver branch carried by an aging warrior. When Cormac shook the branch at the members of his clan, they fell into a deep slumber, and Cormac found himself in the Otherworld. This land beyond the veil is also called Avalon, Island of the Apples, and appears later in the Arthurian legend when Morgan le Fay takes a mortally wounded Arthur to be healed at Avalon.

Druid traditions past and present pay special attention to the magic of the apple tree. The apple tree is, once again, used to represent a journey into the Otherworld, and some contemporary Druids use apple wood to carve wands and staffs to use in rituals involving communication with deity.

In Norse mythology, there is a tale of Loki, the trickster god. When Loki was captured by a giant, he was forced to secure his freedom by offering the giant some precious golden apples owned by the goddess Idunn. These apples granted eternal youth, and were consumed by the gods to keep them vital and strong. When Idunn and her apples fell into the hands of the giant, the gods became old and weak. Loki was forced to use his resourcefulness—and of course, trickery—to recover the magical fruits.

Apples also appear prominently in the Saga of the Volsungs, when a king prays for his barren wife to conceive. Frigga, the wife of Odin, sends a crow to drop an apple in the king's lap, and when his wife eats it, she finds herself pregnant for six years. Interestingly, the Germanic peoples occasionally buried apples in the graves of their dead, and the fruit has been found at such archaeological sites as the Oseberg Ship in Tonsberg, Norway. Perhaps those left behind buried these apples with their loved ones as a gift of eternal youth and life, as represented by the apples of Idunn.

During the Mabon season, you can use apples for divination and magic. Pick them fresh at your local orchard, or buy a few at a farmer's market while they are fresh and in season. With a bit of ingenuity and some apples, you just may be able to see what the future holds for you!

Feasts and Treats

Susan Pesznecker

MABON IS THE TIME of the harvest feast. At the Autumnal Equinox, we celebrate and honor Earth's bounty by feasting on goodies from the home garden, farmers' market, and green grocer. This autumn dinner represents harvest cooking at its best. A mélange of autumn vegetables roasts with a juicy whole chicken. Julienned vegetables in a tart vinaigrette provide a zesty complement to the main dish, while a moist, dense apple cake speaks to the harvest itself. Spread a cloth over a table outdoors and dine *al fresco* on nature's bounty!

Maple Roasted Chicken with Root Veggies

This recipe is an old autumn favorite: it's simple to make, delicious and soul-satisfying to eat, and makes a beautiful presentation. A chicken roasts atop a baking pan of fall's best root vegetables. A drizzle of amber maple syrup and fiery spices caramelizes during the roasting and takes on a deep, complex flavor, echoing the earthly correspondence of the maple and the season.

Prep time: 10 minutes
Cook time: 1½ hours
Serves: 4

6–8 cups assorted root vegetables: potatoes, sweet potatoes, onions, parsnips, turnips, rutabaga, carrots, beets, fennel, etc. I recommend using an onion; after that, try a few you're unfamiliar with
1 whole chicken (about 8 ounces per person)
¼ cup real maple syrup
¼ teaspoon <u>each</u> red pepper flakes, black pepper, paprika, allspice

Lightly grease a 13 × 9-inch glass pan or coat with cooking spray. Peel the vegetables. Cut into 1-inch chunks and arrange in a single layer.

Rinse the chicken and pat dry. Make sure to remove any paper container of giblets from the cavity. Cut away any obvious large pieces of fat. Set the chicken on top of the veggies.

Stir the red and black pepper and allspice into the maple syrup. Use a pastry brush (or your fingers) to drizzle the maple syrup mixture over the chicken, coating the entire bird evenly. Sprinkle chicken and exposed veggies lightly with salt.

Roast in a 325 degree F oven for 1½ hours. After a half hour, baste every 15 minutes with pan drippings and the remaining maple syrup. Remove the chicken after 1½ hours; cool on a platter, tenting the bird loosely with foil. If needed, roast the veggies until they're soft. Serve the chicken and vegetables drizzled with the pan juices.

Julienne Salad

This salad is easy to make, but gorgeous to look at and even better to taste. The watery, feminine cucumber, fiery-Mars carrots and fennel, and a sweet-sharp vinaigrette nicely contrasts the earthy main dish.
  Prep time: 15 minutes
  Serves: 4–6

¼ cup vegetable oil
½ cup seasoned rice vinegar
1 clove fresh garlic, peeled and sliced
1–2 cucumbers; peeled, seeded, and julienned
1–2 large carrots, peeled and julienned
1 small head fennel, trimmed and julienned

At least two hours before serving, blend the oil, vinegar, and garlic in a lidded cruet or screw-top jar. Shake well to blend. Chill.

Julienne the vegetables and toss in a medium bowl. Cover with a damp towel and refrigerate for up to a few hours.

To serve, toss the chilled vegetables and vinaigrette. Season with salt and pepper. (Store the remaining dressing in the refrigerator. As you use it, simply add more oil and vinegar. The garlic will keep—and continue flavoring the dressing for months.)

Apple Cake

This might be the world's most perfect cake. It stirs up with only a bowl and spoon, bakes without complication, doesn't require frosting, and keeps for days. And it's also rich, spicy, and delicious!

Prep time: 20 minutes
Cook time: 40–60 minutes
Serves: 8

2 cups white sugar
1 cup vegetable oil
2 eggs
2 teaspoons vanilla
3 cups flour
1 teaspoon salt
1 teaspoon baking soda
1 teaspoon cinnamon
3 cups finely chopped apples (about 6 big apples; I recommend Golden Delicious or Jonagold)

Grease and flour a 13 × 9-inch pan. Preheat oven to 350 degrees F.

In a large bowl, with a mixing spoon, stir together the sugar, oil, eggs, and vanilla until smooth. Add the flour, salt, baking soda, and cinnamon, stirring just until blended. Stir in the apples.

Spoon into the prepared pan and smooth the surface. Bake 40 to 60 minutes, until a toothpick inserted near the center comes out clean and the edges are beginning to pull away from the pan. Start testing at 40 minutes.

Cool the cake in its pan on a wire rack. This is a moist, delicious cake that keeps well at room temperature. It's also sturdy: ideal for picnics, potlucks, camping, etc.

Hot Spiced Wine

Finish off your harvest feast with a steaming glass of spiced wine. Chill the leftovers—cold spiced wine is also quite refreshing.

Prep time: 10 minutes
Cook time: 30 minutes
Serves: 4–6

4 cinnamon sticks
10 whole cloves
8 cardamom pods
½ teaspoon whole coriander seed
8 whole allspice
8 black peppercorns
2 bottles of good red wine—Cabernet or Shiraz work well
3–4 thin slices of fresh lemon
1 small orange, sliced thin and seeded
2 tablespoons sugar
½ cup brandy
Additional cinnamon sticks

Heat a 6-quart saucepan over medium heat for 4 to 5 minutes. Add the cinnamon, cloves, cardamom, coriander, allspice, and peppercorns to the pan and toast for about 30 seconds. Quickly stir in 1 cup hot water.

Add the wine, lemon, orange, and 2 tablespoons sugar. Simmer for 30 to 60 minutes. Do NOT boil, as this will cook off the alcohol.

Before serving, stir in the brandy. Taste and add more sugar if needed. Strain into mugs and serve with a cinnamon stick swizzle.

Crafty Crafts

Ellen Dugan

Theme of the Season: Harvest and abundance
Colors: Red, orange, yellow, and bronze
Scents: Apple, nutmeg, ginger, and musk
Energy: Prosperity, thanksgiving, and liveliness

Fall Candlescape in a Cauldron

This is a quick way to make an altar or table centerpiece. I have also personally done this same look in my garden's pond for a Harvest Moon ritual. It was haunting, ethereal, and gorgeous. Mini-pumpkins and gourds do float! And when they are intermingled with floating orange leaf-shaped candles and fall flowers, they make an elegant and enchanting table or garden display.

Supplies
Large black cauldron or large black bowl
Water
Three or four mini-pumpkins or small funky gourds
Three or four floating candles in orange, yellow, or red. Look for
    fall-themed floating candles such as leaves or flower shapes.
    (Tealight candles float in their cups, too, in a pinch.)

Several fall flowers, such as fall-colored daisies or mums.
Matches or a lighter

Instructions: Fill the bowl or cauldron with water. Float a few mini-pumpkins or gourds in the water. Add as many floating candles as will easily fit—usually 2 to 4 or more, depending on the size of your bowl or cauldron. Remove the stems from the flowers and set the flower heads (face up in the water so they will float) around the pumpkins and candles. Just before your guests arrive, light the floating candles and enjoy!

Variations: Here are a couple nifty, extra-Crafty options! Do this candlescape in the garden pond or birdbath in the garden at night. Or you could really go crazy and turn off all the lights in your bathroom, fill the tub halfway, tuck the shower curtain to the side, and float those mini-pumpkins, floating candles and flowers in the tub at your next party or coven get together. Your guests will think you are a decorating genius!

Time to complete: 20 minutes or less

Cost: $10.00 to $20.00. Watch for sales on floating fall candles in the late summer months. Check roadside stands and farmers' markets for the gourds and mini-pumpkins. Use colored tealights in their cups if you can't find fancy floating candles.

Fall Pumpkin Fresh Floral Centerpiece

There is something so festive about fresh autumn flowers inside of a pumpkin. It's easy and fun to do. Try it for yourself this fall!

Supplies

A clean, fresh orange pumpkin (smaller than a basketball, but bigger than a softball)

Sharp knife

Spoon

Green floral foam for fresh flowers, soaked in water. Or if you prefer, a small glass jar that will fit down inside of the pumpkin.

Water

Seasonal fall flowers, leaves, grasses, and twigs from your garden. Or take a trip to the local florist and buy several stems of red, orange, and yellow mums, a few roses, and some silk fall leaves.

Scissors or garden snips

Instructions: Choose a nicely shaped fresh pumpkin with a solid symmetrical base so that it sits well. Cut the top of the pumpkin as if you were carving a jack-o'-lantern. Make sure that the opening is large enough for you to add the block of foam or to hide your glass jar for the flowers.

Clean out the pumpkin with the spoon.

Next, put the water-soaked foam inside of the pumpkin. You may need to trim off the sides of the block of foam with a kitchen knife. But keep that block of foam as large as you can. It is squishy when water-soaked, so you will have a little room to play. Drop the block inside of the pumpkin. Pour more water on top of the foam so there is an inch or two of water for the foam and the flowers to pull

up from. For best floral arranging results, keep an inch or two of the foam *above* the rim of the pumpkin.

(If you are using a jar, place the jar inside the opening of the pumpkin and add water to the jar.)

Fill in with your seasonal flowers, such as hydrangea blossoms, sedum, rose hips, chrysanthemums, and roses. Add pretty colorful leaves, dried ornamental grasses, cattails, wheat stalks, and little twigs to give the arrangement height and texture.

If you want to make a shape with your arrangement you will need to use the foam. When you arrange the flowers into the foam, push the stems in carefully. Don't pull the stems back out of the same hole several times, it makes air pockets and the flower stems wont be able to drink from the foam. Snip the stems with a clean pair of scissors or your garden snips and carefully arrange the flowers one at a time. This is a creative process and a fun one. Relax and enjoy yourself.

Add the flowers until you have a round shape on top of the pumpkin (although a tall triangular shape is pretty too!). Don't worry if it's not perfect. Add some twigs or grasses for height, let some colorful leaves drape over the top edge of the pumpkin, and make it funky and fun! This arrangement is about texture and color—not perfection. When you have everything arranged to your liking, you may discard of the lid of that pumpkin or tuck it alongside the arrangement at the base.

If you choose to arrange your flowers in a jar tucked inside the pumpkin, the same rules apply. Add the stems one at a time and enjoy the process. (You will have a harder time getting a shape with a jar though.) Keep the arrangement casual.

The colors of autumn garden mums, roses, sedum, and hydrangea are gorgeous. Enjoy yourself and be prepared, you will probably want to make more of these centerpieces for coven get-togethers and for family and friends.

If you keep adding water to the flowers whether they are in a jar or arranged in foam, the arrangement should last nicely for one week.

Time to create: 1 to 2 hours, including gathering flowers from the garden. I let the foam soak in a sink full of water for an hour, before I gathered the autumn flowers from my gardens.

Cost: $10.00 to $25.00. Again, the cost of this project depends on what you have growing in the garden at home. When I did this project last fall, the foam cost five dollars and the pumpkin bought at a roadside stand cost four. All of the flowers and twigs came from my garden. It's not about how much you spend. It's what you do with what you have on hand. So go on, use your imagination and be artistic and see what you can conjure up. Remember, Witches are crafty people!

All One Family

Clea Danaan

IN THE TIMELESSNESS OF childhood, I understood season changes through the portends of nature. The black and orange fuzz of a wooly bear caterpillar foretold the nearness of Halloween, and legend had it the thickness of her wooly coat forecast how snowy and cold the upcoming winter would be. Apple-picking parties and the sticky crunch of the cider press meant the end of summer and the beginning of the sweetness of autumn. Dew returned to the grass in the early mornings. Fall had come. It remains my favorite season, and now I know this season-shifting time as Mabon.

At Mabon, the light and dark once again sit facing each other with equal sway. We have stepped into a cave: the coolness of the darkness to come soothes our sun-heated brows, but we have not yet descended into the dark half of the year. For many families, Mabon comes just after the return to school or homeschooling lessons. The kitchen counter groans with the weight of the last tomatoes, zucchinis, cucumbers, peppers, and sunflowers. Pumpkins, winter squash, and fall crops are beginning to come in as well. Flowers bloom in reds, oranges, and purples. Here in Colorado, we may have already had our first frost, but the days are still balmy and pleasant, even hot—yet on the wind, I can smell autumn.

There is something particularly alive about autumn even though it marks the first deaths as the tilt of the earth takes the Northern Hemisphere away from the most intense sun. The sleepiness of summer's dog days has passed. The time to snuggle deep in winter's chill has not yet arrived. The perfect weather and bright aliveness make autumn a great time to get to know your local ecosystem. Time to pack a picnic of late summer vegetables and go exploring. Bring along magnifying lenses, binoculars, and nature journals. Let yourself play.

Find a local farm, a nearby hike, a beach, a farmers' market, or a new park you have been meaning to check out, and bring the whole family. This would be a great time to perform a simple or elaborate Mabon ritual. Make your altar out of local found materials: fresh or dried-on-the-vine berries, leaves, stones, moss, sticks, even rainwater or water collected from a stream. Let it be a family art project. The youngest toddler and the most jaded teen will find some way to contribute to the altar and ritual circle. Let your ritual be about interconnections and balance in the family. We've returned from the bustling excitement of summer to the grounding calm of the family hearth. As we dip into the cold of winter, we have our family to keep us safe and warm. Let this point of equinox be a level space on which to stand.

I rarely do formal ritual with my family; the pomp and formality make us shy and self-conscious. We do, however, play together in honor of the seasons. We like to make things together: bread, crafts, gardens, chicken coops. We like to make up songs together and tell stories. We love to notice nature. If your family suffers from the same bit of shyness, or if paganism is new to your family, let your play be your ritual. Make up chants while you garden, bake, knit, craft, or just walk through the woods. Integrate your spirituality into all you do.

Here is a simple chant to sing while harvesting from the garden for your Mabon picnic and celebration:

Richness of the Earth, power of the Sun,
We give thanks for we all are One.

Or chant these favorites:

Hoof and horn, hoof and horn, all that dies shall be reborn.

And

We all come from the Goddess, and to her we shall return, like a drop of rain flowing back to the ocean.

Witchcrafting author Phyllis Curott suggests chanting these two together, the men singing one and the women the other.

Discuss with your family or encourage journaling about your harvest—all kinds of harvest. We harvest food from the garden or the farmers' market, and also we harvest dreams and life lessons. What are you harvesting in your life at this time? The inner harvest might be something obvious, like an article or book getting published or a grown child off to college. What we harvest might surprise us, as when we learn who our "true" friends are when we go through a difficult time. We might not see the gifts of a harvest until much later, when the silver lining to a situation becomes clear.

Personal harvests are just like garden harvests. Every year I plant a bunch of seeds and seedlings. Some germinate, grow, and produce exactly what I hoped for. Some seeds just never germinate, or grow poorly. Sometimes plants sprout, grow tall and healthy, and then don't produce fruit or seed as I had hoped. Even then, though, I always harvest something, be it cornhusks for fall decorations, a bumper crop of cherry tomatoes, or knowledge that a certain plant just doesn't grow well in this climate. Sometimes we harvest not what we expected but something wholly different. Life, as the garden, is like that.

So you've found your outdoor spot to play in, you've brought along a picnic of local fruits and vegetables and some homemade bread, you and the family have created a seasonal family altar, and you've gathered around it to discuss your harvest. Take some time together to look back at the year of sabbats. What have you learned? What did you let go of? Begin? What surprised you?

Mabon Ritual: Power of Dark

Dallas Jennifer Cobb

Bring the "power in the dark" into your home, hearth, and heart.

PREPARING FOR A RITUAL requires clarity of spirit and intent. Meditate on the meaning of Mabon, its traditional associations, and discover what resonates with you. Examine your "dark self" to connect with your own dark power. I don't mean dark magic, or evil, but the darkness inside of you that can be frightening and overwhelming. There is great power in fear. And the dark power of Mabon comes from the deep feelings and thoughts that could imperil us, because if, instead of fearing and denying them, we embrace and make peace with them, we harness their energy, a powerful life-sustaining force.

What do you fear? What do you dread? What haunts you? Perhaps like our ancestors you fear the scarcity of winter, the isolation, lack of light, and the chance of succumbing to the cold. Maybe you fear the darkness that grows inside each of us—depression, anger, disappointment, and failure. Or you could be afraid of illness, disability or death, or a cancer growing within us.

Name your fears, and know your dread. Know what hides within you in the spaces that are dark, lonely, and lacking. Because within these spaces lay the power in the darkness, a power source to be tapped and used to work magic. Magic is the projection of natural energies.

Now, prepare your community. Invite your ritual circle, family, and friends to a seasonal power ritual. Ask them to think about what they fear or dread, what haunts them. Urge them to identify both what diminishes their power, things they need to let go of, and what enhances their power, what they need to invite into their lives. And ask them to bring a special potluck dish for the feast, made from seasonal fruits, vegetables, or grains, especially food harvested from their personal gardens. A traditional Mabon feast might include baked apples, pumpkin soup, spicy curried squash, and quinoa with roasted garlic and herbs, plus a few bottles of home-made wine, apple cider, or juice.

Preparing the ritual space often lends itself to further preparing yourself. During the mundane tasks of cleaning and preparing a space, much magical internal work is done.

Sweep your house physically with a broom, and psychically using visualization and energy-projection techniques. Sweet grass or sage can be burned to smudge a space clearing out old vibrations and spirits. When you are done, the space will be cleared of physical and psychic clutter, dust and dirt.

When the ritual space is cleared, bless it, and bless the ritual and all people attending, in advance.

Decorate mindfully. Spread uplifting energy around and through the home with seasonal items associated with Mabon. Litter the front steps with autumn leaves, pumpkins, squash, and bales of hay. Inside, place vases filled with sheaves of wheat and oats, or gorgeous seasonal blooms like dahlias or calendula all around. Hang colorful Indian corn on the entry door.

Prepare the largest space of the house to accommodate the ritual. Push back furniture to make room for a large circle. Spread a sacred or ritual cloth to establish an altar, and in the middle place a cornucopia of fruits of the sun and soil: apples, hazelnuts, grapes, or pears.

Items Needed

A goblet of grape juice or wine and a plate of cornbread for ritual consumption

Matches

Lavender essential oil

A beeswax candle for each person affixed to a safe candleholder

Arrange the tools needed for the ritual on the altar. As the **ritual facilitator**, greet people at the door with a hug or a smile.

Welcome. Place your potluck contributions on the feast table. And then turn on a light in the house. You bring light to my life, so turn on a light and help brighten my home.

By the time everyone has arrived, the house is ablaze with light. Call out to gather people together in the ritual space, where they can place their ritual items and magical tools on the altar, and find a spot in the circle that suits them.

Creating Sacred Space

Standing together, the circle is cast. Walking the exterior of the circle, deosil or clockwise, face each direction, tracing a pentagram in the air, calling in the elements:

Facing North: *By the earth that is her body,*
Facing East: *the air that is her breath,*
Facing West: *the waters of her living womb,*
Facing South: *and the fire of her sweet spirit.*

Walking another large circle around **everyone** incant:

We summon the elements circling around,
For within this circle magic is found,
We gather in peace and tranquility
We work together, a magic community.

Walk back to your place and step through it, into the middle of the circle.

Here between the worlds we stand [looking around at everyone in the circle]

Children of spirit [hands out to the sides] *and children of land* [hands touch the ground]

What happens here in magic space [circle around fully with arms extended] *Affects all worlds and every place*

Invocation

Great Goddess Demeter, great mother, doorway of the mysterious feminine, we petition you to be with us. Bless us with your light, your growing energy and your deep abiding love for your daughter. As we celebrate the fruits of the earth, let us know you, let us know passion and let us know all that endures through darkness. Please join us.

And join us Persephone, courageous daughter who journeys to darkness. Bestow us with bravery and fortitude for our own dark journey.

Demeter and Persephone, we sip this wine, and taste the sweetness of motherly love. We take this love inside us.

Pass a goblet of wine or grape juice around the circle for everyone to sip.

Oh God Mabon, we call to you. Lost one, stolen one, son of light, the power in darkness. Be with us. Let us know your anguish and sorrow, let us feel your abandonment as we too feel abandoned today. Be with us and teach us to overcome our fears, to find comfort in solitude, and to hold tight to our belief in ourselves. Be with us Mabon as we honor you with this sweet bread.

Pass a plate of cornbread around for everyone to savor.

Be with us Goddesses and God, as we spiral into our own darkness. Teach us to overcome sorrow with joy, find solitude in abandonment, know that rebirth and life come from death, and to know the deep and abiding love of the Mother that is ours. Walk with us as we spiral into the dark.

Light one of the candles and hold it in your right hand.

The Power of Dark

Let this light illuminate what is inside of you, as we take the time-less journey of the seasons. Let symbols resonate, stimulating thought and feeling, evoking your own personal meaning and message. Take from these words what you need to connect to the magic of the season.

At Autumnal Equinox the Sun crosses the equatorial line, and for the first time since Vernal Equinox, the days shrink as the nights stretch longer. Today we experience light and dark in sacred balance, like the scales of Libra.

Known as the Feast of Avalon and Harvest Home, Mabon is a time to honor balance, duality and the cycle of life. It is the Pagan second harvest, a time of abundance, but with winter not long away, it is also a time to store. As we harvest the life-giving fruits of sun and soil, we also bring death to the plant. It is a time for us to take stock.

While the Goddess and God symbolically prepare for their journey to the underworld, we prepare for the darkness, and quiet that lays ahead. Tonight we walk into the darkness, spiraling down, searching within us for the power in darkness, which will accompany us as we journey. We spiral in to hearth and home, friends and family. Spiral in to our dreams, déjà vu, and spiritual selves, rich with visions, intuition and inklings. We spiral in to fear, sadness, loss and abandonment. We spiral in to power.

Tonight we focus on balance, harmony and duality, aware that death is the spiritual gateway for rebirth and life, we no longer fear death, but celebrate it. We honor the dead, while protecting ourselves and our families. Harvesting, we store our abundant crops, securing supplies that sustain us through winter. Within, we affirm and meditate, raising self-esteem and cultivating self-worth, the spiritual supplies that will sustain us.

With your left hand, take the hand of the person next to you. Instruct everyone to link hands.

Hold tight as we spiral together into the dark. Let your hands and hearts see what your eyes are blinded to. Know that the love of the Mother is always with you, and even in the dark, you are safe within community. As we all move through the house together, hold hands, for together we enjoy safety. [Everyone joins hands.]

Walk to the right around the house, entering each room, and ceremonially turning off each light. After each instruction, turn off a light, moving slowly to the next switch.

Feel yourself balanced, as we stand in this moment of time, Equinox. [A light turns off.]

The scales of balance shift as we move into the dark. [Turn off another one.]

Look into your own darkness, and glimpse what you fear. [Another light turns off.]

Every home has a different number of rooms, and a different number of lights. Below are some statements to use for each light you extinguish; use them as needed. Be sure to voice your responses, demonstrating and encouraging participation.

What do you need to leave here? Let go of what no longer works, and leave it.

Name what you fear, and abandon it here.

Say what you dread, and let it be dead.

What are you sick of, now be clear, and as the light extinguishes, leave it here.

When all the lights are off, slowly move the group back toward the space where the circle had originally formed. Remind them to travel carefully, holding onto each other, avoiding any accidental bumps or stumbles.

We go now in darkness, traveling slow, hold onto hands for you don't know,
Where to step and where to turn, but to the circle we now return.

Returning to the room where the altar is laid, take your single candle (still lit) and place it (in its candleholder) in the center of the circle.

Cleansing

Invite the group to circle around the single candle that burns in the candleholder. Carefully prepare a small burner of sage, light it, and begin smudging yourself as you talk:

Mabon is the time to let go, releasing things that don't work or are broken, things that hurt or don't feel right. And the letting go isn't just of stuff, but people, situations and feelings. As you smudge, be cleansed of your fears, your dreads and pains, your hurts. Leave them here. Let this sacred smoke purify us, cleanse body, spirit and ethereal energy.

Personal Magic

When everyone has smudged, return the sage (in its burner) to the center of the circle, taking up the candles, one for each person.

Mabon is a time for completing projects, finishing stuff, harvesting, and storing. It is also a time for taking stock of what we have, organizing and repairing. A time to focus on what we need to heal, organize and repair.
Mabon is a time to look at what you have and be grateful for it. It is a time for working prosperity magic, and welcoming new riches into your lives. Meditate now on abundance, with a focus on what you need. What new habits will you cultivate, what new friends will you nurture, how will you improve your life, health, and self?

Pass one candle to each person. With a finger on the top of the lavender oil dram, tip a little onto your left index finger and anoint your own candle as you speak.

With this oil, anoint your candle, attaching the energy of every-thing you want to seed in your life, and grow. Focus your intent to draw abundance into your life, to fuel the fire that burns deep inside.

Let each person anoint their candle. Whisper:

In deepest darkness, there is always light,
Fire sweet, and burning bright,
Be it spirit or merry heart,
Let the light this moment start.

When all candles are anointed, return the oil to the center of the circle. Spark a match, and light your candle:

All alone there is simple light,
Gathered together we all burn bright,
I give my light and keep my own,
Friends and family light this home.

Lean to the person on your left, using your candle to light theirs, passing the flame around Widdershins, or counterclockwise. Chant:

Passion is power, that grows in the dark,
Magic is power I sew with this spark.

As the flame passes around the circle, let the chanting grow louder as the room grows brighter, taking it to a crescendo. When the flame has traveled around the circle and all candles are lit, end the chant.

Pause for a moment, then the **ritual facilitator** speaks. [Those gathered should follow the facilitator's guidance]

We will close the circle here, then move to the feasting table, where I ask that each of you light a candle there, from yours. Then blow out your candle and take it home to use for your own magical work.

With your candle lit and inside alight,
Move from the circle out into the night.
There are candles on the feasting table,

Each one light one, if you are able.
In the darkness we celebrate,
Family, friends and our good fate.
Put out your candle, use it later on your altar,
And summon its magic when your inner light falters.
Find the power in darkness and hold it long,
We will survive, in community, together strong.

Closing the Circle

Thank you Demeter, Persephone, and Mabon. Be with us as we feast and celebrate your passion. We open this circle, releasing the spirits, carrying our magic into our lives.

Merry meet and merry part, and merry meet again. Blessed be.

Notes

Notes